There's a blue star beaming in the window,
For a loved one far away;
And its light is shining through the gloaming
As we kneel alone to pray.
And we're yearning for his returning
To his home and happy days of old;
While with trembling our hearts are asking
"Will the blue star turn to gold?"

Of our dear ones ever we are dreaming;
In our heart there throbs a prayer:
"Put Thy loving arms about him, Father,
Guard and keep him over there!"
And if some day we hear the story,
How he bravely fought and nobly fell,
We will trust Him who knows our sorrows,
For He doeth all things well.

There is one who heals the broken hearted;
O how much He loves His own!
For He sent His Son from heaven's glory
Here to die for us, alone.
And the bright star in old Judea
Was a token of His love untold;
And He knows all our bitter sorrow
For His own star turned to gold.

Refrain:
If the blue star turns to gold,
Then His love He will unfold;
For the Father loves with a tender love,
If the blue star turns to gold.

— *When a Blue Star Turns to Gold*
Words and Music by A. S. Reitz, 1918

Dedicated to the brave, selfless individuals
who have served, and who now serve, our country.
Thank you.

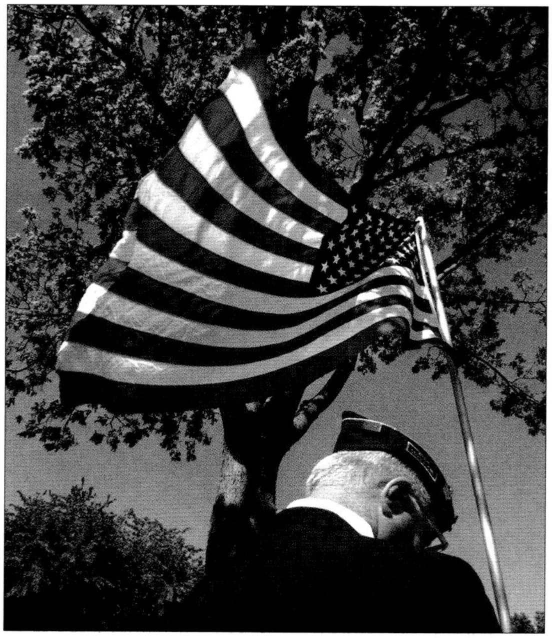

peopleScapes PUBLISHING

Produced and published in the United States of America by PeopleScapes Inc.
Printed in the United States of America by Sioux Printing, Sioux Falls, SD.

First Edition

Library of Congress Cataloging in Publication Control Number: 2004092018

ISBN 0-9673485-5-2

BLUE STARS

A SELECTION OF STORIES FROM SOUTH DAKOTA'S WORLD WAR II VETERANS

☆☆☆

Enjoy the book!

Compiled and Photographed by
GREG LATZA

Designed and Edited by
JODI HOLLEY LATZA

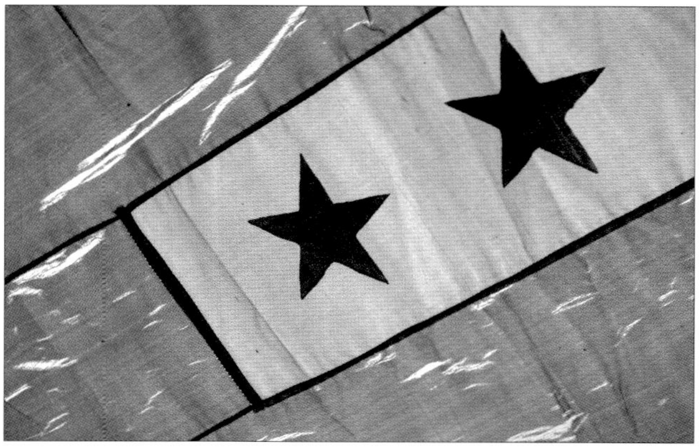

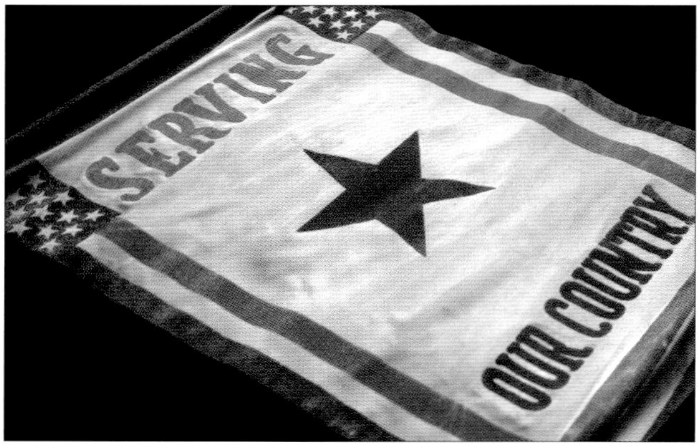
SERVING
OUR COUNTRY

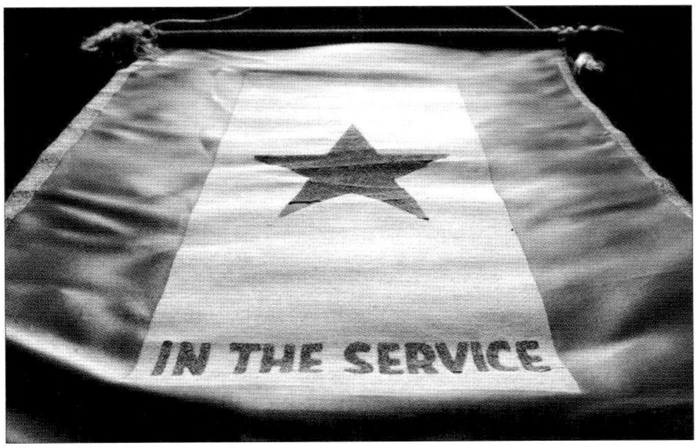
IN THE SERVICE

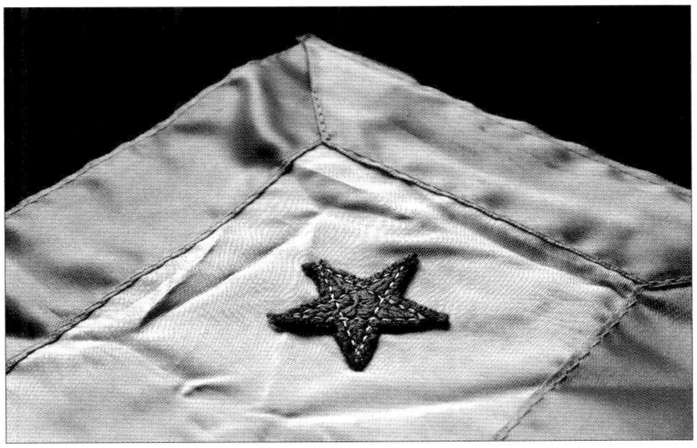

INTRODUCTION ☆ *by Greg Latza*

My assignment to photograph a World War II veteran shortly before Christmas in 1994 began like most others that I had during my years as a daily newspaper photographer. The yellow assignment slip had been dropped into my slot earlier that morning. On the surface it looked just like the hundreds of other portraits we photographed each year. While the practice seemed monotonous at times, the intrigue of meeting someone new and hearing their story kept me interested.

Every once in a while, I had already met the person I was about to shoot, or I knew I had something in common with them. But on this day, I had never heard of Monsignor Francis Sampson.

The reporter was Carson Walker. A few minutes before we were due to arrive at Sampson's house, we hopped into my car and during the short drive we talked about regular stuff — how our wives were doing, what we thought about that day's paper, and all of the other odds and ends that occupy a journalist's mind. It was a slow news day.

I asked Carson what he knew about Sampson and the angle we were covering. He explained that Sampson was a chaplain in World War II, and that he had spent Christmas 1944 as a prisoner. Our story would profile Sampson's memories of the long-ago holiday for an upcoming Christmas season feature.

We walked up to the house and knocked. The door slowly opened, and an old man in dark-rimmed glasses welcomed us in. Since it was my job to make an interesting picture, I immediately started scouting for a suitable setting as Carson pulled out his notebook. Then we sat down to listen.

☆

The conversation that followed can be directly credited as the origin of this book.

Francis Sampson was just an average old man when he greeted us at the door. When he finished talking to us, he was my hero.

I sat in stunned silence as he recounted jumping into Normandy on D-Day with the 101st Airborne, and landing squarely in the middle of a deep stream. His parachute dragged him into shallower water, and he had to dive several times to retrieve his lost Mass equipment. (This scene is re-enacted in the 1962 movie,

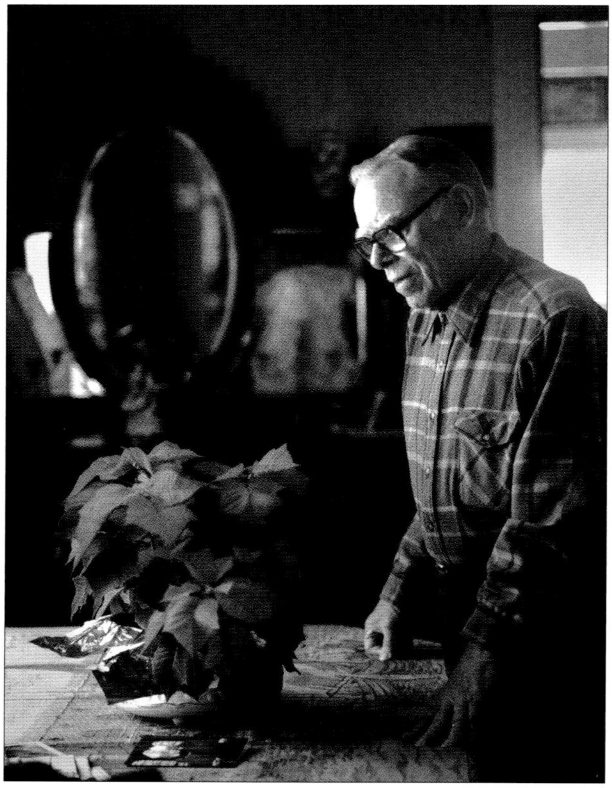

Monsignor Francis Sampson marvels at a poinsettia's beauty in his Sioux Falls home. (Photo reprinted with permission from the Sioux Falls Argus Leader.*)*

The Longest Day — even though the chaplain is British in the movie.) He then spent the next few days tending to a house full of wounded soldiers. While he was there, the Germans took control of the house, walked him down the road, and were about to shoot him until one of their officers recognized him as a Catholic priest.

Returning to the wounded, he survived direct shell hits upon the house as the Americans overran the immediate area. He gave last rites to two of the once-wounded soldiers, now dead from the blasts.

Even though Sampson barely survived those first days in France, he jumped with the 101st again — this time into Holland. He would survive the Market-Garden operation there, only to move on to Bastogne and the impending Battle of the Bulge. It was there that Sampson and several other Americans were captured by the Germans, and they began a long, treacherous march to Stalag 2-A. Their ever-growing column was accidentally strafed and bombed by American planes several times, killing German soldiers and American prisoners alike.

It was Christmas Day when the 800 prisoners walked into Prum, Germany, and were herded into a large school auditorium. With half a boiled turnip and half a slice of black bread in each belly and American bombs falling throughout the city, the soldiers sang *Silent Night*. The building shuddered with each nearby blast.

Sampson gave a sermon to his unlikely congregation that night. He offered hope to a group of desperate men embroiled in a terrible war and did his best to encourage strength in their time of hopelessness.

As I sat and listened to his story, I realized there was no way I could capture the character of this man with a mere camera. Knowing Carson's story was slated to be a short feature, just a few inches long, I could tell he was struggling with similar thoughts.

How were we supposed to give proper credit to someone who had endured the unthinkable? Someone who had risked his life, time and again, for the freedoms that Carson and I enjoyed — and took for granted — every day?

When he had finished talking, Sampson got up and invited us to a room full of memorabilia. We saw medals and a photo album stuffed with the signed portraits of colonels and generals and congressmen. But these items were humbly pooh-poohed by Sampson as he reached for something more dear.

He held out a small cigarette case. It was made by a starving Russian prisoner after Sampson had taken food to him. He showed us a silver chalice, a remnant from the Mass kit of an Italian priest who died in the camp. He shared other small items too numerous to describe, but his focus always remained on the men behind the items, not the items themselves.

☆

It was the first and last time I ever saw Francis Sampson. He died 14 months later at the age of 83. I was shocked to read another detail about his war experiences a couple of years later. Soon after D-Day, he had broken the news to a young soldier that three of his brothers had been killed in action, and that the soldier would be going home. This story became the basis for the motion picture *Saving Private Ryan*.

"Private Ryan" was actually Sergeant Fritz Niland, and Sampson did not make a heroic journey to rescue him. He did, however, arrange Niland's passage back to his parents, after breaking the news to him at Carentan. While the movie is a loose representation of Sampson's experience, it depicts the grim reality of World War II in amazing detail.

The inspiration for one of history's best war movies was living among us, right here in South Dakota. But like most people, on the surface I saw Sampson as little more than a soft-spoken, elderly man.

Meeting Sampson was a very important experience for me. Each time I saw or met men in their 70s or 80s I began to wonder: Were they veterans? Where did they serve? What were their individual stories?

I started to read more books about World War II. I took notice when World War II specials were aired on The History Channel. And when Jodi and I began to publish books about South Dakota in 1999, one of the ideas on my short list was a book about South Dakota's World War II veterans.

☆

The most challenging aspect of publishing a book like this is deciding who to feature in it. There is an abundance of notable veterans to choose from in South Dakota. However, I didn't want *Blue Stars* to be considered as some type of "Who's Who" list of World War II veterans.

Plenty of ink has been used to document the achievements of two of our most famous veterans, Joe Foss and George McGovern. The attention is warranted. Each man served his country well, and for that I applaud them.

The late Joe Foss was a superb Marine pilot. He defended Guadalcanal in the early stages of the war, at a time when power in the Pacific Theater was held firmly by the Japanese. Even though the battle of Midway had already decimated a good portion of the Japanese fleet during the summer of 1942, there was still a lot to do to ensure Japan was rendered ineffective as a fighting force. Toward that end, Foss was credited with 26 downed aircraft and 14 "smokers" — planes so badly damaged they most likely went down. He later received the Medal of Honor for his actions.

But Foss did not work alone. Many other fighter pilots also battled Japanese Zeroes throughout the Pacific. One of those men was Cecil Harris, a farm boy from Cresbard. He had 24 confirmed kills — only two fewer than Foss — but today most people do not know his name. The fact that he began a quiet life in Cresbard as an educator, then returned to a career in the Navy did not diminish the value of Harris' duty, but it did lower his profile. Conversely, Foss chose to live his life in the public arena. He was elected governor of South Dakota, became commissioner of the American Football League and served as president of the National Rifle Association.

Another public figure, George McGovern piloted a B-24 bomber from an Italian air base, flying 35 missions to help destroy Germany's war machine. By all accounts, he was an excellent and dependable pilot, and on more than one occasion he was credited with making life-saving decisions on behalf of his crew.

McGovern served his country well and decided to try politics as a profession. He was denied the presidency in 1972, but in recent years he has worked on behalf of the world's hungry and has made a difference on an international level. McGovern will be the first person to tell you that he was just one of hundreds of bomber pilots flying in World War II. His plane came back riddled with holes, but so did many others.

Noted World War II historian Stephen Ambrose wrote a book about B-24 crewmen and centered it around McGovern and his crew. An excellent book, *Wild Blue* puts the reader in the co-pilot's seat, right next to McGovern.

Would Ambrose have profiled McGovern if he had not been famous? Probably not. The book is more interesting because we all know the person that McGovern became.

But what about most of the other 68,000 men and women from South Dakota who also served in World War II? Several were notable, and some have found themselves in the South Dakota Hall of Fame for their military service. A handful of veterans have written books about their experiences, leaving a valuable record of their service for us.

The vast majority of South Dakota's World War II veterans live modestly in cities, small towns and farms scattered throughout the state. They rarely find occasion to share their experiences with anyone outside their friends and family. I kept this fact in mind as I located veterans for *Blue Stars*. I chose not to profile Foss and McGovern, not because they weren't deserving of it, but because we already know their stories. Instead, I wanted to illustrate how a random sampling of veterans could tell the story of the war through their varied experiences.

☆

It has been my experience that many veterans who wouldn't or couldn't talk about the war just five or 10 years ago have found the courage and desire to talk about it now. In some cases, that ability has been aided by popular movies such as *Saving Private Ryan* and *Band of Brothers*. For others, inquisitive grandchildren or great-grandchildren finally may have brought the subject to light.

I hope that people reading this book will be encouraged to sit down with veterans they know and talk to them about their war experiences. Perhaps they might even write a few pages about it, or ideally, record the interviews on audio or video tape.

For many World War II veterans, there's not much time left for reflection. Every day when I read the obituaries, I see the names of two or three more veterans who will have military honor guards saluting them at their funerals. In most cases, their duty is summarized in one or two sentences. It is incredible to think that for the past 60 years, these few words may be the most that was ever written about the most dangerous and pivotal years of their lives. Don't they deserve more than that?

Some of the strongest movements to record this history evolved as the World War II Memorial was being constructed in Pierre throughout 2000 and 2001. Newspaper stories about local veterans were commonplace in the days and weeks leading up to the September 15, 2001, dedication, and schools across the state used the event as a lesson to teach kids World War II history.

Another notable project involved the work of Sheila Hansen, a middle school teacher in Spearfish. She assigned students to write biographies for each of the 2,200 South Dakotans (including four women) killed during the course of the war.

Prior to the dedication ceremonies, 2,200 white crosses labeled with each soldier's name, hometown and date of

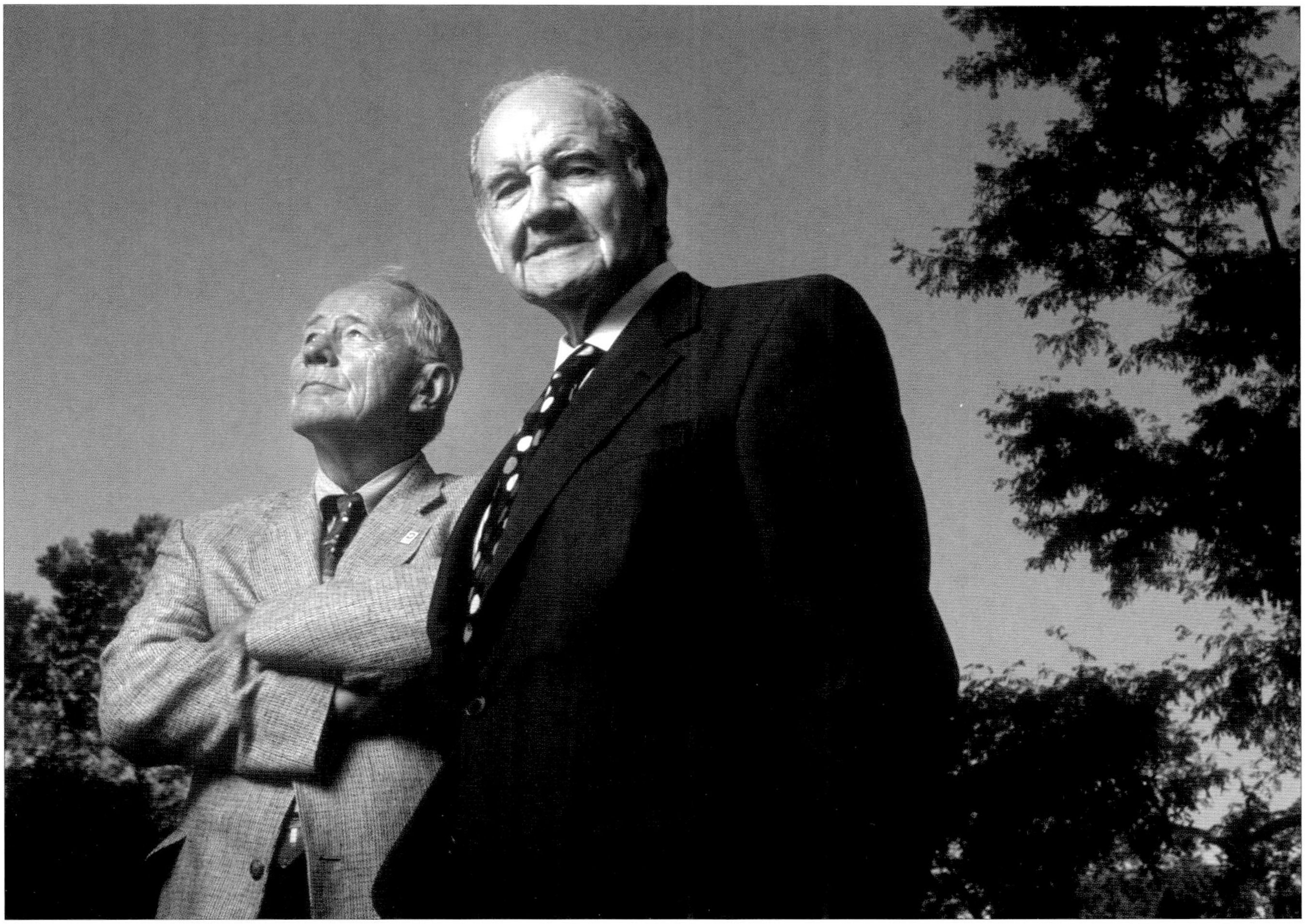

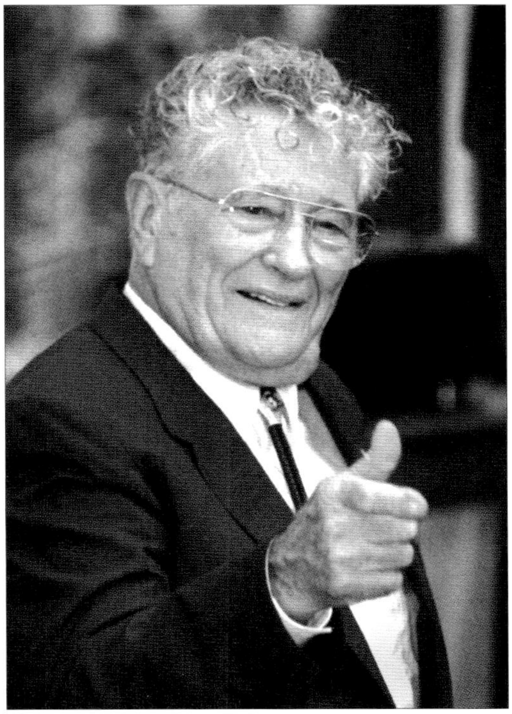

Above: George McGovern (right) and Stephen Ambrose relax on the campus of Dakota Wesleyan University in Mitchell prior to a joint speaking engagement on August 16, 2001. I photographed the pair for a USA Today *review of Ambrose's book* Wild Blue.

Left: Joe Foss gives a thumbs up to family and friends gathered at the Sioux Falls Regional Airport prior to the unveiling of a statue sculpted in his likeness. (Photo reprinted with permission from the Argus Leader.*)*

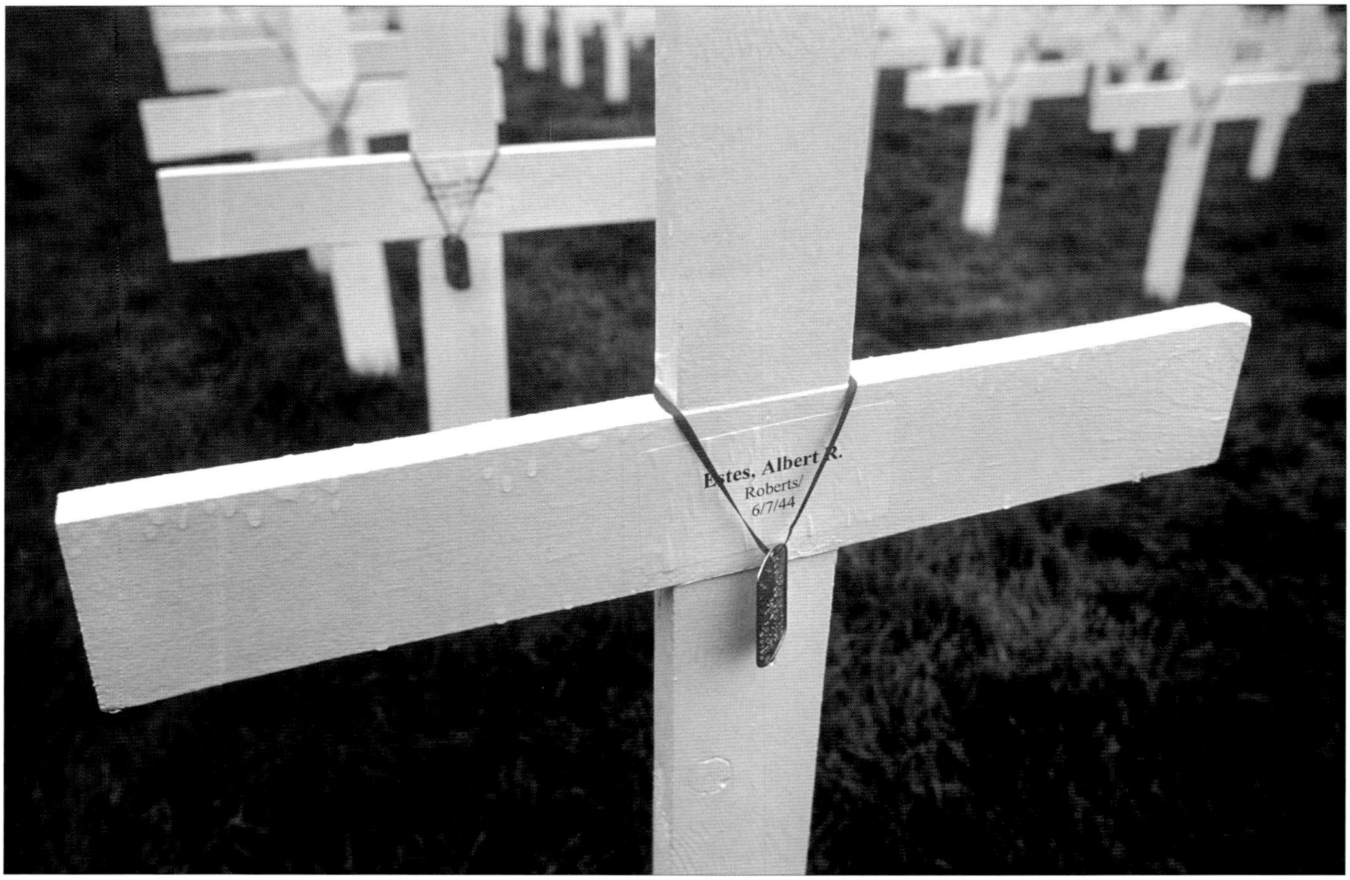

Above: Rows of rain-drenched crosses grace a hill north of the Capitol building in Pierre as part of the dedication ceremonies for the South Dakota World War II Memorial.

Right: A veteran watches the WWII Memorial Parade from under a huge American flag. The Capitol building can be seen across the street.

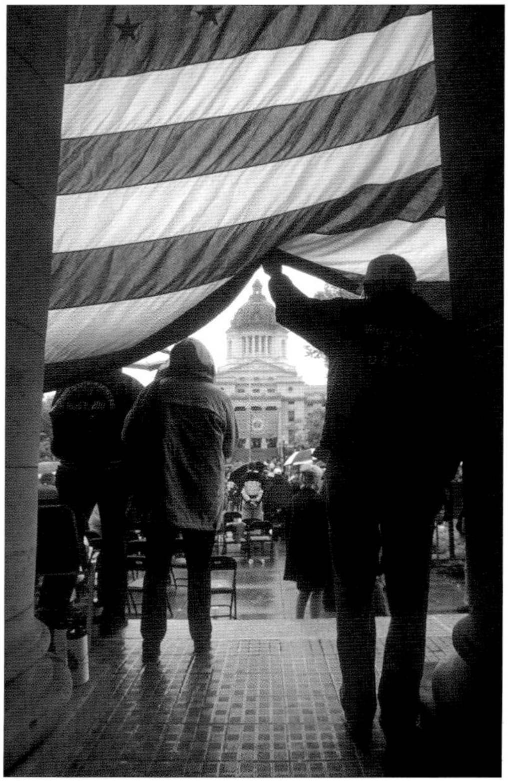

death were arranged in orderly rows north of the Capitol building. Families and friends of the deceased were allowed to take the crosses home with them after the dedication.

It was a very poignant scene that rainy afternoon. Hundreds of veterans walked through the rows with tears welling up in their eyes, while Hansen and several volunteers assisted people in locating individual crosses. The entire display was the most moving thing I saw that day. Many of the vets interviewed for *Blue Stars* were there, and they all said positive things about the ceremonies and the respect shown to them by Governor Janklow and the other dignitaries involved.

That day came 56 years after the war ended. Why did it take so long?

☆

A few times during my search for potential candidates for this book, I was presented with the question: Why only World War II? Why not also create a book about Korean or Vietnam veterans? While that could be a possibility down the road, it is immediately necessary to document the World War II generation, if one hopes to do it at all.

More importantly, these people fought in a war that would have resulted in far-reaching consequences were it lost. The effort of the entire nation was required to defeat the Axis powers, and the resulting success of this war brought a prosperity that was desperately needed after the Great Depression. These men and women came back to build the society we enjoy today.

They returned to South Dakota and built homes and businesses, took their children to church and kept patriotism close at heart. It is my belief that had World War II not happened at all, the mass exodus we've seen from our small towns and rural areas would have occurred in the 1940s, not the 1980s and 1990s. The optimism and hardiness of the WWII generation infused rural South Dakota with an extra 50 years of life. Though they are elderly now, they once carried the weight of our freedom on their strong, youthful shoulders.

So when you're about to curse an old man at the wheel of a slow-moving cattle truck as you follow it down one of South Dakota's dusty gravel roads, think again. It might be Oliver Carlson, a soldier who landed at Utah beach and fought his way across Europe for you.

When you find yourself impatiently waiting for an elderly woman towing an oxygen tank to exit the hospital elevator, don't rush past her. It could be Edna Basler, a nurse who patched up Marines on a hostile South Pacific island, offering solace and support to young men she knew may not see another day.

Don't roll your eyes at the end of your airline flight when the white-haired man in the seat next to you is taking his time getting started down the aisle. It might be Morris Magnuson, a P-47 fighter pilot who once jumped from his doomed plane 100 miles into enemy territory. And you thought missing your next flight connection was a problem.

When you think about staying home from the polls on election day, imagine yourself magically transported to a foxhole on the front line surrounding Bastogne during the Battle of the Bulge. It's December of 1944, and there is a grizzled American soldier next to you. He is hungry. His uniform cannot keep out the sub-zero temperatures. German troops threaten to appear from the forest at any minute, and the soldier has been holding the line like this for several days. Now imagine telling *him* that you aren't planning to vote today because it's raining outside, or because you're just too busy, or because you don't think your vote matters much anymore.

Could you look him in the eyes and tell him that?

Freedom has never been free, and it never will be. Most of us now living in South Dakota likely will never have to make a sacrifice for freedom during our lifetime. But we should never forget we are living among those who did.

☆ ☆ ☆

Author's Note

My goal in creating *Blue Stars* is to pay due respect not only to the people profiled here but also to the thousands of other veterans they represent. As you read this book, keep this fact in mind: For each of the 44 World War II veterans profiled in *Blue Stars* there are approximately 1,500 others from South Dakota who served.

As of 2004, somewhere between 12,000 and 15,000 World War II veterans are still living in South Dakota, about 20 percent of the number who served during the war. Knowing we probably lose close to 1,000 each year is alarming, considering the fact that each of them have stories to tell and knowledge to share.

I did not seek to represent every aspect of the war, nor each and every type of duty. That would be impossible. Instead, I tried to locate people who could be your next-door neighbor (and very well may be). These are people who you might see in the grocery store or at your church. They are the type of people that you've known your entire life, but you probably never knew they served our country during wartime.

The stories you read and listen to here all have been recorded on digital audio tape and transcribed into the text that accompanies each veteran's photograph. At the outset of this project, I decided to record the interviews to accurately represent each person's style of conversation and so I would not miss any details I might need later. At that time, I realized that since I would be recording the interviews, I could offer some of the stories on an accompanying CD. But because editing audio and narrating it properly are skills I do not currently possess, I asked South Dakota Public Radio's Curt Nickisch to help with those duties.

We decided that instead of trying to condense all 44 interviews for the CD, we would instead concentrate on 10 personal accounts which offered a wide variety of experiences. This is not intended to temper the great value of the other 34 veterans or the impact of their stories. We simply thought that elaborating on 10 stories would paint a more complete picture than short snippets of all 44 would. I think you'll enjoy what you hear.

I was surprised to find as many World War II veterans as I did. From the time I started clipping newspaper stories and conducting informal research in the late 1990s until just a couple of weeks before press time I had absorbed the stories of more than 500 men and women. I solicited every newspaper in the state as well as each county and tribal veterans service officer for names. I searched newspaper databases at the library, ran Internet searches and made dozens of phone calls to track down my leads.

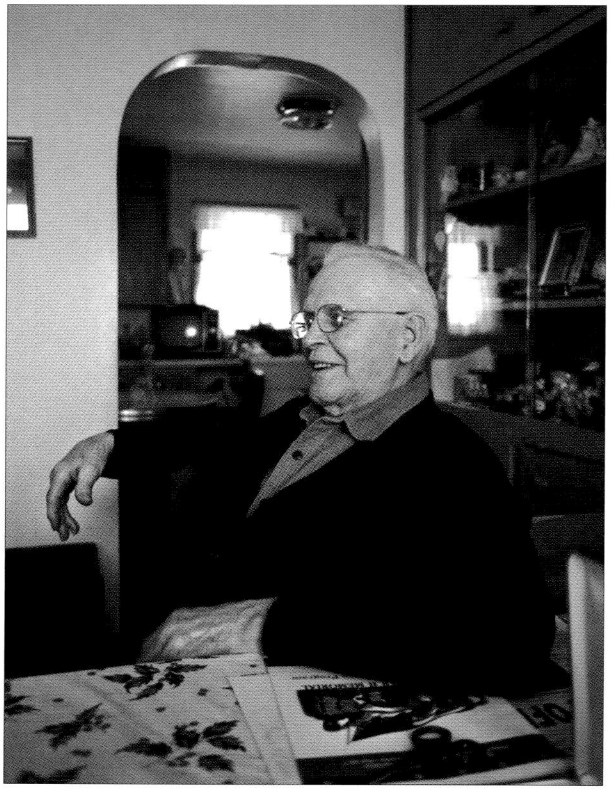

At the dining room table of his Bristol home, Elmer Olson smiles as he recalls a WWII friendship. Most of the 44 interviews for Blue Stars *were conducted in settings like this.*

I compiled a list that categorized veterans by their branch of service, place of residence, and short details about where and how they served. I narrowed my list to include only veterans who were South Dakotans when they left for the war and who eventually returned back to South Dakota to live. I also selected veterans who served overseas to emphasize their participation in a truly global war. This is not to diminish the importance of the thousands of South Dakota veterans who served stateside, or the "home front heroes" who stayed to work on the farms, run the stores and staff the factories while their peers went to war.

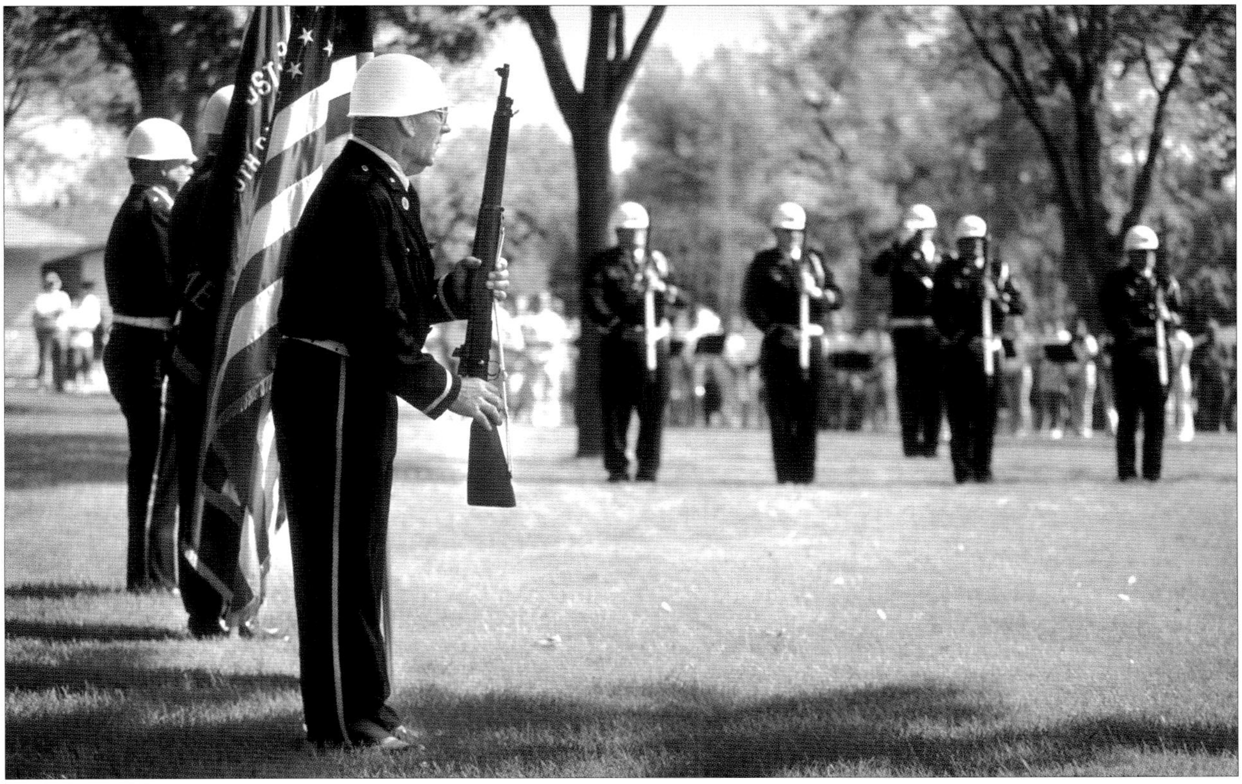

WWII veteran Merlin Schmidt participates in the 2003 Dell Rapids Memorial Day program.

Arranging my interviews in a geographical manner, I traveled to separate regions of the state for two or three days at a time, conducting two interviews from that area each day. Most interviews required about three hours to record the conversation, select and scan vintage photos, and photograph each veteran for his or her portrait.

Back in my office, I edited the audio tape — deleting my voice, coughs, stray words and long pauses — and made a copy to send to each veteran. Then came the matter of selecting the right parts from each interview to explain where the veteran served, how he or she got there, and what events transpired as the war wore on. Interviews have been condensed and arranged for clarity and space limitations, and some of the veterans' words have been supplemented with words I chose to better explain the situation. Words I have added are indicated by italics contained within parentheses.

The most difficult part about transcribing the tapes was that each veteran talked for an hour, maybe two. However, since it took them only 10 or 15 minutes to speak what you read on a particular page, a number of additional details and stories were cut for space. In many cases, I centered on one major story or event. In others, I followed their entire journey through the war.

There were several medals distributed among the *Blue Stars* veterans, but I chose not to focus on these details unless their particular story called for it. Also, the mention of the rank they achieved was avoided in most cases. Most veterans did things that were commendable. Some won medals for it, and some didn't. Some were in a position to ascend the chain of command, and some were limited by factors out of their control.

In all cases, it was my intention to illustrate the many different ways our men and women served during the war — not only the veterans in *Blue Stars*, but also the thousands of others. Some of them didn't see any combat, but their duty helped the others who did.

Many made incredible sacrifices of themselves, and some nearly made the ultimate sacrifice. All of them were — and are — important.

☆ ☆ ☆

JIM PEACOCK ☆ *Sioux Falls*

Moored with six other battleships at Pearl Harbor, the U.S.S. Maryland *was serving peacetime duty. As dawn broke one sunny Sunday morning, Peacock was preparing for Mass aboard the* Maryland. *The date was December 7, 1941.*

The *Oklahoma* was tied alongside us; we were in battleship row. They were setting up for Catholic services. It would be about 8 o'clock for the services.

It was probably 20 minutes to 8 or so. I went up forward where I used to be, to see some of the guys — one deck down, and up in the forward part of the ship.

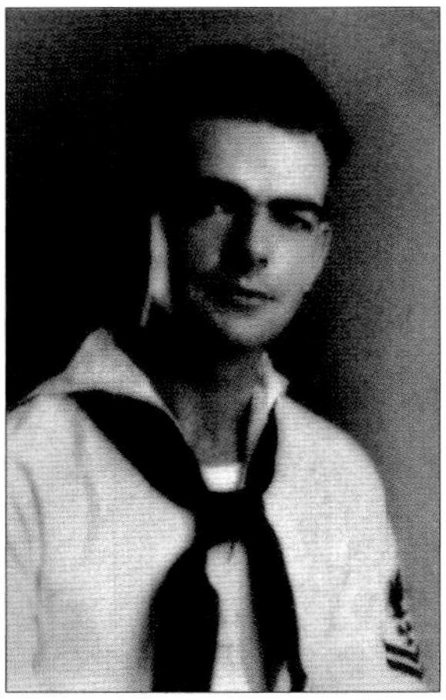

I could hear some awful explosions and could hear the planes like they were flying in on maneuvers and dropping bombs or something. It usually would be just dummy *(bombs)*, but they wouldn't be dropping them on that little airfield — that was Ford Island, right next to us. So I looked out, and here were these planes and they were dropping bombs. Right at that time they blew "Fire and Rescue." That meant that there was something going on — maybe explosions — and they would have to send *(sailors)* over to fight fires on the other ships.

It was just half a minute or so and they blew again. They said, "Battle stations! This is no drill!" and they were Jap planes. We saw them flying by, and then as they would drop their bombs they would strafe the ships, fly back and swoop out.

Your mind just changed to get down to your battle station, and that's where I took off — to go down there. As I was running, the *Oklahoma* got hit with several torpedoes. When the ship started rolling after it got hit with those torpedoes, it lurched our ship when it broke those heavy lines. I got knocked down, and I picked myself up and headed to my battle station, which was the machine shop. It took a little while, but I got down there and there were people trying to get down, dogging hatches. No one knew just what was happening because you didn't get much communication, except to get to your battle stations and that it was no drill.

I was in the machine shop just a short time, and they said they needed engineers to go up and get the circulating liquid for the anti-aircraft guns. The recoil system was getting hot and they were sticking. So we headed up and had to undog our way. After we got most of them going, I think we got a raid that came in, and there were high-altitude bombers. I think they dropped a couple bombs where I had been up there and blew the decks open. At that time the ship lurched again and us guys got knocked down. When I picked myself up and looked over, I said, "You know, the *Oklahoma* is gone."

They said, "Peacock, this is no time to be kidding around!" And I said, "Just get over here and crawl up."

We crawled up and looked over, and it had turned over. You couldn't believe it. You knew what destruction really was. They just opened that ship up and it filled with water and capsized.

Of course, there were a lot of men inside. It wasn't long and we got word to go back and help put lines and men over to try and cut through and rescue them. They tried to cut into the ship and get some of those men. They got a few of them, but they couldn't get very many of them out. There were some that got out through larger portholes or got through some other way and swam up.

Then the water was full of heavy oil. At that time, the ships burned heavy oil. It was like molasses. It had to be steam heated so it could burn, but there was a lot of energy in it. When the ship was blown open, then all that oil came gushing out and then these guys would come up and have to come through this oil.

Then fires moved in, and it turned dark. They had guys with hoses trying to keep that away from the ship. They had guys in different areas trying to help guys that were swimming and get them pulled up if they were still alive.

Ships all over were burning, and some were scuttled; they filled them with water before they turned over.

You knew what fear was, but you were so busy that you did what you were doing. You just couldn't believe that thing could happen like that. Of course, there were a lot of them that were venting a lot of anger, but I never paid too much attention. I stayed busy for about three days and we never stopped for anything.

After about three days, you just had to lay down and get some rest. Gradually they got a lot of the fires out — the smoke was gone — and then they figured out ways

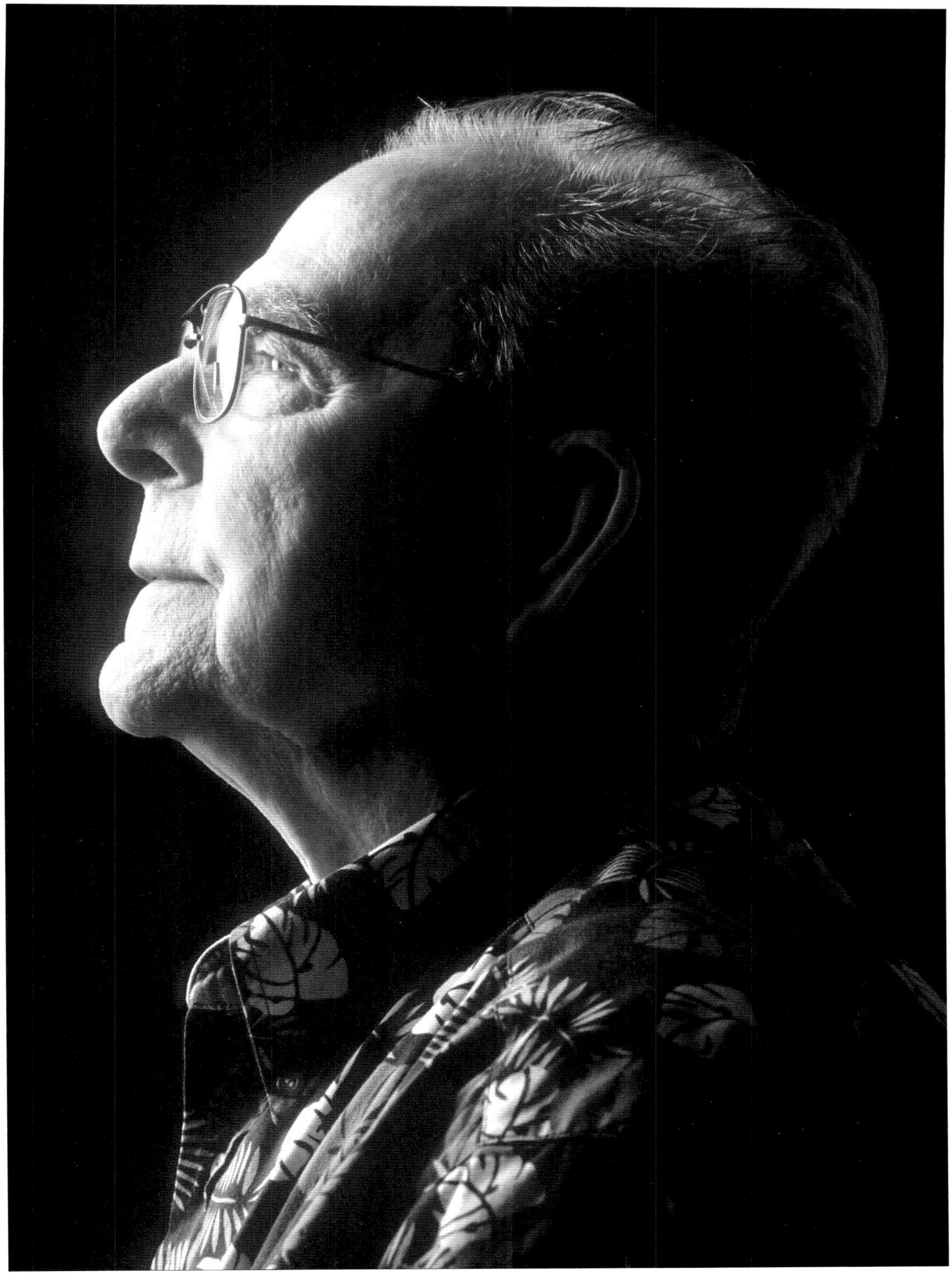

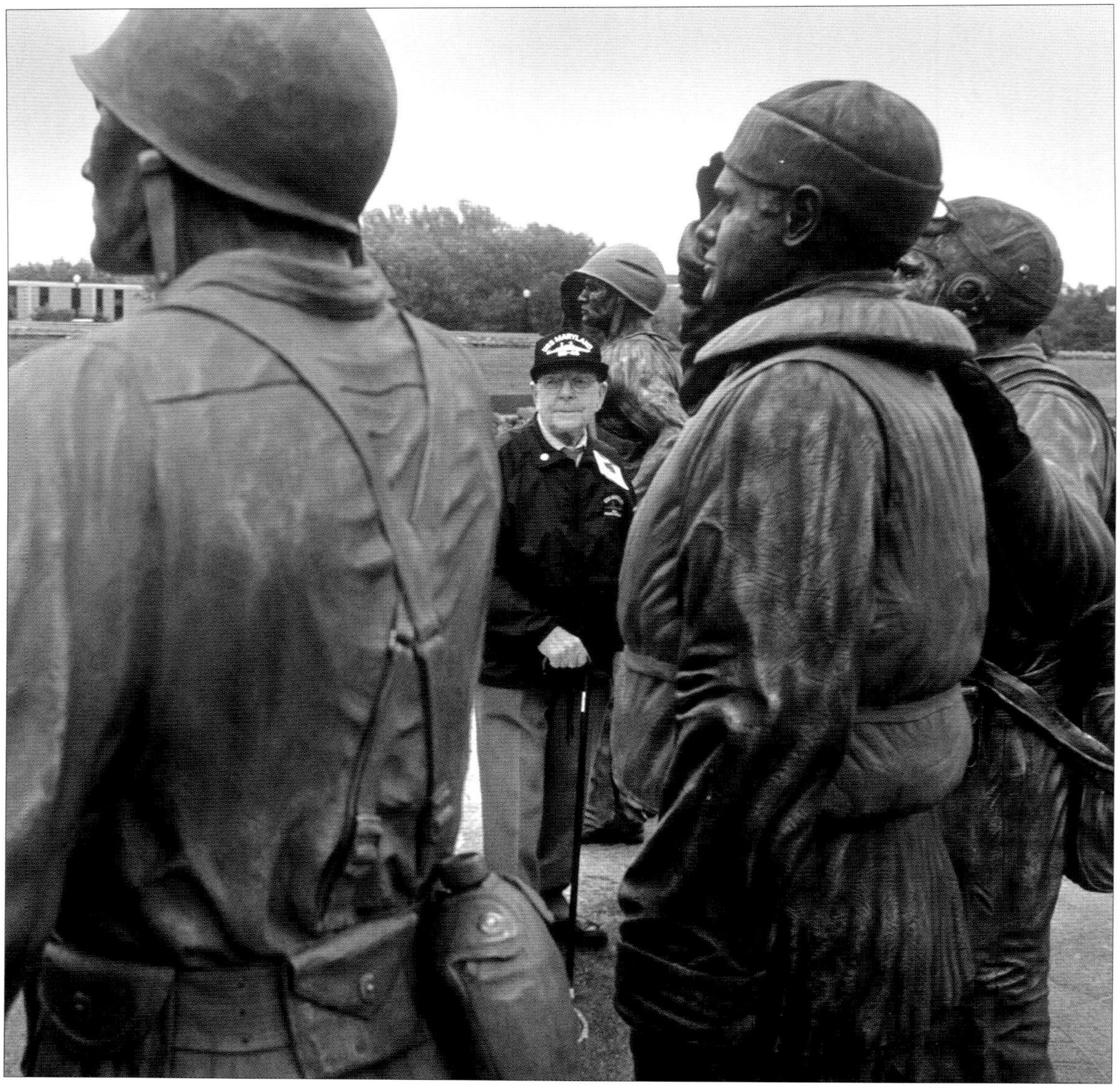

Jim Peacock tours the newly unveiled World War II memorial on the shore of Capitol Lake in Pierre on September 15, 2001.

to try to get the *Maryland* afloat. We had a hole below the water line on the port side. They built what they called a cofferdam around it, welded it underwater, then pumped it out and gradually was able to get the *Maryland* out.

In about three weeks, we were back to the states, into Bremerton, Washington. While we were there, Mary came up, and believe it or not, we got married on January the 31st in Seattle.

Peacock and the Maryland *spent the next two years serving in several battles, as backup in the battles of Coral Sea and Midway, and in an active role in the Tarawa invasion.*

We were back in San Francisco and we were getting some repairs. I was asked to take a transfer, and I was transferred off the *Maryland* at the end of 1943 in San Diego. They picked off different men from different departments of the ship, deck divisions and gunnery and stuff, for these new ships. All kinds of new ships — you didn't know what you were going to get.

Orders came out, and some of the guys came and said, "You're sure lucky — you're picked for the *Missouri*!" I didn't even know they were building a *Missouri*.

You could get lost on a ship like that. The *Maryland* was large, but not as large and complicated as the *Missouri*. It was a new dreadnought — it was the latest. Our main job was to learn where everything was and what your station required. I think we were in New York for several months. I think it was along toward the end of '44 when we were finally getting ready to leave. We got our orders and went to the battle of Iwo Jima.

It was the flagship for Admiral Halsey, and his flag room had air conditioners — on the *Missouri*, you had more modern stuff. You had air conditioning for the magazines, sick bay, plotting rooms and radar rooms. Then they put these portable units on for Halsey, and I used to take care of them. You didn't get up by Halsey in that flag room without special buttons and Marines on each side of you! Everybody would be standing at attention, and he'd say *(to me)*, "You do your work and don't pay attention to me. I'll do mine." He talked to me, and took my wrenches and ratchet a few times.

Both Okinawa and Iwo Jima were real tough battles, and there you started getting kamikazes. The *Missouri* took one on the starboard side, midships, on the upper deck. They had a burial *(at sea)* for that Jap pilot.

We hit the mainland in between Iwo Jima and Okinawa. We went 15 miles off of Tokyo. At midnight we left the fleet with the *Missouri* and a few other heavy ships. We went off 15 miles from Tokyo at midnight and bombarded their factories. They were taking a terrible beating and they wouldn't give up.

We were coming out of there after one of those midnight raids, and they started putting word over that an atomic bomb had been dropped. No one knew what an atomic bomb was. It wasn't over a day or so later, at noon, we pulled in up north in one of the Jap harbors. We shot the whole harbor up. We come out of there and we were heading back, and they dropped the second atomic bomb.

On September 2, 1945, a peace treaty was signed aboard the Missouri *in Tokyo Bay, officially ending World War II.*

At that time, I was pretty well in charge of the refrigerator department. I was down below decks, but the speakers all over the ship were telling every time a boat would come up and a dignitary would board.

We didn't think — with the way they fought to the last man — that they'd ever surrender like this, but they did. You didn't take for granted you were going to win it if you had seen what happened out at Pearl.

After it was signed, it wasn't very long and we were out at sea, headed toward Pearl. We were supposed to go to Frisco, but then we got orders because of Navy Day — the president wanted the *Missouri* and some of those major ships to be in the Hudson River in New York, and he wanted to come aboard.

He was reviewing the troops. A lot of it was just walking and looking. I can remember he was kind of a short guy. I was standing in front, and Truman came down the decks; we were on the aft deck. He came up and took my tie and straightened it out. He said, "Good lookin' soldier!" He talked to me a little bit — I forgot just what he said — and he went on.

The *U.S.S. Missouri* is now moored at Pearl Harbor right close to where the *U.S.S. Maryland* was berthed December the 7th, 1941.

The starting and the stop. ☆

Working for the Corps of Engineers upon his return to South Dakota, Peacock helped build Ft. Randall Dam at Pickstown.

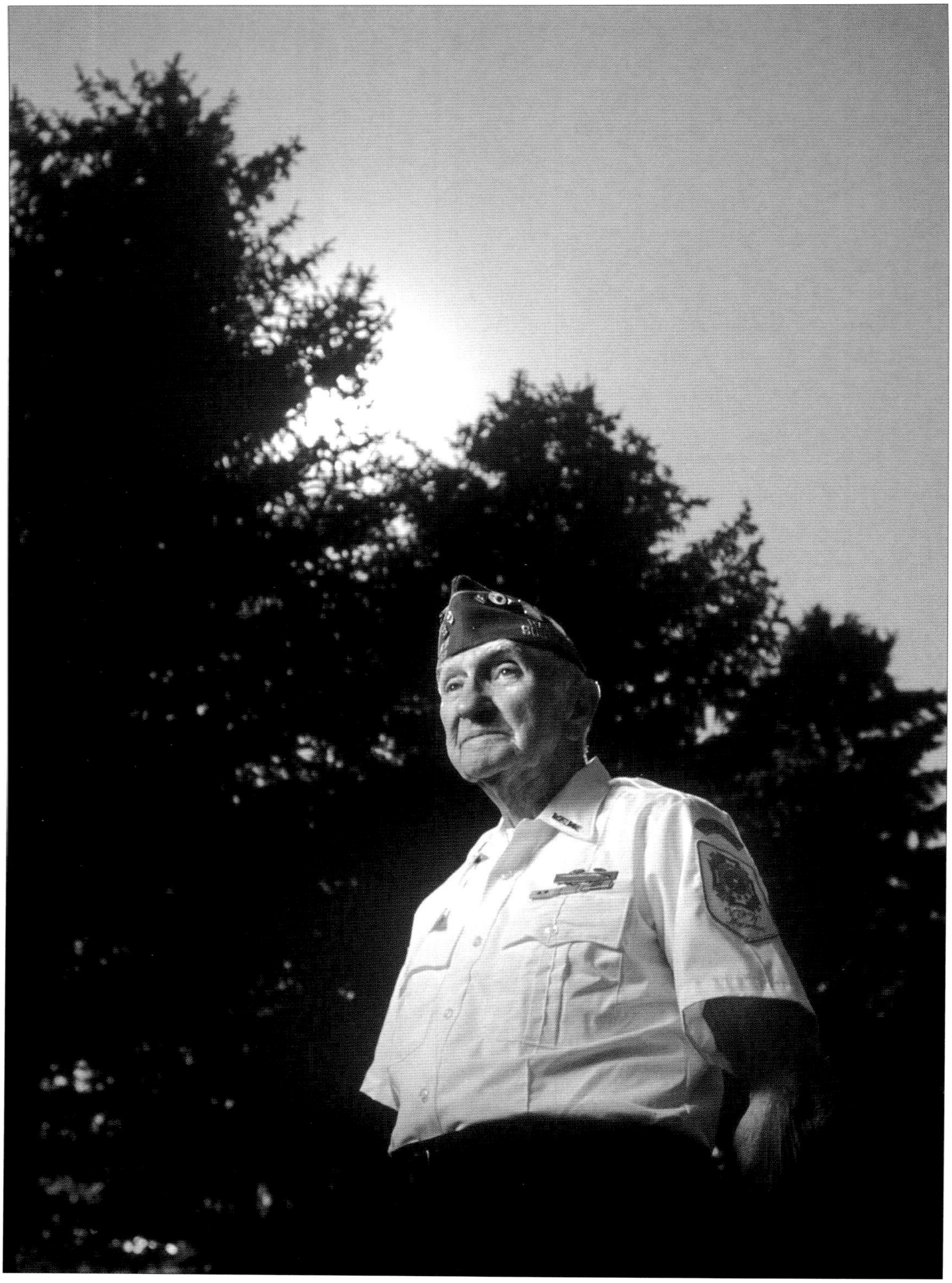

JACK BROOKENS ☆ *Rapid City*

Like most towns in Depression-era South Dakota, Kennebec was hit hard. Jack Brookens left there in 1941 to serve a one-year Army stint. He was training in Fort Ord, California, when news of Pearl Harbor struck fear into the hearts of West Coast residents and soldiers.

I had just gotten to Fort Ord — I had only been there about a week and Pearl Harbor happened. That night, they took us out of camp and went up in the hills and spent the night out of sight of the camp. We didn't know whether the Japanese were going to bomb our camp or not. That morning we went back down and loaded all our stuff up and went to San Francisco.

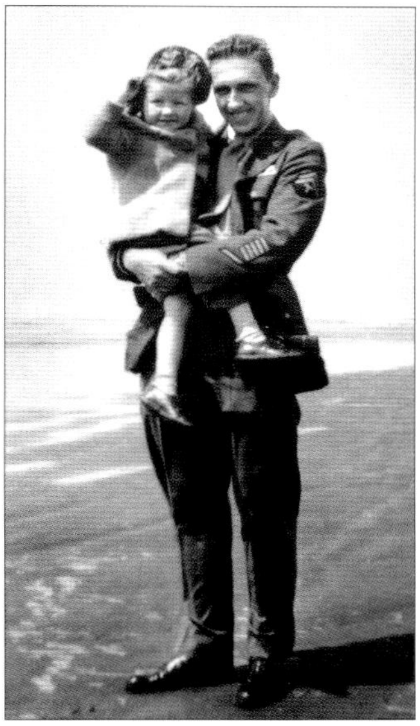

I was in a machine gun outfit, and they had us stationed along the coast there to protect against any invasion by sea. And then we had guard duty on the golf course, protecting against paratroopers landing.

We spent the winter there in California. That next spring, the 164th Infantry, which is North Dakota National Guard, were ready to go overseas. They were there in San Francisco, on board ship, and they were short a machine gun crew. I and my crew got volunteered to join them. How we got volunteered, I don't know. We landed in Melbourne, Australia, and were headed for New Caledonia.

It was all kind of fascinating, because it was all strange to me. I'd never been on the ocean before, or aboard a big old luxury liner like that. Of course, a lot of the luxury was gone out of it. For a little old country boy, why, it was a different experience.

We landed on Guadalcanal on October 13th (*1942*). We'd form a chain line through the water there, unload cargo and rations and ammunition, and pass it hand to hand until they got it up on the beach and stacked it up on piles. A couple of times during the day a Jap bomber would come over and we'd head for the foxholes or try to get behind a tree or something on the beach. They didn't do much, just scared us a little. That was our first initiation to bombing.

They marched us inland. We didn't know where we were going. We got back into the jungle, to a coconut grove, and they finally told us that's where we're going to stop for the night. We had just bedded down, and all hell broke loose. The Jap navy had pulled into the harbor there, and they started shelling Henderson Field, and they had bivouacked us just at the edge of the airport. These shells were whistling over our heads and exploding, and we were trying to hide behind our packs and coconut trees. That was our first initiation to shellfire.

The main duty there was to protect Henderson Field. The Japs had the rest of the island, and we had the airport. Joe Foss was there at the time. He became an ace there. They used to have dogfights right over the island there every day.

We were assigned to a rifle company, and we went on the offensive there. Things were going along pretty good. We were going through the jungle, and we got up on top of a ridge. It was kind of bare — there was nothing but grass on it — and down below it was the jungle. Just as our line came up on top of this ridge, we got fired upon from down below. There was a hole there; I don't know whether it was a foxhole or a shell crater, but it was about 2 feet deep. I piled into that along with a couple of my buddies and our machine gun, and we were at a standstill then. We were sitting ducks. We sat there for 18 days on that line. Never had our clothes off.

I had a close call just after we got into that shell hole. It wasn't very deep, so I decided I was going to dig it deeper. I took my little entrenching shovel, and I was sitting in the bottom of the hole, throwing the dirt out.

All of a sudden, there was a zing, and a bullet hit in the dirt right in front of me. If he'd aimed a just a little bit higher, he'd have hit me right in the head.

One of the guys in my crew dug that bullet out of the dirt. I gave that bullet to my grandson. That was a close call I had. ☆

Brookens serves in the Rapid City Veterans of Foreign Wars funeral color guard. He has provided nearly 2,500 hours of volunteer service in this capacity.

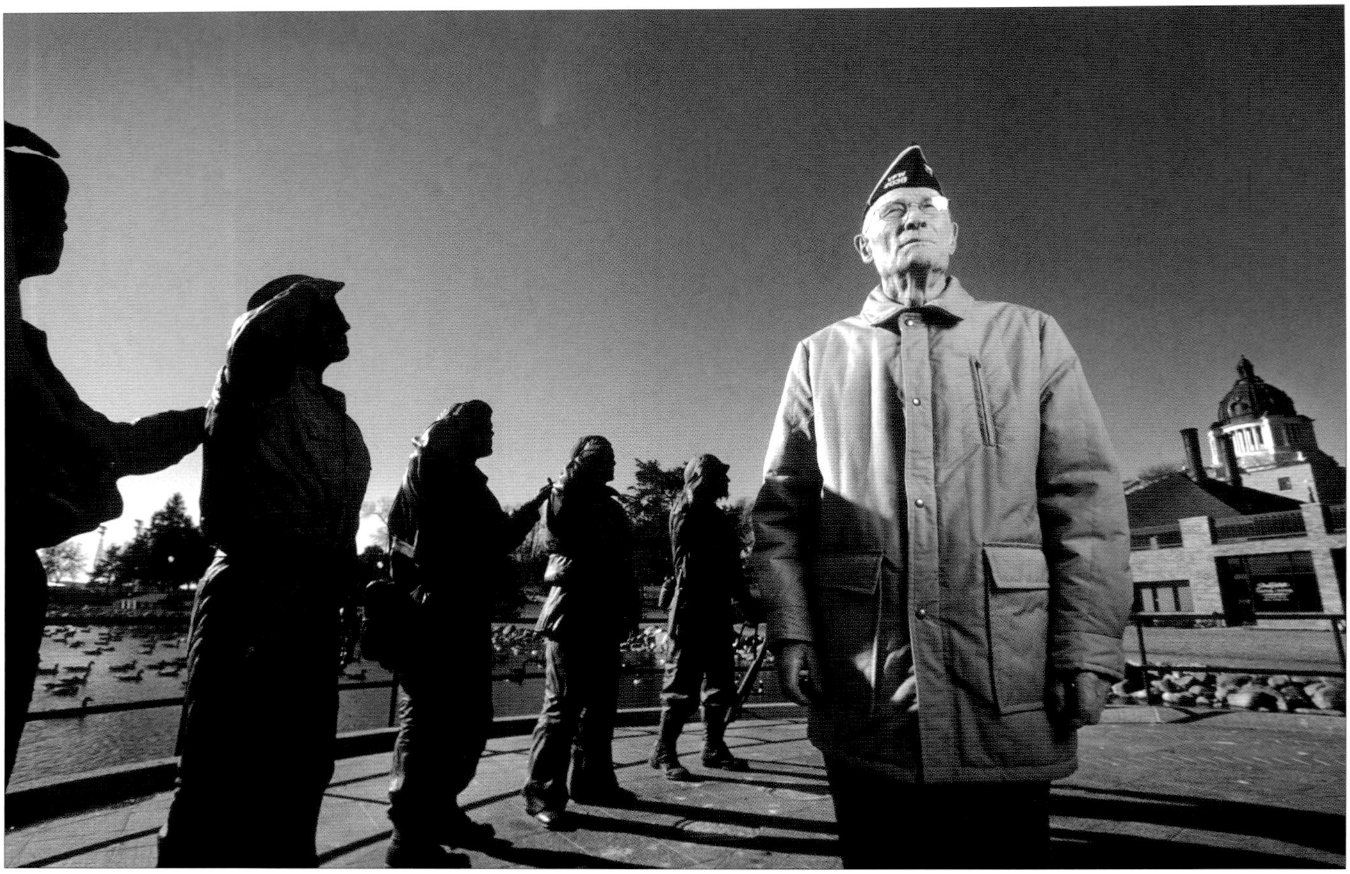

Arnie Gibson ☆ *Pierre*

After his family's crops dried up in the summer of 1940, Gibson entered the Army. He was among the first U.S. troops to invade North Africa in late 1942, and went on to participate in several landings with the 3rd Infantry Division in Europe.

I was in the plain infantry — a rifle company.

It's just like everyday life. You've got a job to do; you do it. But you sleep outside. You wear the same clothes maybe three or four weeks at a time.

If you get a chance where you can get to a creek or something, you can take a bath. If you're in combat, you don't get back and get a rest. You'll be up there maybe for a week, a couple weeks or maybe a month at a time. It all depends on the situation.

You function automatically. You don't think; you just do it. That's just the way it is on the front. If you're going to hit the ground, you're on the ground and in position to defend yourself. You just try to keep your cool.

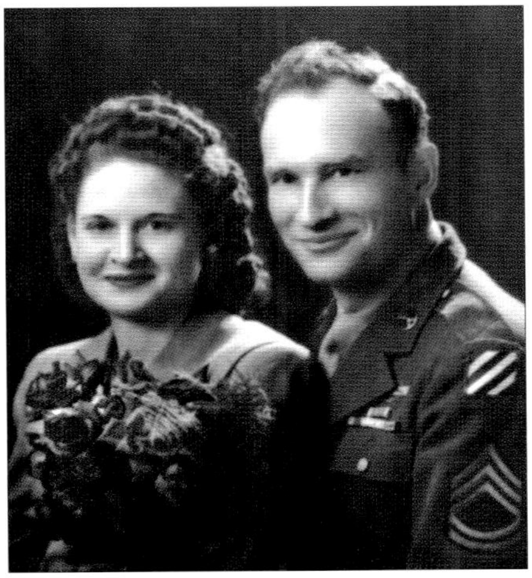

Some guys, until they get seasoned, go wacky. I had a sniper I had to send back to the rear; his eyes were so glazy that you could see he was cracking up. I just told him to go back *(to the rear)*. He was walking just like he was in a trance.

We had one guy who went berserk and ran right into the enemy. He put his rifle at short guard *(as if to thrust it forward)*, swept the fire and just kept loading it to them. They just riddled him full of bullets.

You trained yourself to forget what happened today and think about tomorrow. Otherwise, I think you'd go plumb wacky because of the stress.

There were different characteristics in people that came from different parts of the country. Some of them were efficient, and some of them weren't. And some of them were nuttier than a fruitcake.

(Midwestern soldiers) were real conscientious and real trustworthy. You could send them out on patrols and stuff like that, and they didn't go out there and sit down in the bush someplace and then come back and say they were out there.

That's how my brother got killed. He was in a different regiment. They went out on this patrol on Anzio, and I guess they came around the corner of a building and the Germans opened up on them with machine guns.

He was a damn good soldier. He really did his job. I knew the guys that told me *(he was killed)* — he'd been with them all the time.

I didn't tell anybody. I didn't talk about it.

I got wounded twice. Going up to Montelimar, France, we were put into position around the crest of a hill. Down in the valley, the German tanks were on the other side of a gulch. They couldn't get across because it was 8 feet deep or better. They were really well armed — they put up a hell of a good fight, I tell you. You weren't up against a bunch of kids. They had good equipment and they knew how to use it.

My lieutenant was up the hill about 30 yards and hollered my name and wanted to know where I was at. I hollered, "Down here, down here!" This ground had been burned off and it had brush on it about 18 inches high. We had slit trenches — you couldn't get them dug down because of the tree roots — it was about 6 inches deep. He said, "Stand up where I can see you." I rolled up on my left side and waved. The tanks have those big sights; they can see that. They were only about 800 yards away from us.

While I'm waving my hand, a German 88mm hit this tree. The concussion blew the helmet off of my head, and it went down the hill. I got hit in the mouth, through the bridge of my nose. I got shrapnel in my back. A piece hit me in the arm. I was lucky I didn't get hit hard.

I don't remember how it felt; that's the truth about it. It just goes along with the day. You just fought from the beginning until it was over. ☆

Gibson returned to Pierre and worked as a carpenter. He and his wife, Margaret, were married on March 26, 1945.

Harold Thune ☆ *Murdo*

Performing one of the most difficult and romanticized jobs in the Navy, Thune flew sorties from the aircraft carrier Intrepid, *striking South Pacific enemy installations and dogfighting with Japanese Zeroes.*

I was in school at the University of Minnesota when the war broke out. I wanted to be a Navy pilot and fly off carriers, so I went down and enlisted. They deferred me until June so I could graduate.

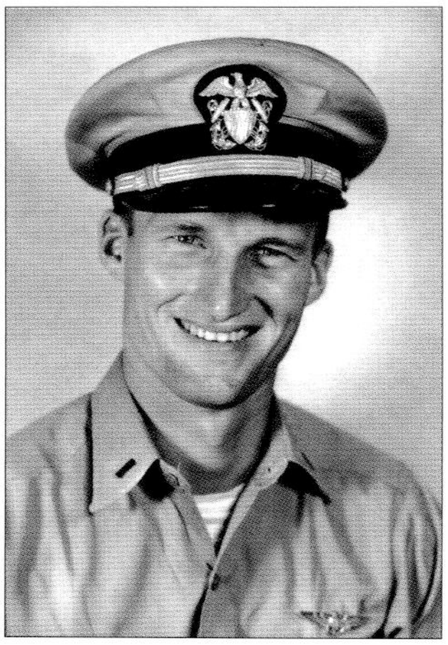

By the time I had graduated from flight training, the corner had turned a little bit out in the Pacific. We were in the beginning stages of island-hopping up *(toward Japan)*.

I enjoyed the Pacific Ocean. When you get out offshore, there is a blue that you can't imagine. The deepest blue. And then at night, you go up *(on deck)* and there's phosphorescence in the water *(green light emitted from disturbed microscopic algae)*, so there's a sparkle to it. You used to go up and just enjoy watching that. And there were the flying fish. So for a kid from the middle of South Dakota to see that water, the expanse of it, the flying fish and the sparkle and all that — it was really exciting.

Our first duty was the Palau Islands, which is just off the Philippines. We covered a Marine landing there.

I have the highest respect for the Marines. If I was in a fight anyplace, I'd be glad to have the Marines there. What a great outfit.

Then we went into Mindoro, which is a big island on the south part of the Philippines. Then we just worked all the way up to the lower Japanese islands.

The fighter squadron had 54 pilots in their full complement, and the dive bombers were about 36 and the torpedo bombers were about 36.

On an operation — if it were to go the way it was designed — the fighters would take off first, then the dive bombers and then the torpedo bombers. The fighters would fly cover over them. The F6 that I flew was a marvelous airplane. The F6 could carry the bombs just as easily as the dive bomber, and it was a little faster.

The purpose of the fighters was to escort the bombers in and to stay there and nullify or knock out any air opposition. After the bombers had made their runs, you'd join up and escort them back. But it wasn't too often that things went according to plan. There was always something that threw things off.

If you were going in to soften things up, and you were going to an airport or aerodrome, they would have maps on those. You're going in to strafe, to try and knock out planes on the ground, to blow up the hangars if you could and hit a fuel dump or something.

When you went in on those, you weren't up against somebody that was after you, so when you got into the dogfights, that's when it became more intense. Then it was a matter of maneuvering, and it depended a lot on who had the superiority when you met. You always wanted to have altitude superiority if you could — because you could always sell that altitude for speed, make your run, and then you could sell that speed back for altitude again.

You train until the thing becomes reflex. If you have altitude advantage, you can dictate a little bit; you aren't as vulnerable. But if you've got someone with an altitude advantage against you, then the maneuvering becomes a lot more crucial to what you're going to try and do to counteract it.

Although you had tactics that you worked with as a squadron, the minute the dogfight started, everything went out the window. So it kind of came down to man-to-man. The section leader and the wingman tried to stay tight together, because that way you always had somebody to be with and to work with. But in the dogfights that kind of went away too.

The Jap Zero was a superior airplane in the earlier part of the war to the planes we were flying out there — the F4F — but when we came out with the F6, which I flew basically most of the time, it was a much better plane. The Zero could still out-turn you, but you had probably a little bit more speed than they had.

You don't get yourself in a position where the guy can out-turn you. You make your run, get out. What the Japs liked to do was, if you're coming in on them, is to do a loop. But they could turn a tighter one than you could, so they ended up on your tail.

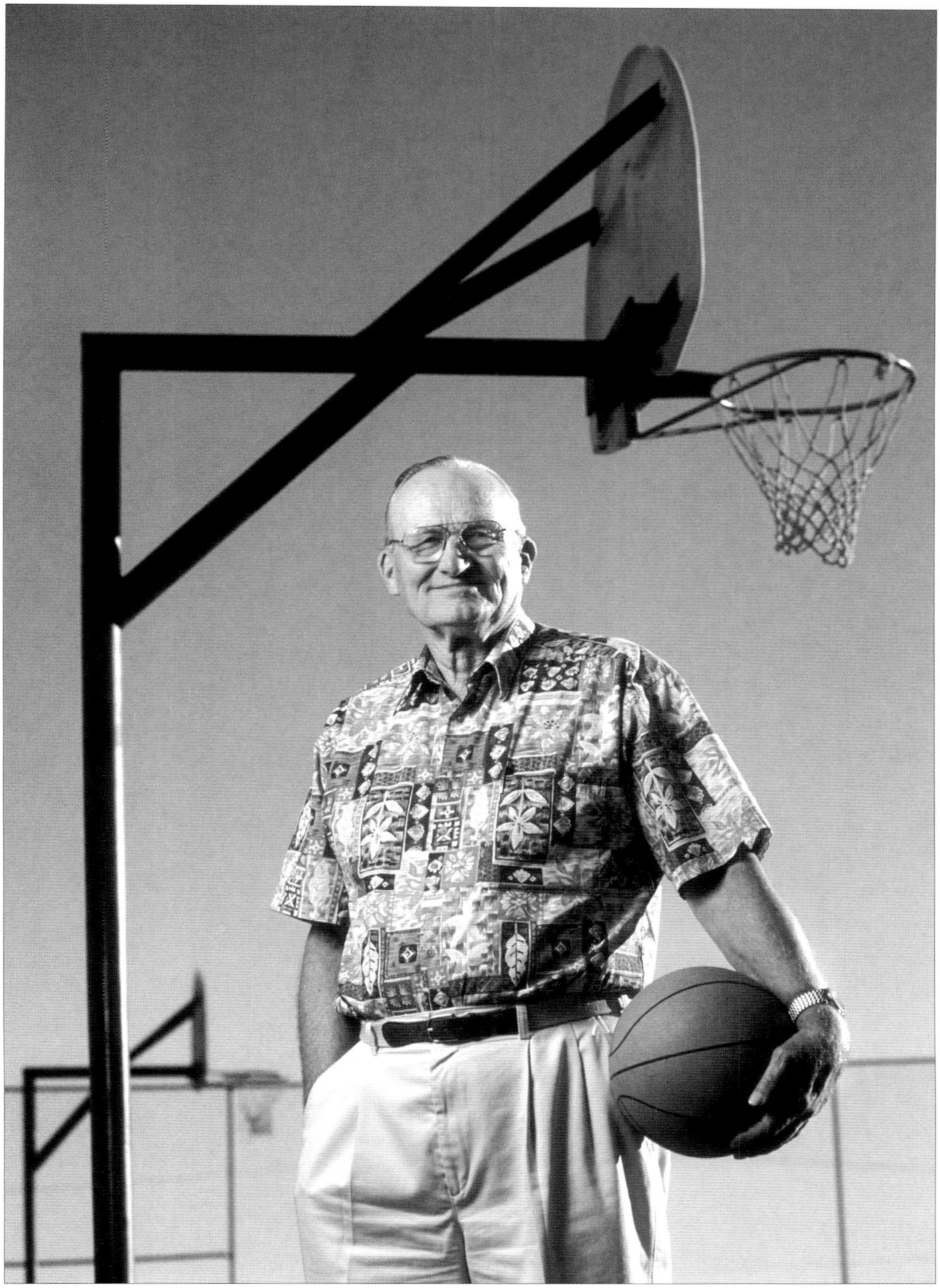

I got into a situation like that where I was right on the tail of *(a Zero)*, and he starts into this loop. Immediately I thought, "If he gets around, he's going to be on my tail." I got ahead of him on it and was able to get him that way. That was just an automatic response to training and knowing what that other airplane could do. Those things had to become a part of you, about like when a pheasant gets up here *(and you shoot it without thinking)*.

I had four shot down. Five, you were an ace — I just missed being an ace. Our squadron, in the time that we were out, shot down 177 planes. We had quite a good record as far as the squadron is concerned.

I shot down one plane, and the pilot bailed out right smack in front of me. Do I take him, or don't I? We had talked about that in the ready room. I think a lot of guys figured it's better not to. Because if they've got some dead ones coming down, then any of ours that come down alive are really going to get it.

And so I backed off. It wasn't quite like shooting another person, but it really wasn't any different. Just from a standpoint of decency, and the way I was raised, you wouldn't do something like that. You'd have to have a little different mindset *(to shoot a helpless pilot)*.

We had guys from every state, although we had three from South Dakota: Robert Gowling from Mitchell, Cecil Harris from Cresbard, and myself. Cece was on his second tour of duty. He had been down at Guadalcanal and had shot down a couple planes. He was the only experienced combat guy. Harris was not that senior, but the skipper realized this guy had some knowledge that we didn't have. So he put him in as flight officer for training the squadron. The tactics that we used were far different than what the book said. It was good that we had Cece.

What makes a Tiger Woods? What makes a Michael Jordan? Nobody knows; it's God-given. Harris was that way with an airplane. He could do more stuff in an airplane than any man I ever saw. He wasn't flashy about it; he was just good. I was glad he was on our side! There was no matter of defense with Harris — it was offense. And he took it to 'em. He wasn't arrogant; he wasn't boastful or anything. That's one reason probably why only a half a dozen people in South Dakota even knew him. *(Harris ended the war with 24 confirmed kills, just two behind Medal of Honor recipient Joe Foss.)*

There was never any bragging, but there was a lot of camaraderie. We had an excellent basketball team on the ship. At first we played on the elevator *(platform used for lifting planes to the top deck)*, but that was kind of small, so some of the guys down in the hangar deck rigged up some baskets. So if we cleared that off, we had a fair-sized court. It was almost bloody, but we had great respect for each other.

We had 54 pilots in our squadron, and we lost 12 of those guys. Some of them were good friends. But you couldn't dwell on that stuff; you had to keep moving.

In what was called the second battle of the Philippine Sea — when the Japs were coming in to try and knock out MacArthur's landing — we escorted the bombers in and we went up against the big battleships the Japanese had. They had two of them bigger than anything we had, and our bombers scored well on that.

At that time, my wingman and I were escorting torpedo bombers in. Our torpedo bombers peeled off and were going down on the deck to come in, and so we went with them. I have never seen anti-aircraft fire like that. I wondered how in the world you could possibly fly through that and not get hit. It was just like a circle, like a great big can, and it seemed like every spot in there was a place where an anti-aircraft shell had exploded. Every place, just those little puffs — they had *(smoke)* that was green and blue and black.

Our carrier was hit by kamikazes. I think there were about 75 or 80 men that were killed on that. They were both planes that hit it. With one of them, the bomb never released from the plane. He just flew her right into the ship. One bomb went through the flight deck before it exploded. It exploded when it hit the hangar deck, and it shot shrapnel to both ends of the ship — even through the room where we slept, clear up in the prow of the ship. Shrapnel had gone through the walls of it. The fires were so far along to being out of control, that they were afraid that the captain would have to abandon ship. It didn't knock the carrier out so she couldn't go, but it knocked it out for any use.

We had just taken off and we were going on a strike into the Philippines. We had headed west, and I never did see *(the attack)*. A couple of guys — I don't know whether they looked back or what — said that they saw

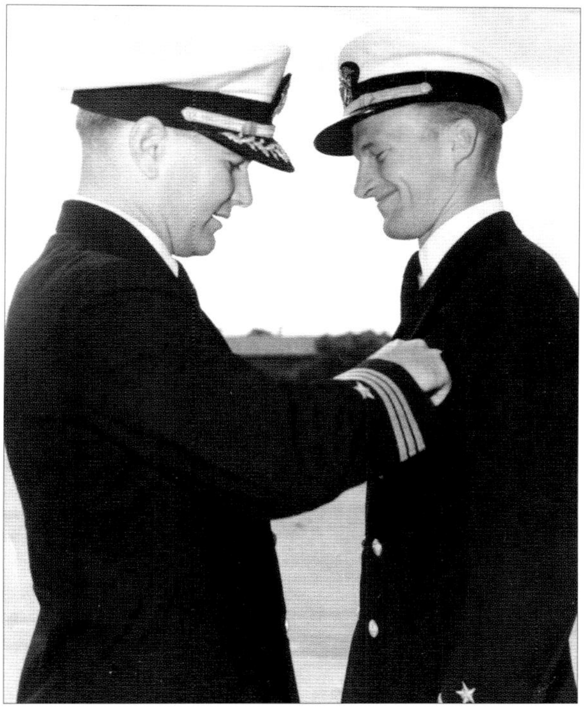

Harold Thune receives the Distinguished Flying Cross for downing four Zeroes in one day.

smoke coming up from the carrier. We went into some of the inner islands of the Philippines to bomb. We couldn't go back aboard, so they diverted us to Leyte. The Army there had just secured the beach area for the Army Air Force, so we went down and landed on that.

When the carrier was hit and we'd landed in the Philippines, we island-hopped back to Peleliu on the Palau Islands, and the next day we were going to hop to Ulithi *(where the carrier was anchored)*.

We stayed overnight and got up the next morning to take off. I was about third in line to take off, but when I went to take off, I blew a tire. In the back of my mind *(I thought)*, "I've got to get this thing up to Ulithi, because the ship is going home. If I can just get this off, I'll worry about landing it when I get up there." I just about had flying speed, and I was trying to horse the thing to get it into the air, and she just started dragging down. The flat tire then pulled me off the runway. Along the runway were some boulders and stuff. As I went off the edge of the runway, my belly tank hit one of those boulders and she was just in flames. So when she settled down over there, I started tearing off my seat belt and shoulder harness and bailed out of the plane.

I was standing there on the side of the runway, and the guys were taking off. They had to keep their eyes on the runway, so they couldn't see me standing there. When everybody took off, a couple of the guys said, "Hey, we've gotta go back and find out what happened to Thune!" The skipper said, "He didn't have a chance; that thing was in flames the minute he went off the runway. There's no use going back." So they wouldn't let anybody come back.

I was burned a little on my arms and around my face and neck and stuff. The Army sent a jeep over and picked me up and took me to sick bay.

They wanted to keep me in sick bay. I said, "I can't stick around here. Is there something going up to Ulithi? I've got to get up there!" I didn't want to stay in sick bay. I wasn't hurt that bad. It so happened there was an admiral flying in, and he was on his way up to Ulithi too. I got on and rode up with the admiral.

Because the ship had been hit and there wasn't anyplace for the squadron to stay, they had thrown up tents just off the landing strip at Ulithi. I walked over to the *(skipper's)* tent. I walked into the tent and he looked up at me. I don't know if you've ever heard the expression "his mouth dropped open" — well, his dropped open. He had sworn I was dead, and here I was, all bandaged up.

I had some stuff out on the carrier, and they had some launches running back and forth. So I went out and I got on, and when I got there, here was the enlisted men's basketball team practicing. I walked in, and you'd have thought I was their brother! They wanted to know, "How bad was I burned? How bad was it?" and all this. Although we fought on the floor, we had great respect for each other.

The time on the carrier — although it was war, and you can't say there was anything good about war — it was an experience to work in that situation. Today my carrier, the *Intrepid*, is sitting in New York Harbor *(serving as a museum)*. And sitting down on the hangar deck is an F6 with the wings folded and 24 Jap flags painted on it.

And above it : "Lieutenant Cecil Harris." ☆

Thune served as teacher, coach and athletic director at Murdo for over 20 years. He still lives across the street from the school.

Howard Lee ☆ *Volga*

Lee was teaching high school in the fall of 1941 and had no idea that his world was about to be ripped apart, both by impending war and family tragedy.

As the war started in December, I knew I was not going to be able to continue another year of teaching, so I stayed out. At this time I had already lost my first brother *(Leonard)*. He was killed in Myrtle Beach, South Carolina, in a training accident, as he was also a pilot.

He died about a week and a half before World War II started. He died on my mother's birthday. My mother was having a birthday party; that's when she got the news. Son number one.

As World War II started, I decided to go with the Navy. I started active duty on December 7, 1942, just a year after Pearl Harbor.

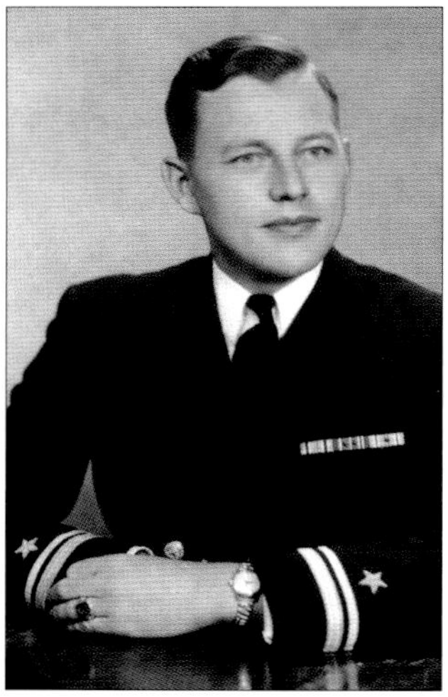

I went to midshipmen's school at Columbia University in New York, and they had a program they called the "90-day wonder" program. Anybody with a college degree — they needed officers in a big, big hurry. I became an ensign in jig time, and was assigned to the cruiser *Boise*.

We left New York after some training exercises and headed for the Mediterranean — North Africa. I was in communications, coding and decoding. That was a very interesting field to be in. From North Africa, we had a massive buildup there to go and take the island of Sicily just to the north. We had about 3,600 ships on that deal, plus all the troops that we were able to carry otherwise too. They had to do the landing. It didn't take too long to take the island of Sicily, and then we went on to Italy. When we were pretty well secured there and back in the Mediterranean, we got communication that we were to be reassigned to the South Pacific. This was 1943.

We came back to New York, and a lot of the mail had caught up to us. One of the first letters I opened was from my mother. The first sentence I read was, "We had the memorial service for Walt last Sunday." That's the way I got the word. The Red Cross message had never gotten to me. And with the war going the way it was, I didn't have a chance to go home and see my parents.

The first place we headed for was New Guinea. I knew that's where my brother had lost his life. New Guinea is about as wild as can be. The jungles were full of snakes and everything else that go along with it. Mosquitoes — great big mosquitoes — and so on. We made progress fighting the Japanese, but with the suicide pilots and so on, it was really a crazy, crazy deal. Sometimes the suicide pilots would fly in real low, so our radar would not pick them up. One time I could see the face of a pilot; he didn't go for us, he went for someone else in the harbor.

The only description of the temporary cemetery where he was located was there was a grove of trees and a stream and a couple other physical characteristics. *(A fellow soldier, also from Volga, had found Walter's grave first.)* And so I went on that basis and went ashore when I could. Between fighting the Japanese — either their ships or the planes — we were pretty busy.

The first trip was not successful. When we made our way back to the ship, we got to the harbor and there was another air raid warning. Lo and behold, our ship was pulling out of the harbor. My home 8,000 miles away from home was leaving, and I had no idea when I'd ever see it again. About two or three days later our ship came back, so it was home sweet home again.

I made another trip into the harbor later on, and I was hoping to find some arrangements. This time I didn't really have permission to pursue it like I'd done before. I chanced it without the actual authority to make that trip.

I got to the location and found the cemetery and I figured that this might be it. Row after row after row after row, it was just something to really see.

I ended one row and started another, and there was my brother — something I hoped I'd never find. I knew it had happened, and yet, you had to find it. ☆

Lee took advantage of a program that enabled a third son to come home and serve stateside if two brothers had been killed in action. He spent the last six months of his naval career in San Diego as a communications instructor, then returned home to Volga and began a career in banking.

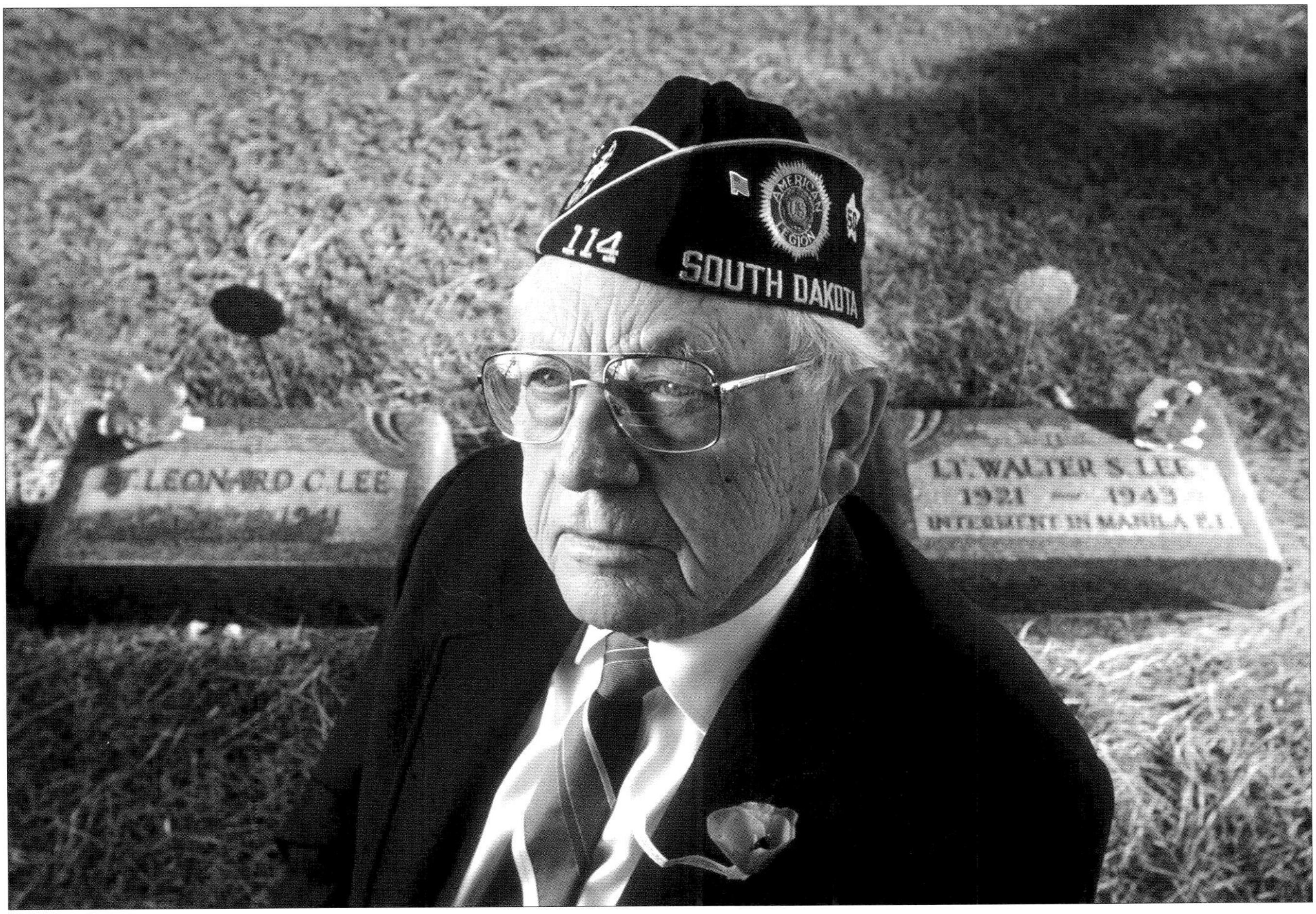
114
SOUTH DAKOTA
AMERICAN LEGION
LEONARD C. LEE
LT. WALTER S. LEE
1921 — 1943
INTERMENT IN MANILA P.I

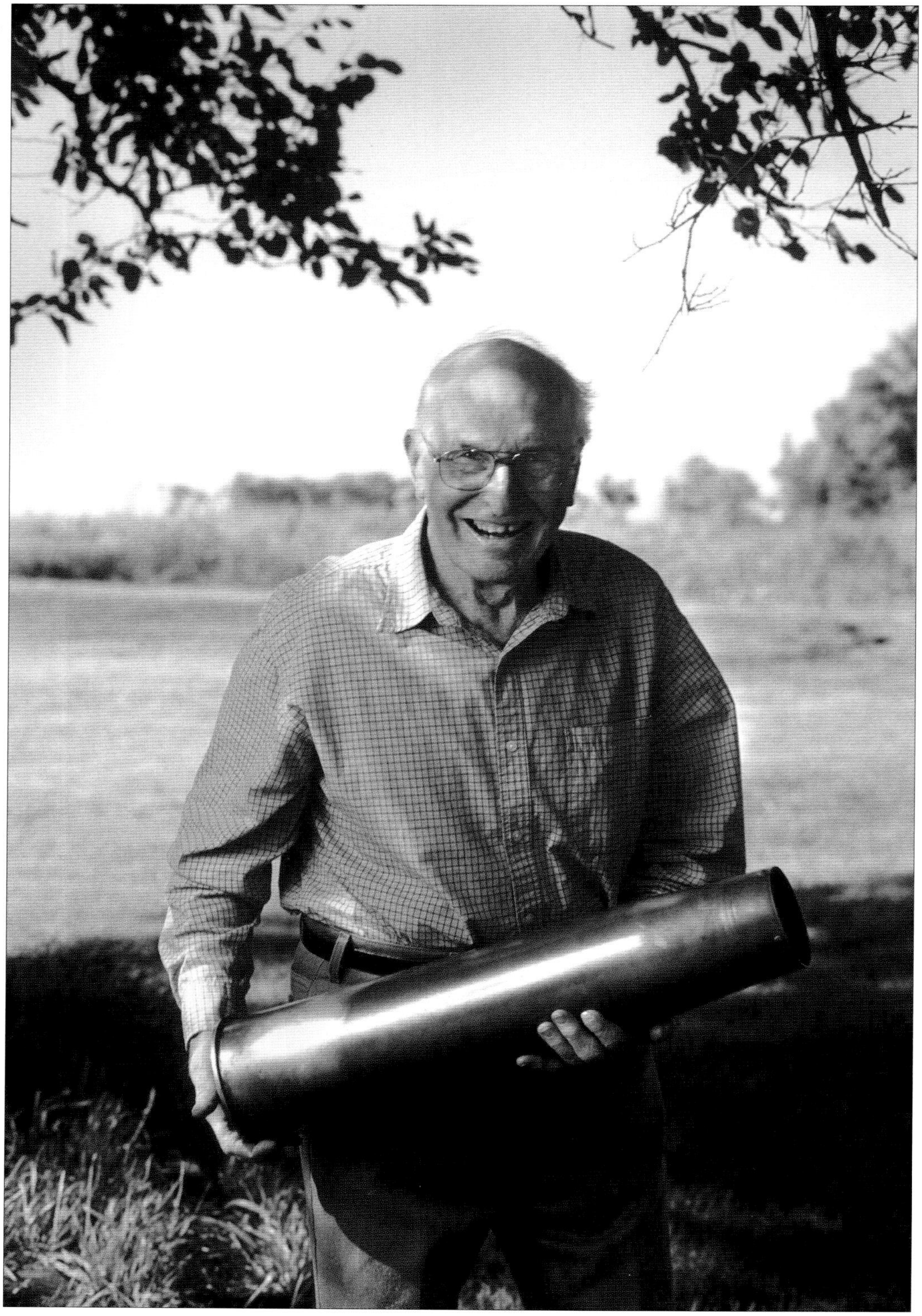

OLIVER CARLSON ☆ *Beresford*

Carlson landed at Utah Beach in June 1944 as part of a 105mm Howitzer crew, and pushed his way toward Germany with the 90th Infantry Division. He credits his strong faith for his unlikely survival.

Pearl Harbor was on December 7th, 1941, and we were in church. When we came out of church, I came out the west door and somebody came running over to me and they said that Pearl Harbor had been bombed. Then I got thinking, it won't be long until I get my call.

I went to the mailbox, and there laid a card that said, "Greetings from Uncle Sam. You are to report to Sioux Falls Medical Center and get your physical." I took it home and I laid it on the table, and I said, "Mom, here it is." I often wondered what went through her mind about that time.

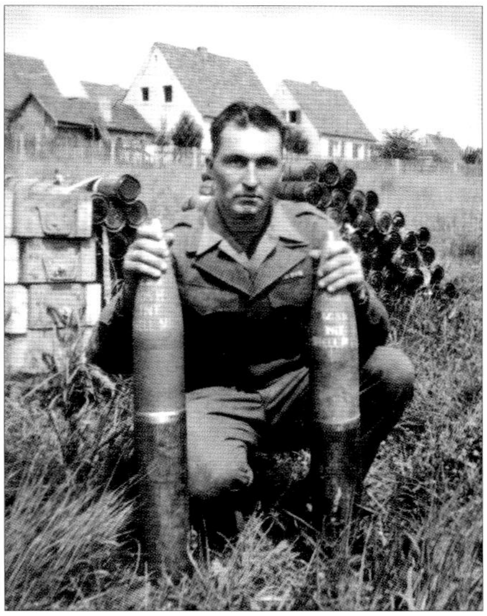

Within two months I was on the way to Fort Leavenworth. We went from there to Camp Barkley, Texas, where we got our basic training. That was the Texas-Oklahoma Division. In World War I, the 90th Division consisted of mostly Oklahoma boys and Texas boys. But because of the death loss and the shock on the communities where they all came from, they decided to take them from the whole United States.

I think it was the latter part of March *(1944)* that we got on the ship, and we set sail for destination unknown. There were 90 ships in our convoy, and every seven minutes the ship zig-zagged, because it took seven minutes for a German submarine to get lined up to fire on a ship. Twenty days from New York and the Statue of Liberty, we got to Liverpool.

Then it was a trip into Wales; we had some more training there. It wasn't long until we got on the ship to head out *(for D-Day)*. They still didn't tell us where we were going, but we knew exactly what the story was.

We sailed along the coast of England for six days, then the ship headed straight toward France. It was the seventh morning after we got on that we were firing into the country of France. The morning of the invasion, the 101st and the 82nd Airborne landed out ahead of us.

There was a plane that come in at us and somebody hollered out. They said, "What is it?" *(Someone else answered)*, "Friendly aircraft." They said, "Are you sure?" About that time, he dropped a bomb into a ship — the second one that was over from us — and killed 26 doughboys in one shot there.

Then it was our turn getting off the ship. *(Soldiers climbed from larger ships into the smaller landing craft while still offshore.)* A shell exploded alongside the landing craft that I was already on. I was on a firing battery; I had to get off before my friend Joe Snead did, and he was up about three stories. He seen that shell explode and just about hit me, and he said, "Ollie, if I don't see you here, I'll see you over there *(in heaven)*." And I said, "Joe, it may be soon."

With that, our landing craft headed to the shore. Shells were hitting everywhere. There was a dogfight overhead, and there was one of our planes that had been shot down and was coming straight at our truck. I said, "Oh, we're going to get it right away." But then he cut off about two blocks away and exploded.

The dead laid everywhere — and I mean everywhere. I think we lost more men on Utah Beach than they lost in and around Baghdad in this last war.

We pulled into position. I was a gunner on that 105, and those had shells that weighed 50 pounds. The projectile weighed 33 1/3, to be exact.

We fought through the hedgerows for quite a few days. For the first six weeks, I never slept outside of a foxhole because of the terrible danger of getting hit by shrapnel.

As we went on, we finally went to what they call the Battle of Hill 122. We took and lost that hill five times. That's the only time that we ever were warned that we might have to back up.

Prior to that, one of our boys shot himself in the foot. This other guy was a coward, you understand. I'd just like to know what he said to his family when he went home. They come over and they told me, "Carlson, you're it to be chief of section." I said, "No, you wouldn't give it to me in the States, I ain't going to take it now. If I die with two or three stripes on my shoulders, it don't really make any difference to me." Why I refused that was *(because)* I knew if the infantry lost enough men that I would be called upon to pick some of our cannoneers, and that's something I almost couldn't do. It was just about impossible for me to take a friend and send them up on the line and be pretty dead sure they wouldn't come back.

We moved on to what they called the Battle of Falaise, France, where we encircled 200,000 *(Germans)*. It was about 6 miles deep and about 6 miles wide. And we caught them in there and almost closed the trap, and they refused to surrender, so we started firing until our guns got hot.

That was a sad day for one of our little forward observers. He flew right straight out in front of my gun and he hollered, "Fire!" and a shell hit him and exploded and blew the plane out of the sky. I felt real bad about that, but there was nothing you could do.

Finally, after about three or four days we secured that valley. Joe Snead come to me and he says, "Ollie, I'm going to go down and see what the valley looks like." I said, "I don't think I will, because I know about what they'll do with us in case they catch us in a place like that."

Well, I finally changed my mind and I went down there with him, and I've never seen so much death in all my life. Dead laid everywhere. Most people don't realize that the Germans had a lot of horse-drawn equipment. There was one place where there was six horses dead in their harness and the man that was driving this ammunition cart — he was killed, of course, and a piece of shrapnel severed his head. His head was laying in one place and his body was laying in the other. The dead were laying all over.

I had quite a few buddies die around me. One time a shell exploded, just about covered up a guy, and he came flying over into my foxhole. He trembled like a leaf. I said, "Riggs, would you have been ready to meet the Lord if that one would have got you?" He trembled and said, "No." I said, "You better get ready, the next one might." And just like that, two shells hit right alongside of the foxhole, about 20 feet *(away)*. About two weeks later, we were walking side by side along a creek with our mess kits. And all at once I heard the roar of a plane, or planes. I looked back behind me, and you could always see the dust coming above the bullets. I let out a yell and said, "Riggs, look out!" and I run to the side just as hard as I could. As they went over — they happened to be two of our own planes that didn't know we were there — I looked over and I seen him laying dead over there. A bullet went through him.

Many times after a close call, I said my mom and dad were praying, and that's what I attribute it to. Mom and dad must have been praying.

(After the Battle of the Bulge had receded), we headed toward Bastogne. There wasn't a building in Bastogne that wasn't hit by gunfire of some kind. After we moved out of that town for 3 or 4 miles, I had to go back to Bastogne on an errand. Me and another guy visited a Belgian family, and there was seven boys in that family. There was only one left — the Germans had killed the other six. They cried when they were telling it. I couldn't talk Belgian, but we used a lot of sign language and we got along great. Then we went back and slept in the barn and we went back to our guns in the morning.

The only thing that I thought of in the Battle of the Bulge — when it got so terrible cold — was if I got wounded and lay there without any detection and froze to death. I was concerned about that.

One night we pulled into an area, and the Germans were scattered everywhere. It was so pitch dark you couldn't see your hand in front of you. About 2 in the morning, I went and laid down after I got my artillery piece lined up for the morning firing; I laid down by a fence. In the morning, just as I was going to get up, I looked over and here laid a German right by me — with a gun. He jumped up and he threw his gun and he surrendered to me. He could have easily killed me. There again, another miracle. I don't think he wanted to fight no worse than we did. I would have loved to have met him later on in life and thanked him for what he'd done.

The day that Roosevelt died, we were ready to make an attack that morning. Our trucks were all lined up, ready to head out into the field of battle and get set up to fire.

One guy run by our gun and hollered, "Roosevelt

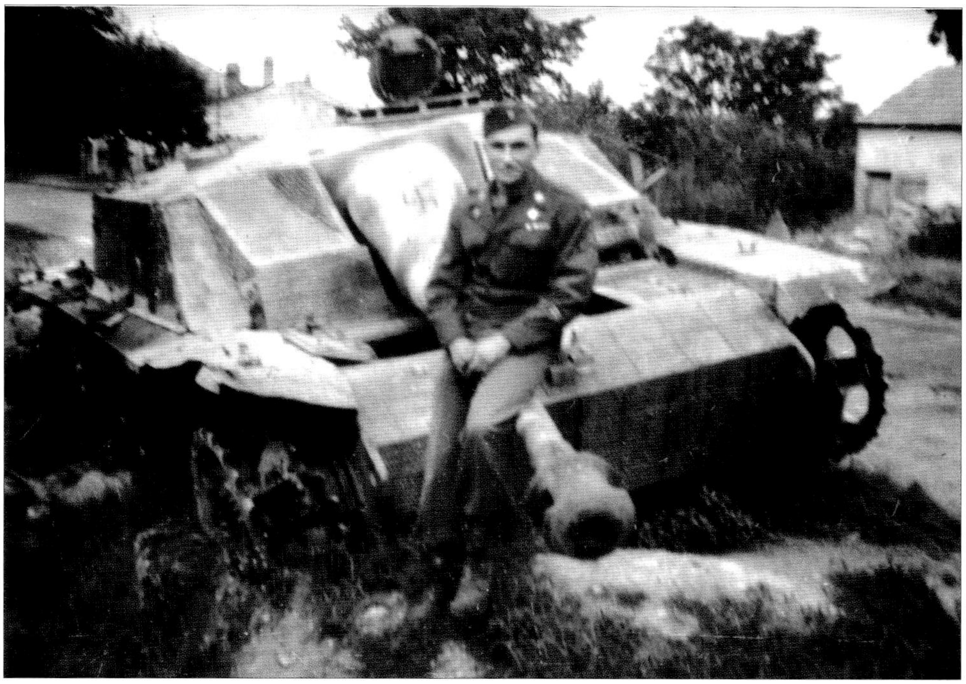

Carlson perches on the barrel of a destroyed German tank.

died!" The thought that went through my mind was that a lot of these boys around here are going to die before the day is over, and the world ain't going to know anything about it. But a leader is gone, and the whole world knew it just like that. Every day we just thanked the Lord for another day of safety.

There was a slave labor camp that we took. I told a guy next to me, "If I never make it, it'll be worth it to see these people liberated because of the treatment they got." They were poor, and they were sick and starving. They went behind the lines, and we went ahead.

We had fought the German Panzer divisions all the way across Europe. There were thousands of German boys that came in and surrendered to the 90th.

The war was over, and I laid down on the bank and I cried like a baby. And I just said, "Lord, is this possible?"

Joe came and said, "Ollie, I can't believe it. It's a wonder we can even remember our own name after what we've seen." I'll be honest with you — I didn't expect to make it. And most of my buddies didn't. Both Joe and me come home without a scratch after 11 months at the front. It's a miracle; that's what it is.

I thought, "I'm doing this for my country," and I never wished that I wasn't there. I never regretted doing the job that I was assigned to do. I done it willingly.

I was willing to give my life if that's what it took, but it wasn't easy. We all had fear, but I never was to the point where I was beyond control. I had a peace about it. I never worried about dying.

When I was on maneuvers in Louisiana *(back in training)*, I sat down by a tree. I was just thinking about the future, because we knew that the battle of Europe was to be held at France. And a poem come to me, just out of the blue, but I know the Lord put His hand in it.

And that poem was:

Day and night God cares for me,
No matter how rough the road might be
But with God's care I'm ever at ease,
His care for me shall never cease

Life's road may lead to the battle front,
My life the enemy may seek and hunt
But with God's care I'm ever at ease,
God's care for me shall never cease

And it never did. ☆

Carlson farmed after the war, and he still operates a trucking business in the Beresford area.

DAVE BALD EAGLE ☆ *Takini*

In 1876, Chief White Bull fought Custer's 7th Cavalry in the Battle of the Little Big Horn, dealing the U.S. Army one of its worst defeats. Sixty-eight years later, in 1944, grandson Dave Bald Eagle jumped from a plane on D-Day as a U.S. Army paratrooper with the 82nd Airborne Division and was promptly wounded by four bullets.

We were ready. We were ready for anything. I didn't care what happened; I wasn't scared to fly or nothing. There was nothing I was afraid of.

I was probably the quietest one in the bunch. You could hear the moaning *(on the plane, prior to the jump)*. We were hearing guns all over. Guns, bombs, everything. Just noise. All over, machinery.

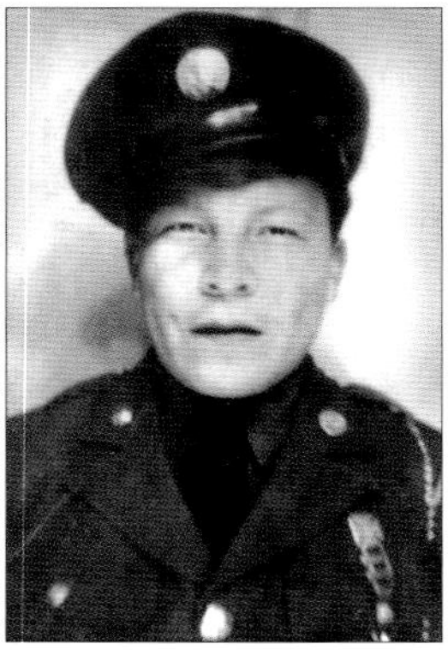

What we went through *(on the plane)* was worse than what we were going to see *(in the coming battle)*. We never thought, "Why, what if we wrecked?" or anything. We never thought of things like that. We knew we were coming home, that was all we knew.

We jumped in Normandy, and that was the end of my war right there. I didn't even get to see part of the war. I was shot down. I can remember coming out of the plane, but I can't even remember hitting the ground. I was hit in the leg, shoulder and hand. And I got hit in the head. You could see where it hit and went through *(my helmet)* and didn't go through the lining. Lucky. I always consider myself the luckiest trooper in the whole outfit.

Practically the whole battalion was shot out from under us. A lot of them dropped during the night, but we were dropped about daybreak. They dropped us in the wrong place; we were right on top of *(the Germans)*. We had no chance. The last time I saw some of my buddies alive was in the plane. A lot of us were hit in the air. Just a few — not very many of us — lived. They just picked us off. That was the last of my soldiering.

They would have left me for dead, I imagine, but this one British guy in the medical department came over to feel my pulse, and it was still beating. He told them to rush me in right away. I came to in the field hospital.

(My friend Johnny) lived to give me his Purple Heart. At the time, he told me, "Could you give this to dad and mom?" I said, "Come on, John, you're coming home with me. You deliver it to them." We were both in this hospital. And here, he died. Just a few minutes after he said that.

This nurse, she was there and she heard that, and she gave me the box. That was the hardest thing I've ever done, to deliver that Purple Heart to his family. They were in St. Paul. They knew he wasn't coming back.

I just went right on up and knocked, and a lady came to the door. She seen me and just like that, she fainted. The old man came over and picked her up.

"Come on in, son," he says, so I walked in. I was on crutches then. When she came to, the first thing she said was, "I knew you right away. That's the reason it shocked me. I knew Johnny wasn't coming back." They knew me so much because he was my buddy. He always talked about me. They knew it was me, his Indian buddy.

They practically knew me when I walked in. Of course, they knew Johnny wasn't going to be with me. Later, I took that box out and I told them, "Johnny told me to give you this."

They showed me pictures of him and his sisters having a lot of fun. It makes you kind of emotional, you know, makes you cry.

It was kind of hard; he wasn't the only one. There was a lot of them that was good friends of mine that was in that outfit.

For a long, long time I couldn't talk about it. To this day, I could never see the movie they made about it, *The Longest Day*. My boys, they're in the 82nd Airborne. They asked me to see it. But I don't want to see it — too many buddies lost in that. Even to this day, I think about some of those guys.

As you get older, you wonder why you're living. It seems like you could have been dead. I guess they did leave me for dead. ☆

In the years following WWII, Bald Eagle acted in 17 movies, working alongside the likes of Errol Flynn, Clark Gable and Marilyn Monroe. In 1958, he performed with Casey Tibbs' Wild West Show at the World's Fair in Brussels, Belgium, where he met his wife, Josee. They ranch near Takini on the Cheyenne River Reservation, where Bald Eagle serves as chief of the Minneconjou Lakota Sioux (Mnikoju Band of Hohwoju).

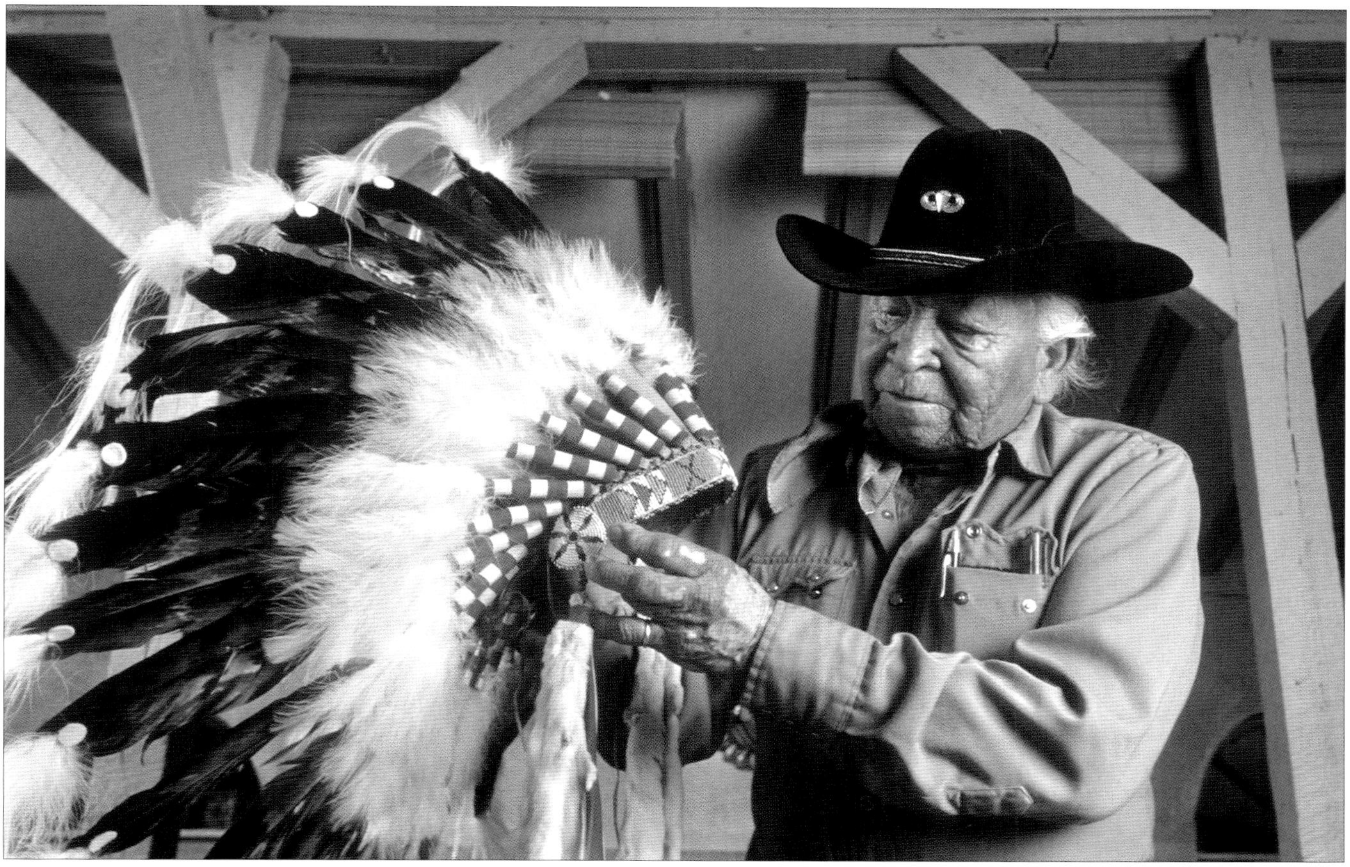

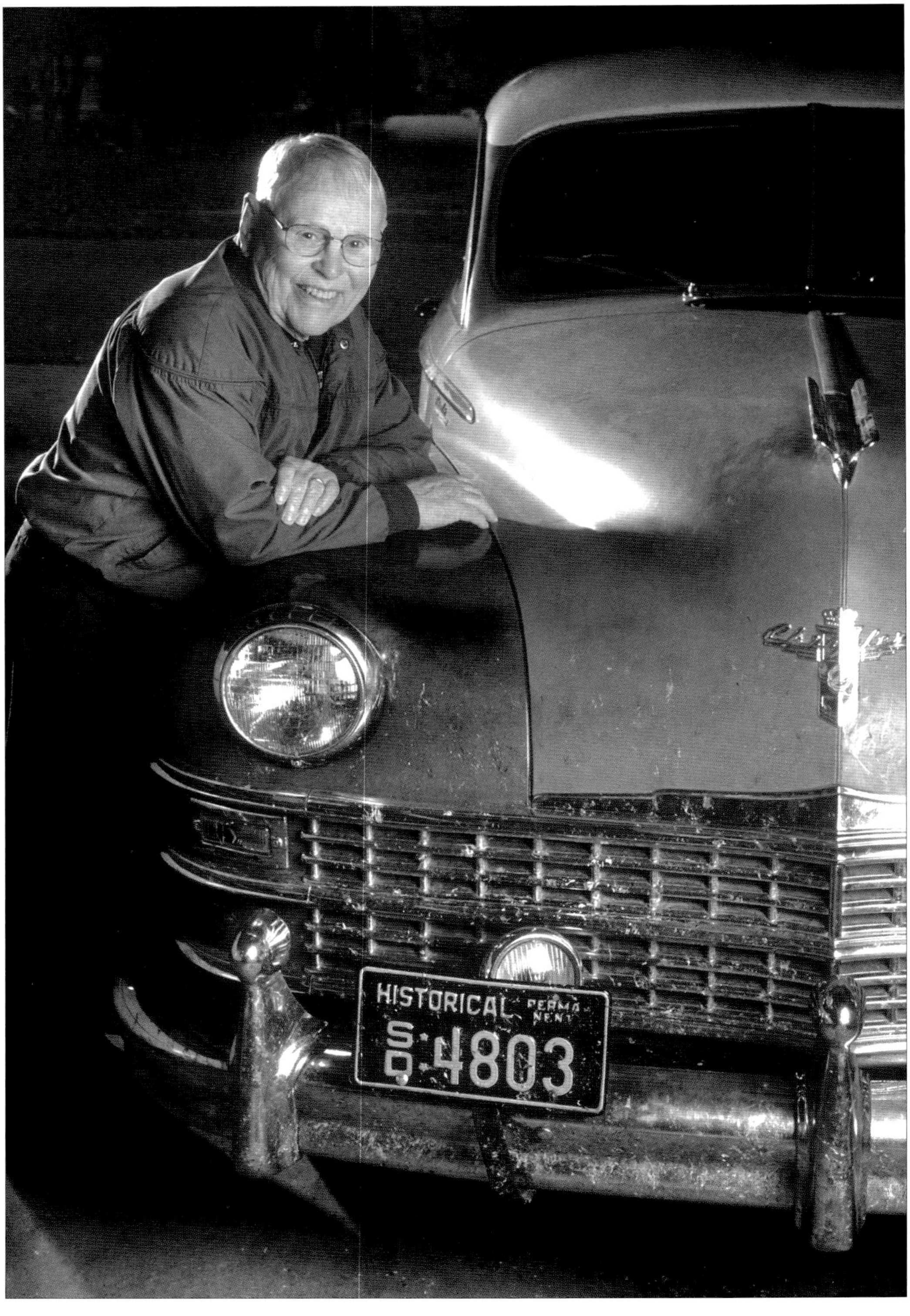
HISTORICAL PERMANENT
S D 4803

FLOYD SHORT ☆ *Lemmon*

A policeman's son, Short joined the Navy after the Pearl Harbor attack and in early 1943 ended up on the most modern aircraft carrier to date, the Essex. *His duty was to repair planes that malfunctioned or were battle-damaged.*

We went aboard ship right after the first of the year in '43, and after a shakedown cruise, we headed out for the Pacific. We were brand-spanking new. I mean everything was new — including 90 percent of the crew!

Our first action we saw was at Marcus Islands, about 1,000 miles off some of the Japanese Islands. Then we went down and hit Wake. We sent the aircraft in and they would do their work. They tried to keep the ship about 100 miles offshore, because if they got to us, why, they got everybody. We had destroyers, and we generally had a cruiser with us.

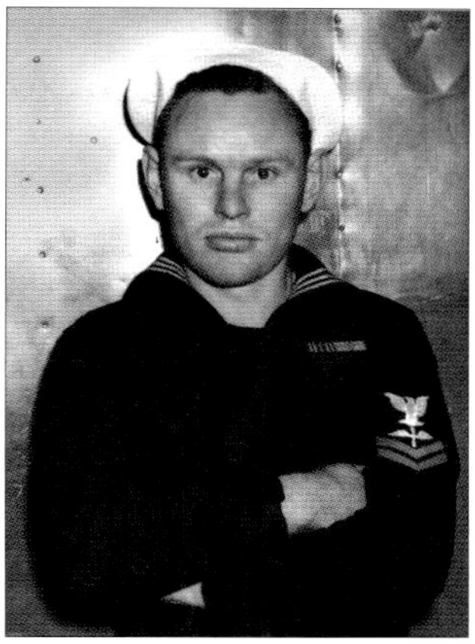

Hydraulics and rigging was my specialty; that's what I did. If we had a shell or bullet that had hit the hydraulic system *(on a plane)*, it was my job to fix it. They couldn't fold their wings if they were out of hydraulic fluid. Also, the moveable parts were fabric — the plane was metal, but the airfoils, elevators and ailerons and rudder were all fabric. It was my job to keep them sewed up. I'd be out there with a needle, sewing them back together, and then "dope" it — that was a shellac.

We listened to music. When we were out in the Pacific where we could get her, we'd listen to Tokyo Rose all the time. She played good music. She played jazz music, which is my favorite. She'd tell us we might as well turn around and go home — that our sweethearts at home were all sleeping with somebody else and all that kind of dang stuff. She had quite a lingo.

We were with the *Enterprise* and got word that the Japanese had a big concentration of shipping in Rabaul Harbor. On November 11th of 1943, the ship really got baptized with fire. We got all our planes back on the deck, and we'd got them fueled, and all of a sudden here were the Japanese. Some of our guys had themselves a Japanese Zero before they got their wheels up. They went off the ship firing.

They came in with torpedo bombers. That's as close as I ever got to them. There was one that came down on our port side. You could see both *(Japanese crewmen)*, and I know that gunner was as scared as the rest of us.

When the smoke cleared away that day, we accounted for 65 Japanese planes — we shot down 50 within sight of the aircraft carrier. We lost two planes that day, but we got both pilots back. We were right in the middle of it. It seemed like it took all day, but it didn't. We had one piece of shrapnel come through the fantail into the metal shop, of all places. While I was aboard ship, that's the only time we were ever hit. When you knew that the enemy was pretty close, it scared you, especially when they were coming in on you. You're apprehensive. You don't know what the hell is gonna happen.

We lost more people from accidents than we did from enemy. Usually, planes will take off and they'll sink below the bow of the ship and then you'll see them coming up again. This character, he'd get airborne and he'd pull back and he'd go up about 75 feet. They kept hammering at him and hammering at him not to do that. And he did that once too often. He stalled, and he had two depth charges in that damn thing and a crew of three. *(They were going out on submarine watch.)* When that went off, a man's ear fell in front of me. It just blew all three of them completely apart. I had to take a good friend out of a plane that had been hit. He was dead. I had another friend, and he forgot where he was and he walked right into a propeller, and it sliced him up like a piece of sausage.

In 1944, we made the first run on Truk and Saipan-Tinian. It was at Saipan-Tinian that we saw our first kamikazes. Now we didn't get hit, but we had two of them come down on us. One of them was on our starboard side and when he blew up, he blew debris onto the flight deck. The other one, he missed us by a mile. I don't think he wanted to die that day, but he did.

I'm proud of my service. I've always said that I wouldn't take a million bucks for what I've been through, but I wouldn't give a dime to do it again. ☆

Short owned a Lemmon dry cleaning business for 35 years, then served for 20 years as a county veterans service officer.

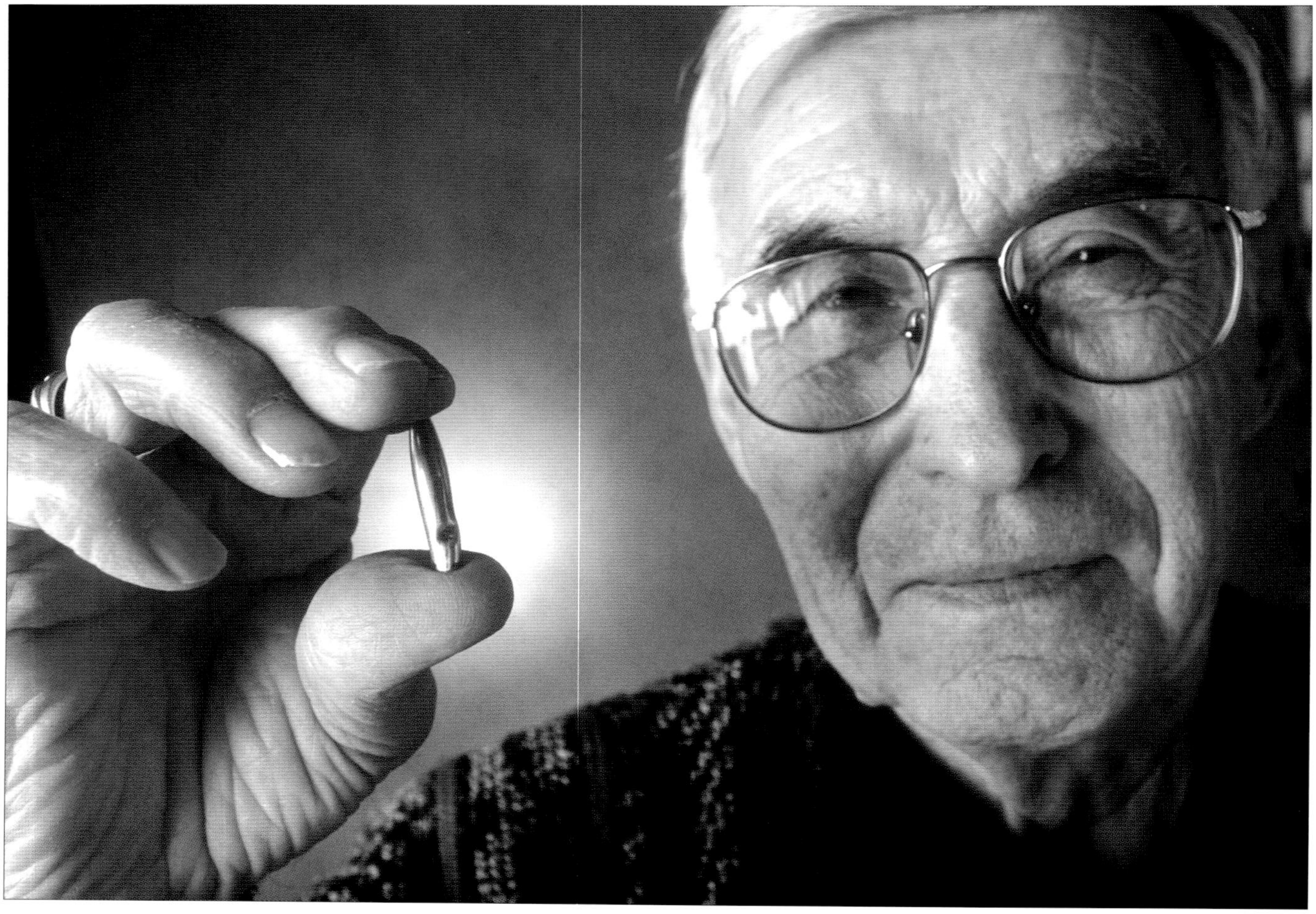

JACK HYDE ☆ *Huron*

In May 1943, one year after graduating from Onida High School, Hyde began learning the finer points of high explosives and pontoon bridge building while training as a combat engineer. He enjoyed the work but got a rude awakening upon his arrival at Bougainville in the South Pacific.

The old colonel lined us up on shore and said, "Boys, you are now in the infantry." Well, I didn't like it very well. And then to top it all off, they threw a BAR at me, a Browning Automatic Rifle, and I'd never seen one before. I had to learn to how to take that all apart and put it together, and it's got a lot of firepower. I was the tallest one in the bunch, and that's why they threw that BAR at me. It drew quite a little bit of fire, because *(the Japanese)* didn't like those automatic weapons.

They had so many casualties there on Bougainville, and they needed infantrymen, so that's what happened.

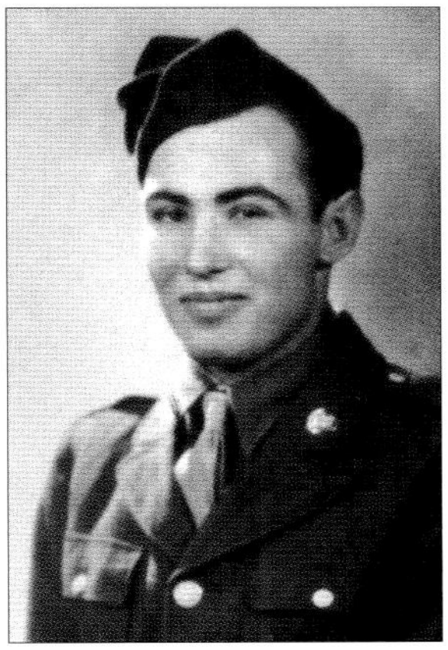

We made the initial landing on Cebu, and of course we had quite a battle there. Cebu was the whole island, and Cebu City was the second largest city in the Philippines at the time. It rained every day. I got malaria, but I never came down with it until I got back to the States. I had several attacks of malaria.

You never knew when you were going to run into *(Japanese soldiers)*. They were scattered all over. They were always up above us and looking down at us, from up on those hills. At night, they'd shoot tracer bullets down at us from anti-aircraft guns. It was some deal. We had several guys killed right there by where we were. It was a shame. I don't know how we ever survived. A lot of them didn't.

They had tunnels in these hills, and they stored their ammunition in them. *(The Americans)* drove one of our tanks up there and started shooting into one hill, and it was all full of ammunition. Blew the whole hill up and buried a whole squad of our men going around the outside edge of it. Buried them alive. It blew the tank over, upside-down, and they sent us up there at night to guard that darn tank. Two or three of us, all alone up there. If you don't think THAT was scary to guard that tank. They were afraid the Japanese would come up there and blow it up.

We had those Japanese come through the line with TNT on their backs, suicide guys. Right through our lines, and they'd blow up. Can you imagine anyone doing something like that? They blew themselves up in those tunnels, too, when we had them surrounded. You could hear them. I think they put a grenade at their stomach and it just blew them up. Some of them tried to run out, and naturally, we had to shoot them. We didn't know what else to do.

We could see the Japanese off in the distance, and they could see us. We were wandering around waiting for orders to move up on them, and all of a sudden, boom, the sniper got me. He must have been a long ways off, otherwise that bullet would have gone right on through me. It just hit me and knocked me right down. A medic was right there and put blood plasma in my arm. I felt kind of fortunate, because I knew I wasn't dead and I knew they were going to carry me out of there, down to the hospital. This doctor colonel came in and he looked at me, and said, "Well, we'll put a different cast on you, and put you on the ship, and you can go home." That made me feel real good.

I was in the hospital for eight months after I got back from overseas. My brother had gotten killed the 14th of March, a day before his birthday, over in Mindanao in the Philippines. *(Jack's injury occurred one month after his brother's death.)* I didn't know until I got back to the United States. He was out in the Leyte port when we were there. He knew I was there but I didn't know he was out there, and they wouldn't let him get off the ship to come and see me. We were right on shore unloading DUKWs *(amphibious trucks)*.

I called my mother when I got back to San Francisco, and she said, "Did you know Neil was killed?" I sure didn't. That was a shock. There was just nothing you could do, you know. He's gone. ☆

Hyde spent 33 years as a mail carrier in and around Huron. He keeps the .25-caliber bullet that shattered his shoulder on a watch chain. It is his most prized war souvenir.

HOMER PARCE ☆ *Letcher*

Playing cornet for the 147th Field Artillery in Mitchell, Parce found himself and several other Letcher bandmates heading into the Pacific shortly before World War II began.

My dad picked up an old mellophone someplace. That's what I started on, and later changed over to trumpet. It wasn't very long that I was playing in the Letcher City Band, too. If it wasn't band, baseball or church, I pretty well *(stayed)* at home. Along about '38, a bunch of us joined the National Guard Band in Mitchell. At that time, we went to a meeting once a week. We got all of one dollar. No one got very rich at it.

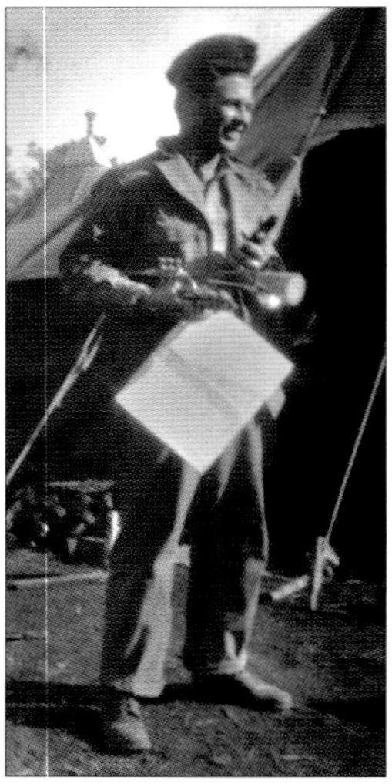

When we were called into the Army, we went right on with our music. We had weapons, but we didn't really know how to use them. I don't think any one of us joined with the idea of going to war; we just joined because we liked to play in the band.

We left the United States November 22, 1941. We pulled into Pearl Harbor and we saw that big line of battleships that the Japanese sunk. We were only there two days. We were out in the ocean someplace when Pearl Harbor got hit. We were supposed to go to the Philippines, but we wound up going to Australia instead because the Japanese took over the Philippines pretty fast.

I don't think any of us were worried. The Japanese reported that our ship was sunk several times, but we kept on going. We ran out of food; we ran out of water. Once we pulled up beside a cruiser and they pumped some fresh water into us. And then we stopped at the island of Fiji and picked up some food.

We didn't do what you would call concerts, but we practiced. If we made mistakes, we'd start over again. The troops were all around us, because that's the only entertainment there was. We played quite a little bit.

We landed in Brisbane, Australia. We were the first American troops EVER to land in Australia *(during World War II)*. Then we loaded back up and went around the northern tip of Australia and landed at Darwin, which was just a small community. After we'd been there three or four weeks, the Japanese bombed it about once a week for a month. We were 15 or 20 miles from there; we could see the planes and we could hear the bombs.

We got up there and there was absolutely nothing to do. No town to visit, we didn't even have a canteen. And so we did a lot of entertaining. I'm sure the band was never appreciated as much as it was during that six-month period. When we went someplace to play, which was three or four times a week, there was a big crowd. The Australians would say, "Play *Alexander's Rag*, Yank!" That was about the only piece they knew that we knew. They requested things like *In the Mood*. At that time, the Japanese were bombing Australia and we had our guns laying right beside us. We carried rifles at all times then, because they really expected the Japanese to invade northern Australia.

They sometimes used us as a work battalion. They'd put us to work unloading barges, working a warehouse, guarding a gas dump or something like that. If the Army wanted a place for a gas dump, they just pushed the house out of the way and dumped it. Anyway, they put me in charge of this gas dump, I suppose it was a couple hundred 50-gallon barrels. This was in the Philippines. All I had was a .45 pistol. Anybody could have taken that gas dump away from me. There I am, walking around this place, and all of a sudden 25 or 30 Filipinos stood on the outside, jabbering. Their house had been where this gas dump was. Finally one of them approached me, and through signals *(he said)* they were looking for something. I told them to go ahead. They measured here, and they measured there, and pretty soon they got a spade and they started digging. Out of the ground they pulled a pot. It was plumb full of silver money they'd kept hidden from the Japanese for four years. I walked up, looked at it, and I suppose they were afraid *(and thought)*, "I suppose he's going to take that away from us now." I reached in and took one piece for a souvenir and told them to go.

About all I'm good for anymore is *Taps*. I don't practice or anything anymore, so I just pick it up and what I can do, I do — and that's it. ☆

Parce farmed near Letcher after the war. On occasion he still plays Taps *for local military funerals.*

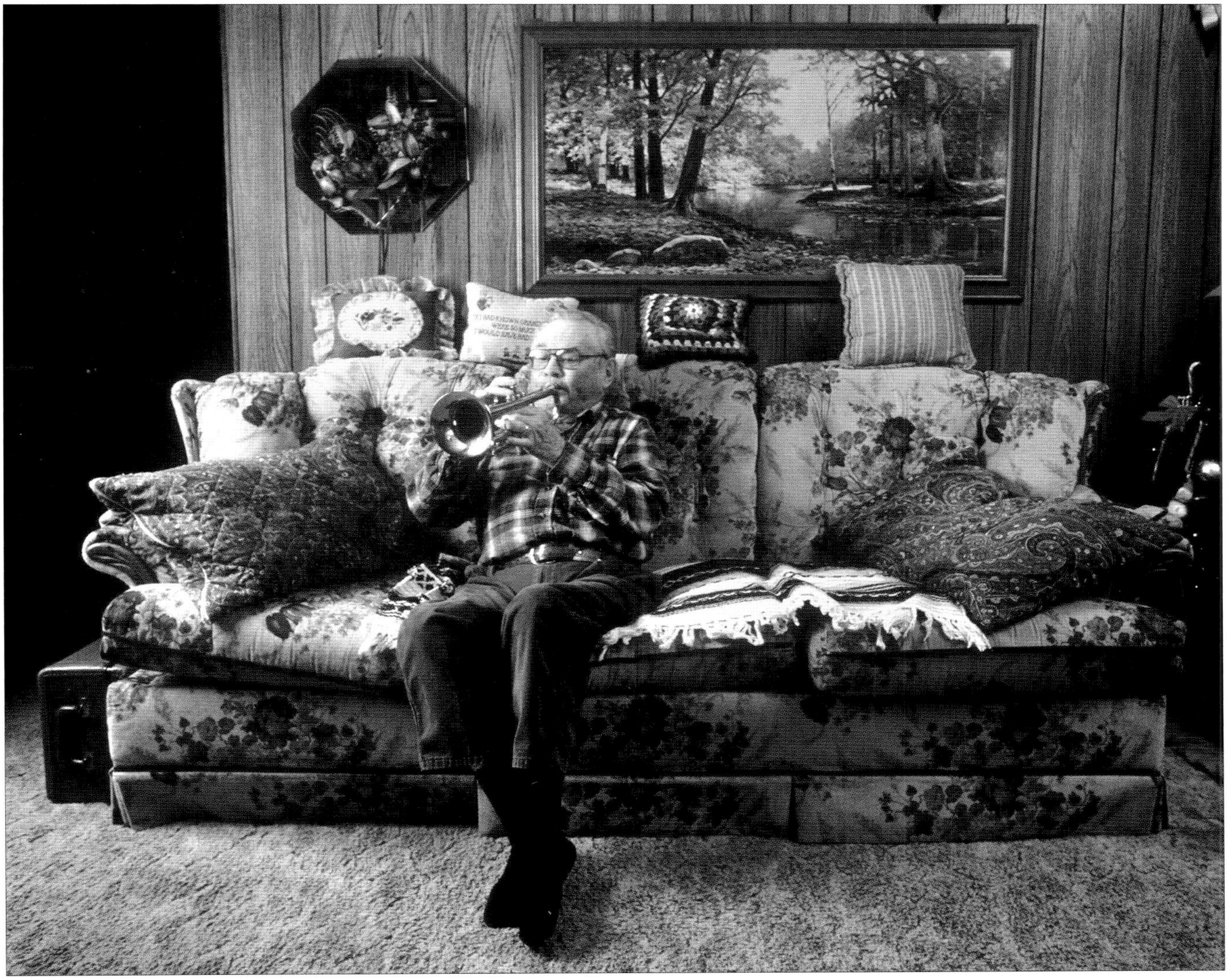

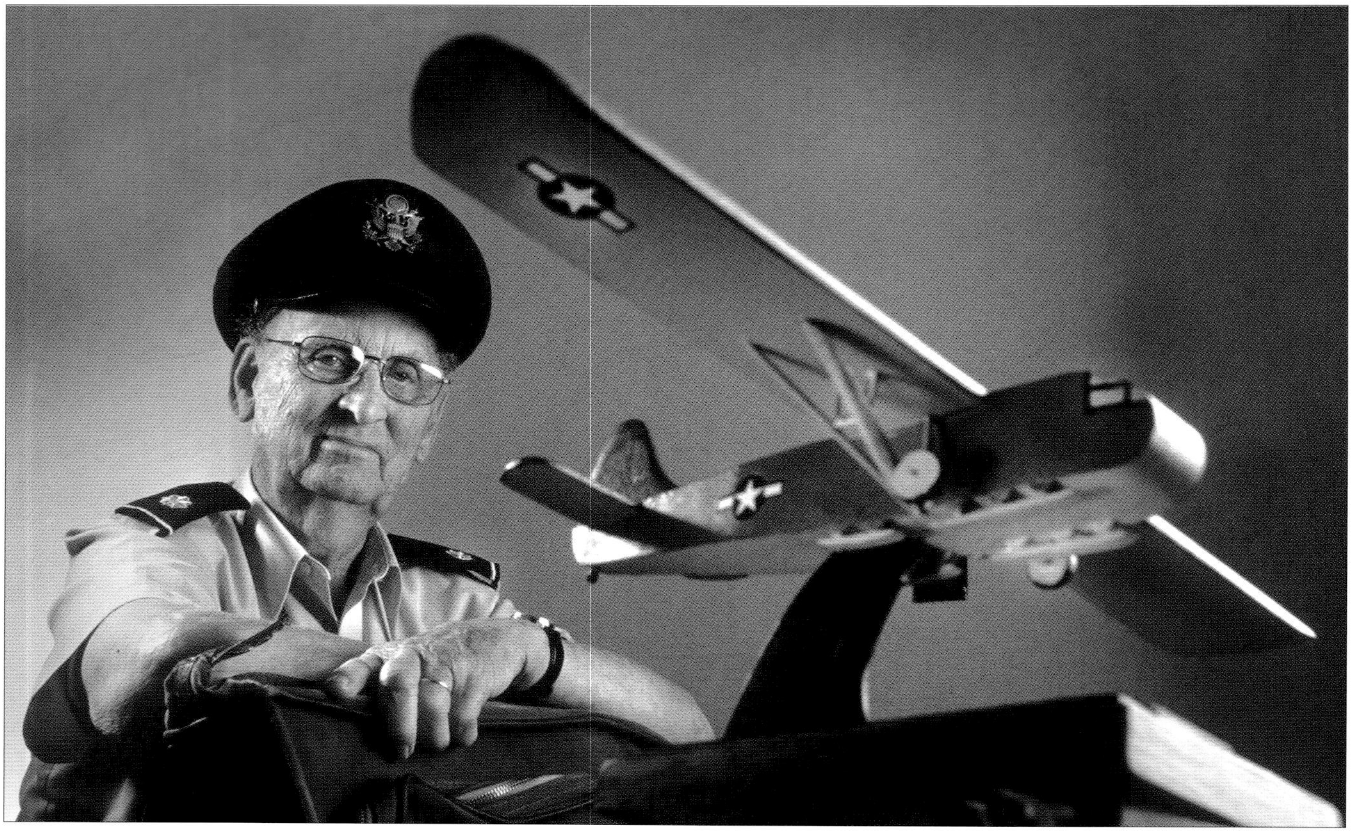

Nelson Lagendyk ☆ *Avon*

Most war scholars agree that the duties of a glider pilot, which involved crash-landing a plane, followed by combat, were some of the most harrowing and dangerous performed during the course of World War II. On the eve of D-Day, Lagendyk knew that he was about to embark on the adventure of a lifetime.

Well, we stayed up all night. We couldn't sleep, of course. Our gliders were stacked on about the first third of the runway, and our ropes were curled around in front of our gliders, 300 feet of nylon rope and a C-47 in between each one.

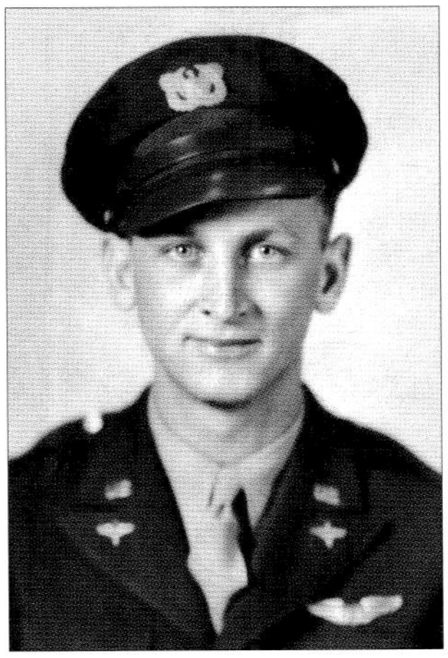

They started taking off. They have a jeep on the side of the runway to let the pilot know how much of the 300 feet they've taken up so they can slow down a little bit when the ropes are getting taut.

My release let go. There I'm sitting. Doggone it, I've trained all this time and I couldn't go? I was pretty disappointed. Then they run out another C-47 and that one took off. My co-pilot, he looked at the release there and he kicked it. And by golly, it held!

We were toward the end of the flight. We took off and flew to about 1,500-foot altitude, and went across the Island of Wight, in southern England there, and then 70 miles across the channel, on the left side of the Cotentin Peninsula. And then we went 10 miles inland at 300 feet. At 300 feet, we avoided anti-aircraft fire, but of course we were still subject to rifle fire and small-arms fire. And we didn't have any parachutes, because the big brass had figured out that going in at 300 feet, the parachutes wouldn't open up if we had to bail out. So why waste good parachutes! The glider pilots were the only pilots that flew without parachutes.

We got about 10 miles inland, near St. Mere Eglise, France. I saw a pasture up ahead there. The tow plane, they flashed the green light at me. When I saw the green light and I saw the pasture, I saw a few gliders in there already, and I hit the release. As we were coming to the approach, I didn't see them, but Rommel had his asparagus, those were poles set up at the end of the field.

I had a jeep in my glider, and two Airborne men and a .50-caliber machine gun on the jeep, and some 57mm ammunition in the jeep too. When I sat in my seat, the bumper came across my back, so I didn't want to hit anything solid, because the jeep would crush me.

My co-pilot — there were big trees ahead of us, huge trees, tall trees — he thought that we were going to hit those. So he hit the parachute release, the drag chute.

I was coming in about 70 miles an hour, and that dropped me into that doggone pole. It took off my undercarriage, and we came down pretty hard, 'cause the wings folded up.

We were kind of collecting our thoughts a little bit there when we were on the ground. A machine gun nest was on the end of the field by the woods. They opened fire and they stitched my glider fuselage, and pretty soon a couple of *(bullets)* came through my Plexiglas window there. I turned around and hollered, "Get out! Hit the ground!" So we all piled out and hit the ground.

There was a woods on the east side, and on the west side was a hedgerow. One of the 82nd Airborne men that I was taking in the glider had been in combat before, and he was scared stiff. He says, "Head for that hedgerow over there." I said, "No, you head for it." He says, "No, YOU head for it!" Pretty soon I made a zig-zag path and dropped in the hedgerow. They saw I was safe, so they came. The machine gun fire was coming from the other side there, and there were snipers in the woods too.

As we got our bearings, a German soldier came out with a potato masher — that's a hand grenade — and he was going to throw it in the glider. One of our guys shot him, and he landed on his chest *(on top of the grenade)*, and the explosion blew him over on his back.

After the field was cleared — the infantry had come up on the road, up to our position there — we wanted to get the jeep out of the glider. He was laying there, and I could see right down to his spine.

His face was pure white, no blood in his face. ☆

Lagendyk served in the Air Force Reserves for over 30 years, retiring in 1977 with the rank of major. He and wife Leonora owned and operated the Variety Store in Avon for 48 years.

Darrel Christopherson ☆ *Vermillion*

A welder on the repair ship Vestal, *Christopherson was next to the battleship* Arizona *at Pearl Harbor when World War II began for the United States on December 7, 1941.*

They swore me into the Navy on my 17th birthday, on February 12th, 1941. I was assigned to the *U.S.S. Vestal* at Pearl Harbor. I had no idea in the world what the *Vestal* was, or as far as that goes, where Pearl Harbor was at, other than that it was in the Hawaiian Islands.

They took a draft of us and they had an oil tanker that was going to Honolulu. We were seven days at sea on that oil tanker, my first time at sea. All we got to do was chip paint, scrape paint and paint. Once you got it chipped and scraped and painted, then chip it and scrape it and paint it again.

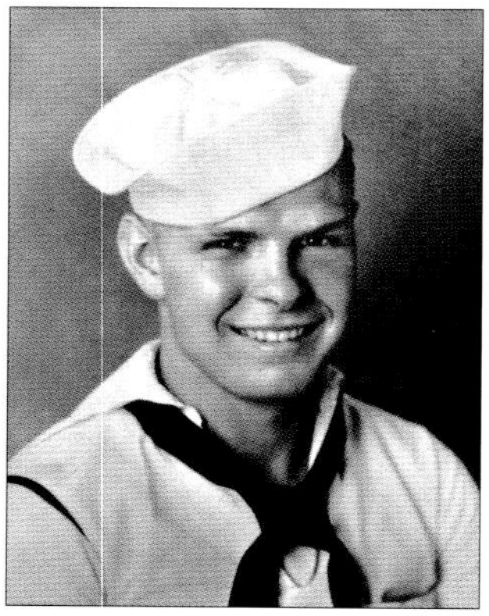

We got to Pearl Harbor, and they picked us up and took us over to the *Vestal*. We pulled up to it, and it looked like an old scow. It looked like something they pulled out of World War I, which they practically had, because it was built in the early 1900s. As it turned out, this ship was one of the best repair ships in the fleet.

On about the 5th of December, we got orders to go alongside the *Arizona*, which was tied up there at Ford Island, and we were going to do some minor repair work. We got alongside of her on late Friday, and on Saturday we just cleaned up and nobody was going to start work until Monday morning. I had had some minor surgery, and they had me in sick bay for a couple of days.

On Sunday morning, airplanes started coming in. We could hear those airplanes and figured it was a mock attack. The Air Force every once in a while would pull a mock attack on Pearl Harbor. But then one of the guys stuck his head out of the porthole and he sees these airplanes up there with a big red meatball painted on them. He says, "Those aren't ours! Those are Japanese!"

There wasn't anything we could do. We didn't have any guns on there — we had one 3-inch anti-aircraft gun that jammed after the third round. We had two 5-inch bag guns that were for surface targets and useless as far as aircraft. So all we could do was sort of watch and stay under cover — stay back in where you wouldn't get shot because occasionally they would strafe.

We got hit twice while we were alongside the *Arizona*, and to this day, I don't recall either one of those bombs hitting us. One of them hit back aft and went out the bottom, and made just one big hole all the way through. The one that hit us up forward hit down in the storeroom that we kept metal stored in. It blew up down there, and it started a fire in a storeroom that had a bunch of baled rags in there. And those baled rags are just like trying to put a fire out in hay bales. You can't do it. Finally, after about three trips down there fighting fire, we got enough water in there to keep the fire out.

Our skipper had been blown over the side from an explosion from the *Arizona* when it got hit, and our executive officer was running around hollering, "Abandon ship!" Fortunately, our skipper never got injured seriously when he got blown over the side, and he swam back to the gangway and he came back aboard. The first thing he wanted to know was where everybody was going, because everybody was back there by the gangway waiting for boats to get off. He says, "Abandon ship? Hell, we're going to get underway." So we cut the lines tying us to the *Arizona* with fire axes — nobody over there could get to the lines to throw them off for us.

We were just pulling away from alongside the *Arizona* when it got a bomb that went down and exploded in her magazines, and that's the one that really tore her apart and put her right down on the bottom.

As soon as we had up enough steam, we run the *Vestal* across the channel into what they call the Aiea mud flats, and that's where we sat for the rest of the attack. Once we got away from the combat ships, they left us alone. In fact, I think those two bombs we took were probably meant for the *Arizona*, and they would have been near misses except that we were there and they hit us.

I've seen the movie (Pearl Harbor). You've got two hours of love story and 45 minutes about Pearl Harbor. Believe me, I never seen anybody get any loving there during that attack. ☆

Christopherson spent 20 years with the Navy, followed by 23 years with the Vermillion police department.

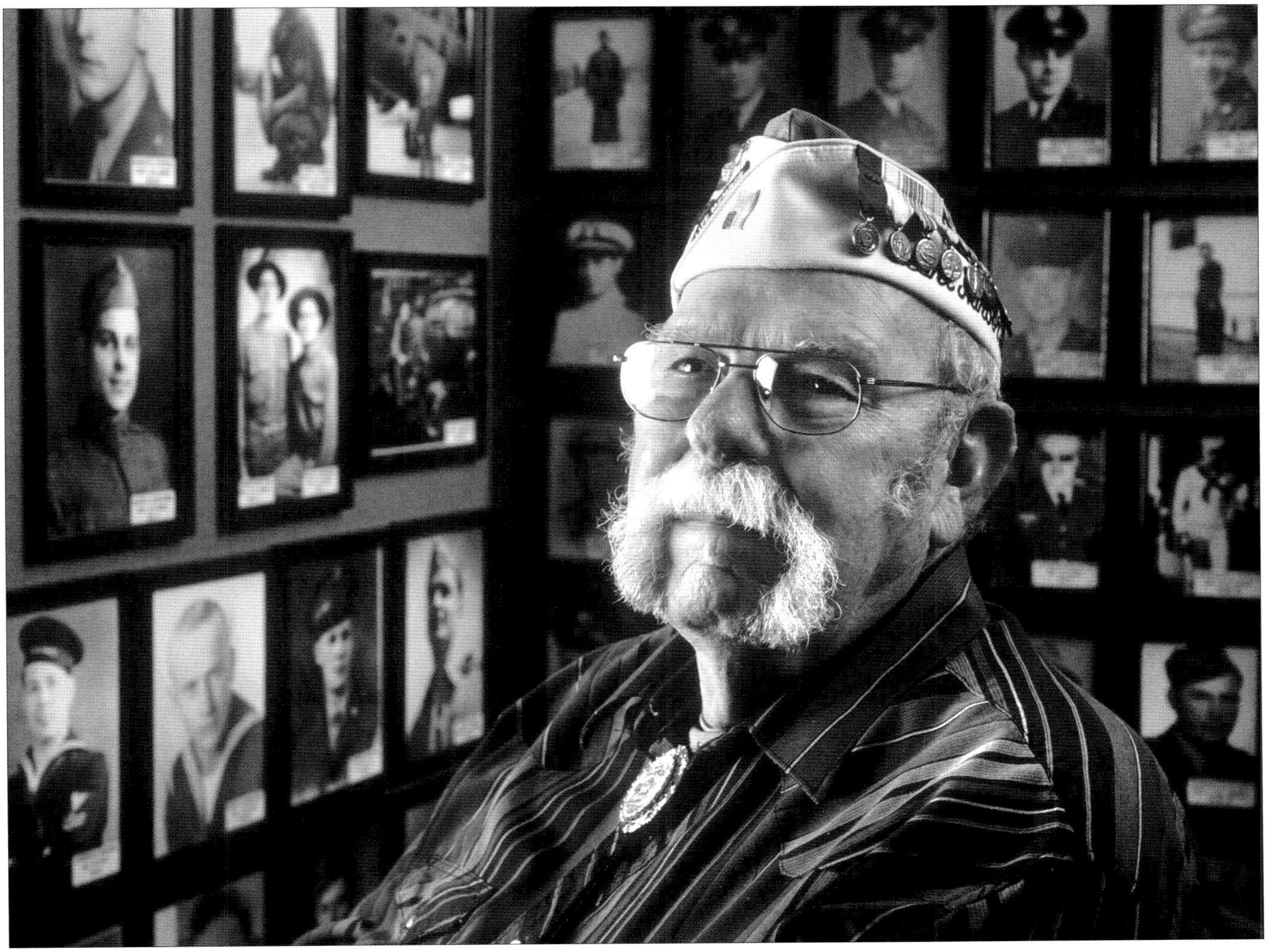

CECIL SANDERSON ☆ *Brookings*

As commander of Company L, 377th Infantry, 95th Division, Captain Sanderson and his men were engaged in heavy fighting along the Moselle River near Metz, France, in late 1944. He was approaching a concrete bunker when a German officer emerged from it with a pistol and killed a Free French soldier nearby.

There was a cement *(barrier)* around the fort, and I was in back of that. I told this German officer to come out with his hands up. It was in the fall of the year, and there were a lot of leaves. I knew he had a pistol, because he shot a Frenchman there with it, but when he came to me, all he had on him was a holster. The pistol was gone. After the dust cleared away, I went kicking along in those leaves and I found that pistol.

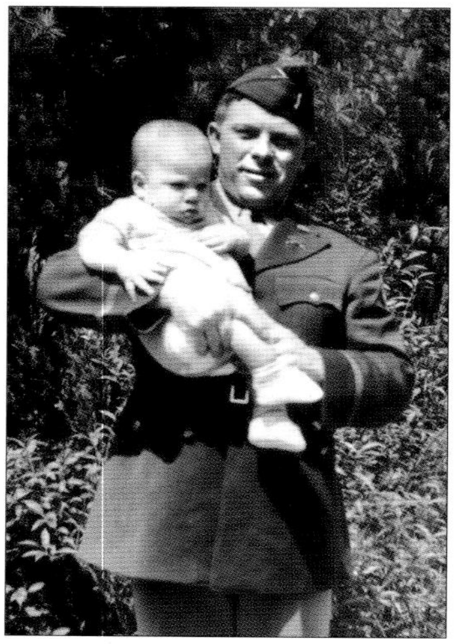

The rumor was that if you were caught with one of those as a prisoner, they'd put you out of your misery quick with the thing. I didn't intend to be a prisoner anyhow, at least taken alive. So I carried that P-38 most of the time. The last bullet that went out of there was the end of a Free Frenchman.

I didn't know he was a German officer at the time. When we were taking him back as a prisoner, the local people recognized him, and women came out with brooms and anything they had handy. (*The officer had earlier taken some of the men from their village to be shot.*) They were well acquainted with him locally. I had to run him back and get a number of my company men to go with me to protect him so we could take him out as a real prisoner.

Those Free French, they were out to do all the damage they could to the Germans. They were hunting for them. They went where they could do the most damage, but they didn't use much military smarts. There were two of them with our company. They weren't part of our company, they just went with us.

You also had in your company what they called scouts, two men, usually. The Germans would generally let the scouts go through, waiting for the main company. I moved much of the time up with the scouts, up in front. I was dressed just like the regular GIs. If you were out there portraying yourself as an officer, you got picked off. My company radio was clear in the rear. I could call in fire; we could call in air power, mortar fire, and whatnot, you know. You couldn't command a company when you're sitting in a foxhole. I didn't mind taking my chances with the regular GIs.

Your first responsibility as a company commander was to safeguard — do the most damage you could to the enemy and without any casualties to your own folks.

One interesting thing happened. We had some of our men, in order to keep from being detected, upstairs in a particular building. There were some Germans down below, and they didn't know our men were upstairs. If they'd made some racket or something, why, they'd have been taken care of by the Germans that were lunching down below.

Some of the boys wanted to go retrieve their folks that were upstairs. They went in there with the lead flying and took care of the German soldiers that were down below and retrieved our ones that were up above. So, there were some dead Germans that didn't finish their lunch. There wasn't much of an alternative if we were going to retrieve the rest of our company.

The only thing I came out with was a hearing loss. When we were up next to the Siegfried Line, they were putting those mortars over. I was approaching several buildings, and I was just walking through the garden on kind of soft material, and one of those mortars came over. I didn't know what happened. It knocked me out; I never knew there was a mortar over. They drug me into the house there, and I could see their lips moving but I couldn't understand what they were talking about. My hearing gradually returned about halfway so that I could do more than just write instructions on a pad.

It was a good experience, I guess, but I wouldn't want to have it a second time. ☆

Sanderson returned to civilian life as a county extension agent, serving in Hamlin and Roberts counties. He donated the pistol and his other WWII memorabilia to the Brookings County Historical Society Museum in Volga in 2000.

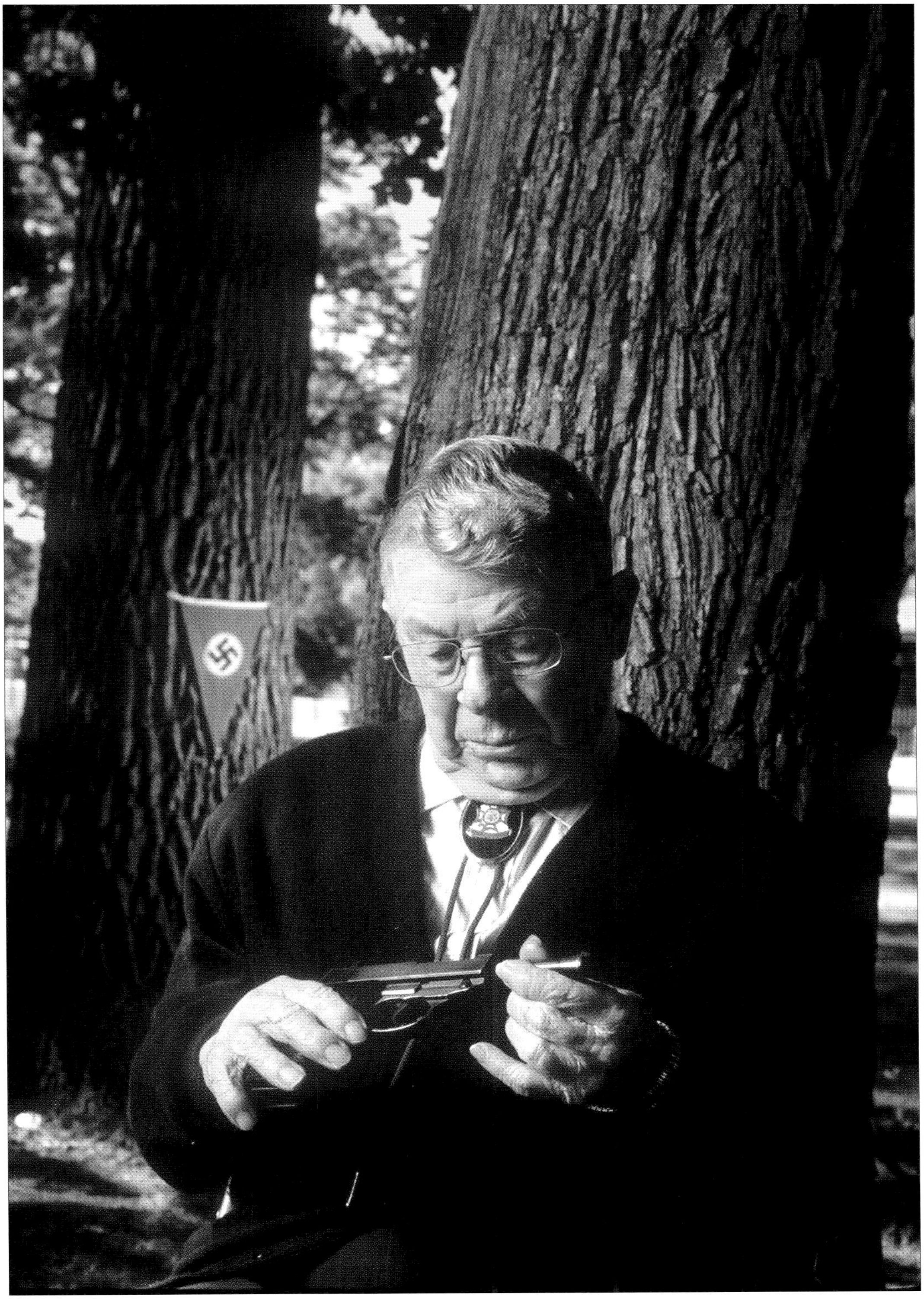

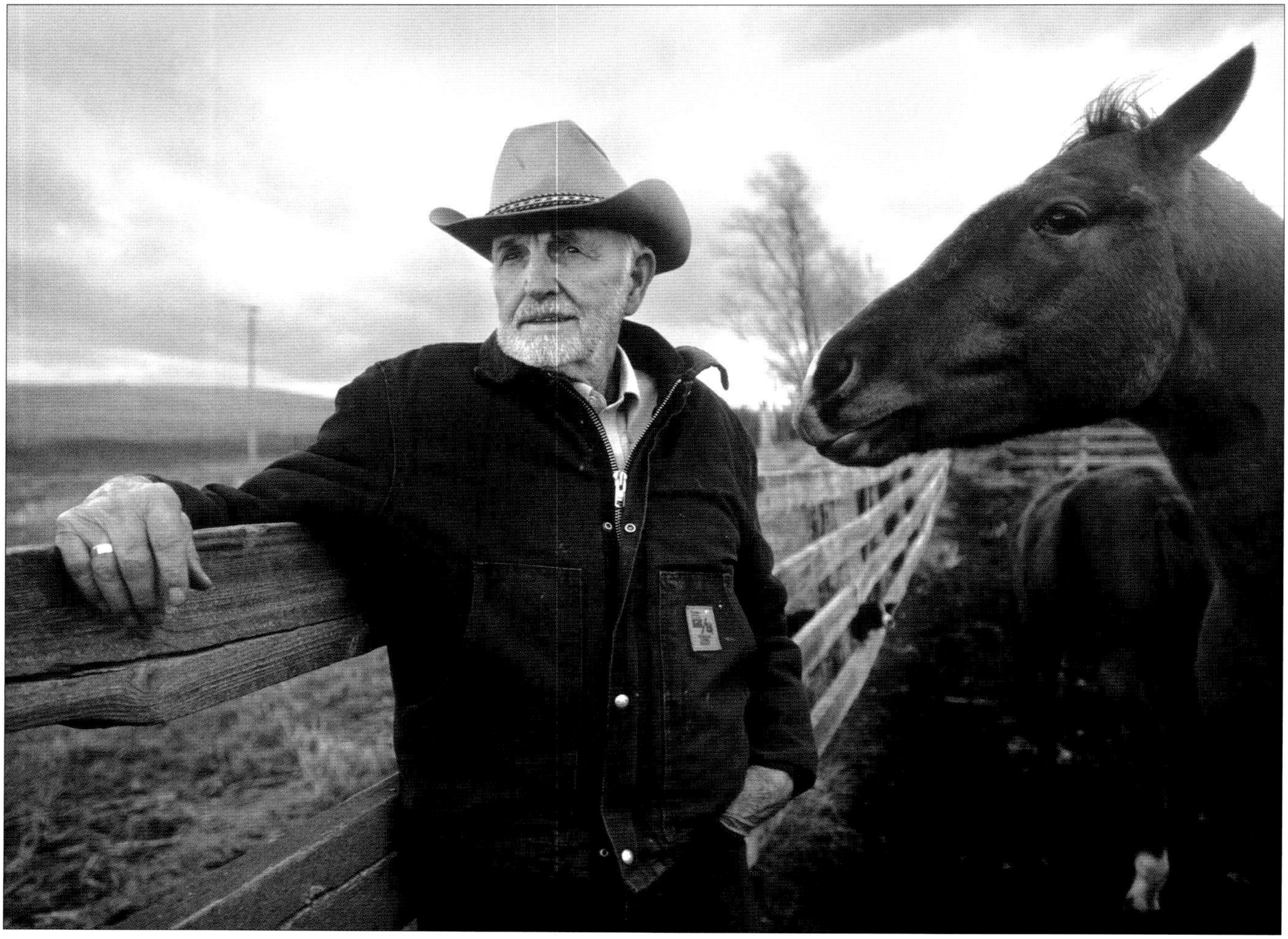

Bill Abernathy ☆ *Gann Valley*

As a soldier in the renowned 101st Airborne Division, Abernathy spent the war serving in the division's 321st Glider Artillery Battalion. He made a seaborne landing in Normandy, an airborne landing via glider into Holland for the Market-Garden operation, and weathered bitter cold and feisty Germans in Bastogne, Belgium, during the Battle of the Bulge. The 101st had recently liberated the Dachau concentration camp and penetrated Hitler's Eagle's Nest at Berchtesgaden when Germany surrendered.

We were in England nine months before the invasion. It was pretty country there, not too far from Oxford. There was a castle up on the hill, and they kept horses up there. We didn't see much sunshine, but it was not too cold. They didn't have enough gliders for everybody — we went in on a ship (*on D-Day plus one*). It was the *Susan B. Anthony*, and they sunk it right off the shore. It was like it hit a cement wall. They said it hit two mines. It was completely under in 45 minutes. Nice ship, too. They unloaded us on destroyers, and then we went in on LCIs (*Landing Craft Infantry*). They dropped these big ropes off the side of the ship, and we went right down on the destroyer. It happened really fast.

It was several days before we all got together again. We spent some time attacking Carentan. There was quite a lot of artillery there.

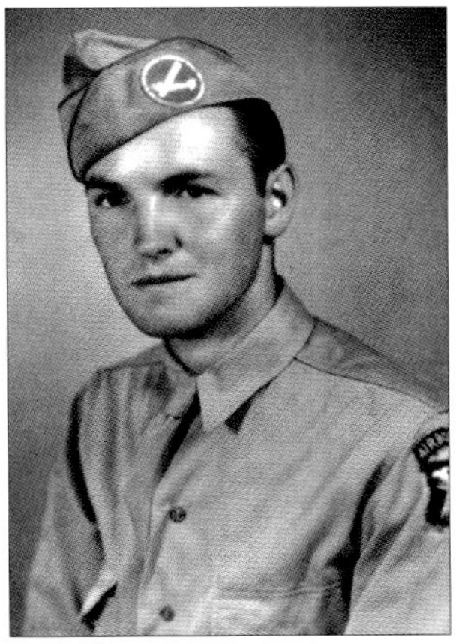

We went back to England sometime in July (*to prepare for the Holland attack*), and then we had replacements, of course. We had a lot of dry runs. They'd take you on just a moment's notice and you'd go to an airfield, and they'd tell you your mission, and then it didn't happen. This happened about three or four times before we went.

In Holland we were supposed to keep a road open, and (*the Germans*) would cut it behind us. The idea was to keep the road open so the British armor could come up there, but it never happened. The British took a real hit up there. (*The Market-Garden operation was made famous in the book and movie,* A Bridge Too Far.)

We were in Holland 72 days, and we were all about half nuts when we came out of there. We finally got out of Holland in time to go up into Bastogne. I don't think we were pulled out of (*Holland for more than*) two or three weeks, and then we were told around 6 or 7 o'clock in the evening (*that we were being rushed to Bastogne*). And 30 minutes later we were on our way, so we didn't have time to think a whole lot.

I never got right into the town when we first got there; I was a ways out of town. We spent Christmas there. I remember the Germans dropped us lots of leaflets and told us, "I wonder what the people at home are doing," and all this. We were pretty near out of ammo. There were some tough times there, real tough times. Some of our guys that got hit, they took them into the hospital in Bastogne and said it was worse in there than it was out where we were. It was pretty well smashed up, but not any worse than a lot of towns in France.

We liberated Landsberg (*a sub-camp of Dachau, one of several Jewish concentration camps in Germany*). That's bad doings there. We had run across a work camp or two where people lived pretty bad and were underfed, but not like (*Dachau*) was. You could lay two of them side-by-side on a stretcher and not crowd it any; that's how heavy they were. We weren't there only a day or two and then we went on.

The road was full of prisoners when we were going toward Berchtesgaden. It was real beautiful country there. We traveled with the 506th, and I guess we were probably about the first ones there as far as I know. We went up in there, and we carried loot out of that place like crazy the first day. We drank some of that good booze — I remember that — a pretty happy time, really. That was the fun part of it.

You can't imagine the stuff that was in there. I remember there was silverware, beautiful tablecloths; it was something else. I think the next day they brought the French army in there, and they wouldn't let us in there any more. I think we still have an ashtray that I took out of there. Some of the German cavalry came in there and surrendered, and we had horses to ride for a while. It was just before the war was officially over. ☆

Abernathy and his family have ranched between Gann Valley and Fort Thompson since the war's end.

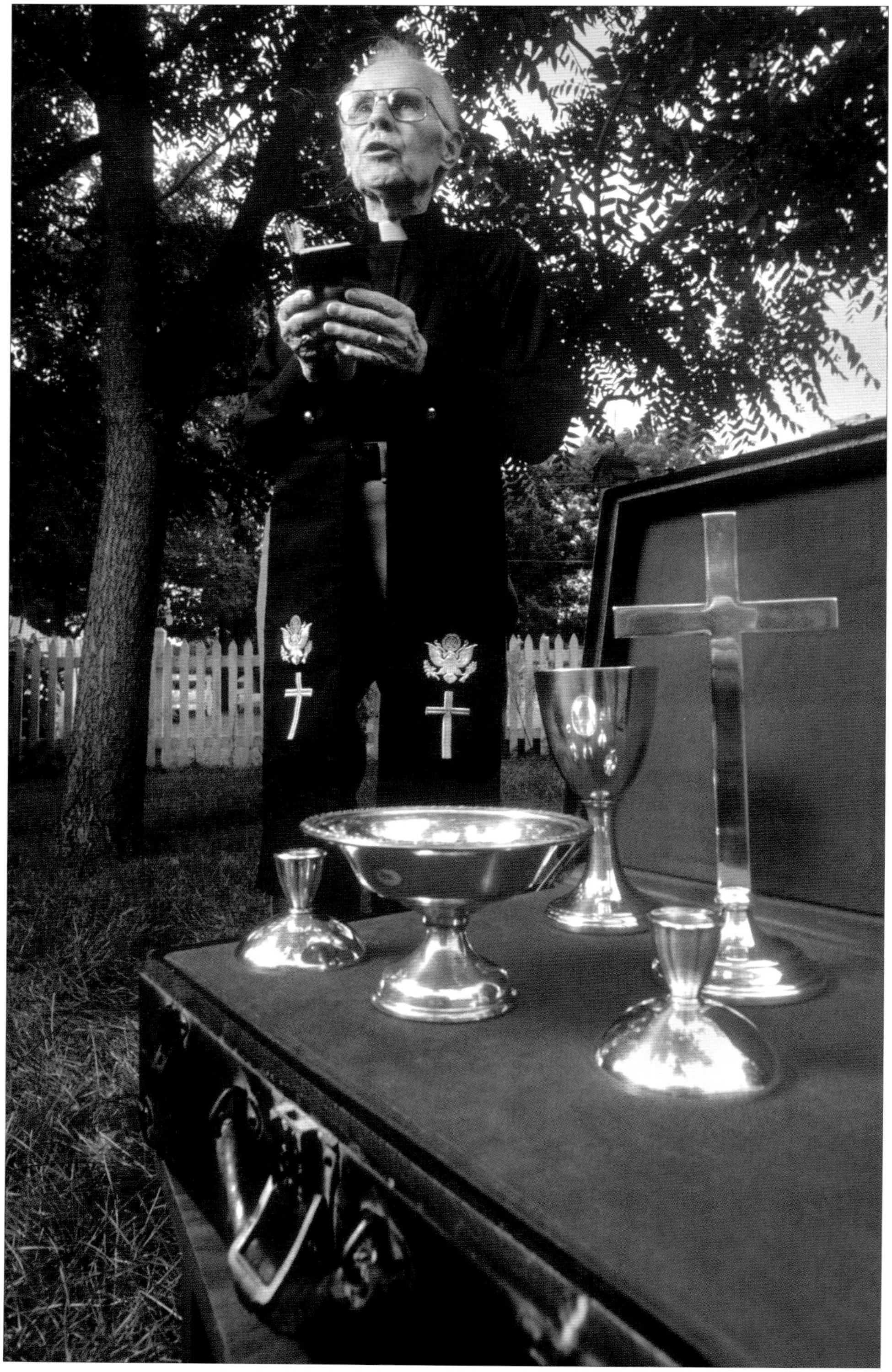

RICHARD DIEDE ☆ *Madison*

The 10th Armored Division sailed for Normandy in September 1944, with Diede as one of several chaplains. He later became Division Chaplain, but not before surviving several harrowing events in France and beyond.

Because I was young, I was assigned to what they called a "hot outfit," which was the 10th Armored Division. We went over on a troop ship, did a lot of zig-zagging. I got on the ship and woke up at 7 o'clock in the morning before we took off and lifted my head, and I was sick, sicker than a dog. I fed the fish for three days. It took us 12 days to go over.

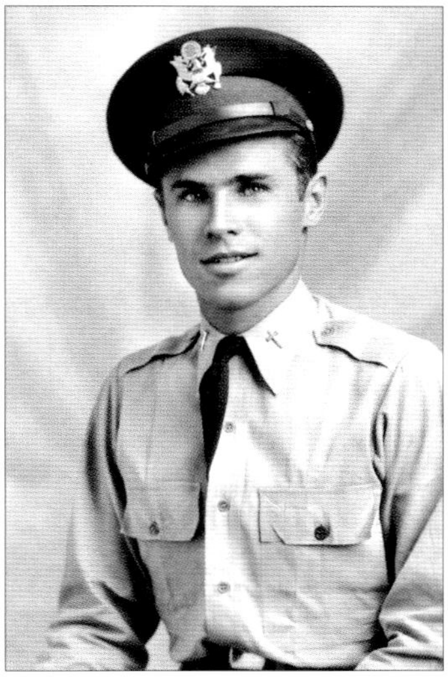

One of the first things we did was to clean mine fields. One of the first bad experiences I had was to be lost in a mine field. You didn't know whether your next step was going to be your last one. Here we were, the organist, my driver and myself. What were we going to do? My driver said, "Chaplain, you go first and we'll follow in your footsteps." He was six years older than I, but he always thought there was a guardian angel looking over me. Well you know, you couldn't say, "No, I'M not going. YOU go!" — your name would have been mud. So I went — we got through. The next day or so, someone got careless and they ran, and of course he stepped on a few of the mines and there were several killed.

You don't know why somebody was killed and you were not. You used to think as a clergyman that you knew all the answers. You found out that you knew very few of the answers to life and why things happen.

You didn't have a ready-made church as you contacted the soldiers and the officers. You set up your services; you went to the different units — Combat Command A, Combat Command B, and so forth. You contacted the 1st sergeants and said, "I'm going to be in the area and I'm going to set up for services. You get the word out to the men." And that was our church.

We had services in barns, services out in the open and in the mud, next to tanks. We had very few services in cathedrals. There were a lot of local ministers where we were that didn't want us in their church.

The 10th Armored usually had about 10 to 12 chaplains. *(Our duties included)* setting up services, visiting the wounded and sick and tending to them.

I worked with the Graves Registration Bureau when they came to gather up the dead and the like. I knew where quite a few of them were, so I directed them. That was not a very pleasant job. These were temporary burials, you must understand, and they were later transferred to permanent burial grounds. They had just dug a trench; I couldn't even see the end of it. Here were the soldiers, minus arms, legs, holes in the back, etc., etc., all along the side *(of the trench)*.

I don't know how many I buried that day or how many I had services for. I thought, "This is all that they get, after having served their country?" I told my senior chaplain, "Don't send me back anymore."

We could choose where we wanted to be, and most of the time I was at the front aid stations. Occasionally, I would go with an ambulance to go and pick up the wounded. Any chaplain could administer to either Protestant, or Jewish, or Catholic. We had three different prayers that we could use to administer the last rites.

We had good men, good chaplains. You didn't push your denomination. You didn't say, "I'm a Lutheran," or "I'm a Methodist," or "I'm a Congregational." That was a no-no. We were inter-denominational, of course. Minister to anybody and everybody in the service.

Most of the time I had good attendance at my services because I was where they were. It's like I always said about my ministry: I never felt I was a great preacher, but I was a friend. I believed in being a friend to anyone who was willing to want a friend. I think that drew more men to my services than my preaching. In fact, I was called "Smiley" at times.

I ended up being Division Chaplain. I'd have gotten a double promotion if I'd stayed in the service, but I felt two years was long enough. I wanted to go home. ☆

Originally from Alpena, Diede ministered in several churches after the war, finally settling in Madison.

Tom McDill ☆ *Custer*

The day after attacking Pearl Harbor, Japanese forces worked to occupy several South Pacific islands. McDill was in the Philippines when the Japanese invaded and was forced to endure the legendary Bataan Death March.

To start out with, I was on guard duty, walking a post for six hours a night, two nights out of three. Then they activated a signal company on the base there at Nichols Field. I transferred into that, and it was kind of on-the-job training for a telephone lineman. That's what I was doing when the war started.

The next day *(December 8, 1941)* they started hitting us with bombers. They didn't waste any time. We moved over to Bataan from Nichols Field across the bay, and we were over on the west side of Bataan. Well, all the telephone lines were right along the roads. Of course when they bomb, they bomb the roads and they'd usually cut the wire. Then it was our job to go out and fix the wire again.

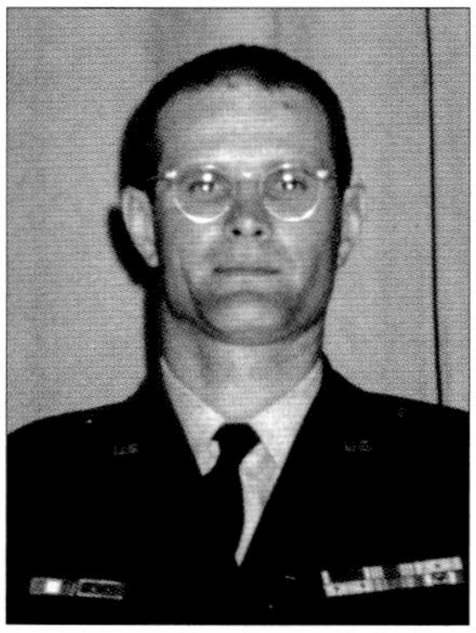

They started landing up on Lingayan Gulf, and they had a front up around San Fernando, Pampanga, there. We were back of the front lines a ways, but the artillery — our 155s were in back of us — when they'd shell, their shells would go out over us. And then we got shelled and bombed, too.

We got surrendered in about April of the next year. Hell, we were out of food, practically out of ammunition; we were out of everything. There wasn't much choice. In fact, there wasn't any choice, I guess. We had to walk down from where we were on the west side of Bataan, then up the Manila Bay side. We didn't know where we were going, had no idea where we were headed for, or how long we were going to be walking there. Of course, the worst part was not getting fed. We didn't get anything to eat, and you had to fight for anything to drink when you had a chance to get some.

They beat on us whenever they took a notion to, and they shot some of them and bayonetted some of them along the way too. Being killed would be the biggest fear. Some of them got to where they couldn't walk, and that's the ones they usually shot. They could kill anyone that they wanted to, and they did. You had to keep moving. I was a farm boy; I was in pretty good health and pretty tough, and glad that I was.

Once you got into the prison camp, although they were pretty bad living conditions, at least you were a little safer from the army troops going by all the time there. They had been fighting with our soldiers, so they didn't give a damn. Once you got into prison camp, there was a certain amount of accountability.

You were always in a 10-man group. The idea was that if anyone in that group escaped, the others got shot. What the hell was the use of escaping there? We were on a pump house outside the perimeter of the camp on the river, and we were pumping water out of the river up to a tank in the camp. We worked on that pump for about a year, I guess. That wasn't too bad; we were outside of the camp, and we got our food right out of the Japanese mess hall instead of the mess hall up in camp. We were getting contraband from across the river at night *(from Filipino locals)*. We'd get in cigarettes and candy and stuff and take it up to camp, sell it in camp and then we'd buy more from across the river at night.

I was almost two years over in Cabanatuan. Most of the work detail over there was working on a big farm raising vegetables, corn, okra. When we plowed it, why, you just lined up a line of prisoners with pickaxes, and that's how you plowed it.

We had malaria a lot of times. Malaria, dysentery — that was pretty common. We didn't have medicine, it would just have to run its course.

After three and a half years *(when the war had ended)*, it was a pretty happy day. Some of our Air Force started coming over — B-17s — and they started dropping food and medicine into our camp. We would eat so damn much American food, we'd get sicker than hell.

Oh, I've had nightmares once in a while about it, but it's got to be where it's so far back now, it seems like a bad dream, mostly. ☆

About 68,000 American and Filipino troops were in the march and imprisoned. More than 13,000 of them did not survive the war. McDill worked in a handful of camps and weighed 105 pounds when the war ended. He ranches in rural Custer.

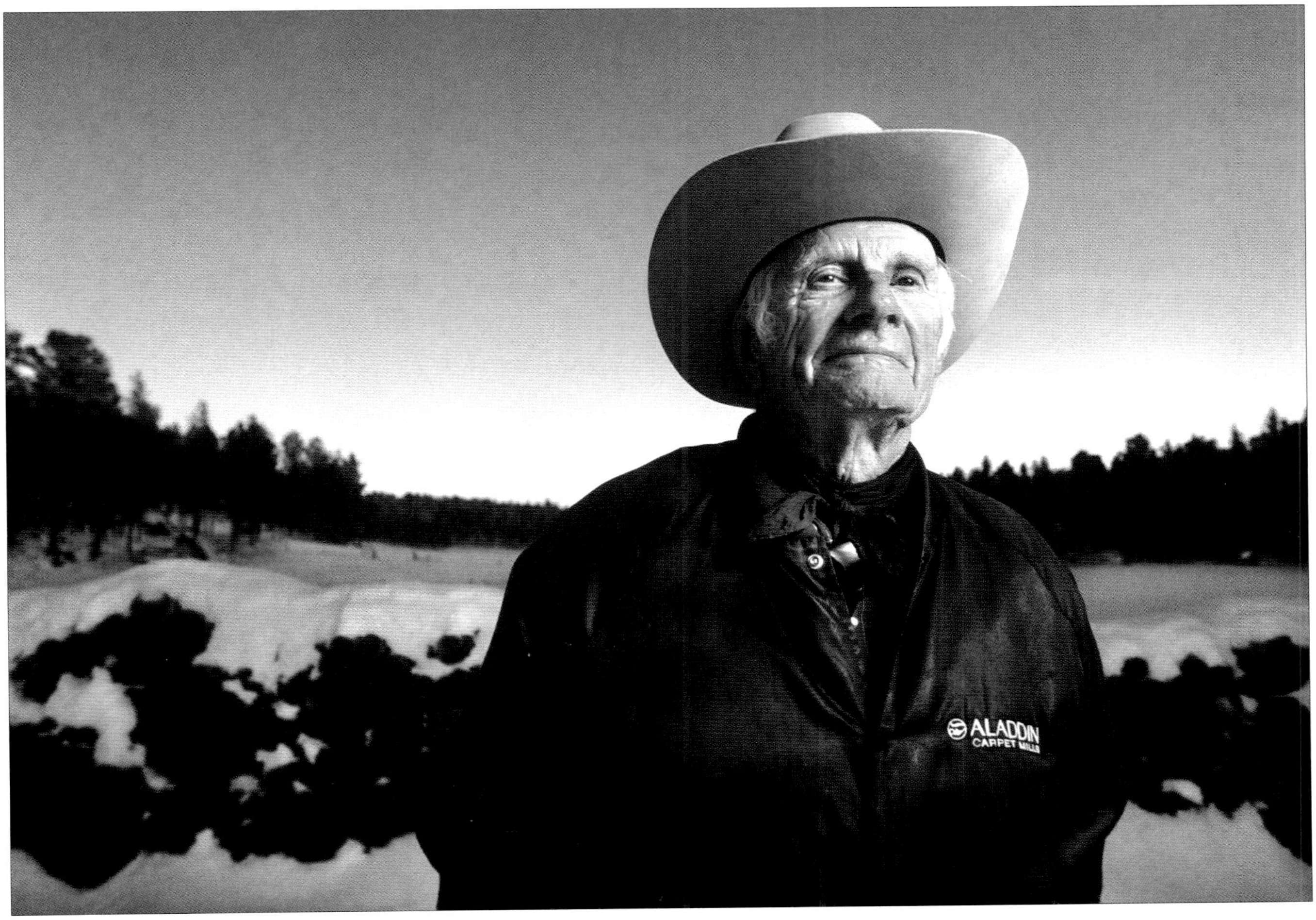
ALADDIN
CARPET MILLS

Dave Moore ☆ *Vivian*

Moore was part of the great influx of American troops into France as the war gained momentum in early 1945. He manned a machine gun in the 6th Armored Division.

I left in August of '44. I was inducted at Fort Snelling, Minnesota, and took my basic training at Fort Hood, Texas. When we were training, we were trained to go to Japan, to fight in the islands. And then the breakthrough *(Battle of the Bulge)* came; all of a sudden they needed troops there. We landed at Greenock, Scotland, on the 17th of January.

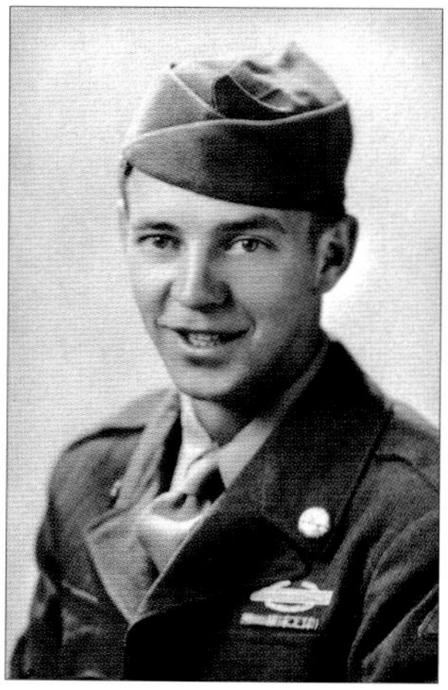

I hadn't been out of South Dakota until I went to the Army. I was bewildered by the amount of damage. When we went through Bastogne, the houses were all destroyed. We spent three or four days in this little town in Luxembourg; I remember we walked around, looked at the town. That's where I saw the first German dead. They were still laying around town, covered with snow. They had their temporary cemetery down in front of a barn where we had our kitchen. The night before we went on the line the first time, they had church for us. We had that in the haymow of the barn.

I got assigned to a machine gun section. It was the 4th or 5th of February. They walked us up the road — I don't know how far we went — to find a crossing to go across the Roer River, which is the border between Luxembourg and Germany. We got up in a wooded area on the German side after we crossed the river on a foot bridge about three or four feet wide with rope sides on it, just tied from a tree on one side to a tree on the other side.

We run into one of those armed pillboxes out of the Siegfried Line that the Germans had manned. They had their artillery zeroed in on that pillbox, and when it just started to get dark, why they started to shell us. The next morning, we had probably two or three feet of pine tree boughs in front of the machine gun.

I could hear German troops talking. When it got daylight, I could see them — I suppose they were 100 yards out in front. At about 10 o'clock they told us to leave all our equipment and bring the wounded out. They had shelled us all night, and I knew we had lost a lot of men. I had no idea how many.

Along with two other guys, I started to carry a guy out on a stretcher. We got partway back to this place where we crossed. We got about halfway down the hill and a big shell lit behind us. We dropped down in the snow when we heard that shell coming in, but we didn't drop down quick enough. The guy across the stretcher from me got hit, he got a piece of shrapnel in his back, about two or three inches long; right between the shoulder blades. It's been a long time ago, over 50 years ago, and I still remember what that looks like. I have no idea who he was, where he was from, or whether it killed him or not.

I crawled over there to him, unbuttoned his shirt collar and jacket — he sounded like he was choking — the first aid man came from I don't know where, and the two of us took that guy back across the foot bridge. It's a funny thing about combat. Sure we were scared, but I don't remember that we had a horrid fear of it.

I remember some soldier walking by the halftrack and saying that Roosevelt died. I remember we were all wondering what would become of the war after President Roosevelt was gone.

Nobody wanted to get hit; I've made it through this far, I ain't going to get hit the last week or so. There's always got to be somebody that's last.

We could get the feeling that the Germans were on the run. I remember how relieved we were when we got the word *(that the war was over)*. I still remember that morning. I remember taking that steel helmet off. I just remember how good it felt to get rid of that thing. It weighs about three pounds, and we wore those things forever and ever, it seemed like to us.

The older I get, the more I admire my mother's courage. It must have been immense. She was not a very big person, she was not very well. Her health was not good. She must have been torn up inside to send her oldest boy off to war. ☆

Moore returned to Europe in 1996 and visited the battlefields and cemeteries along the path he took in 1945. He worked as a banker in Vivian after World War II.

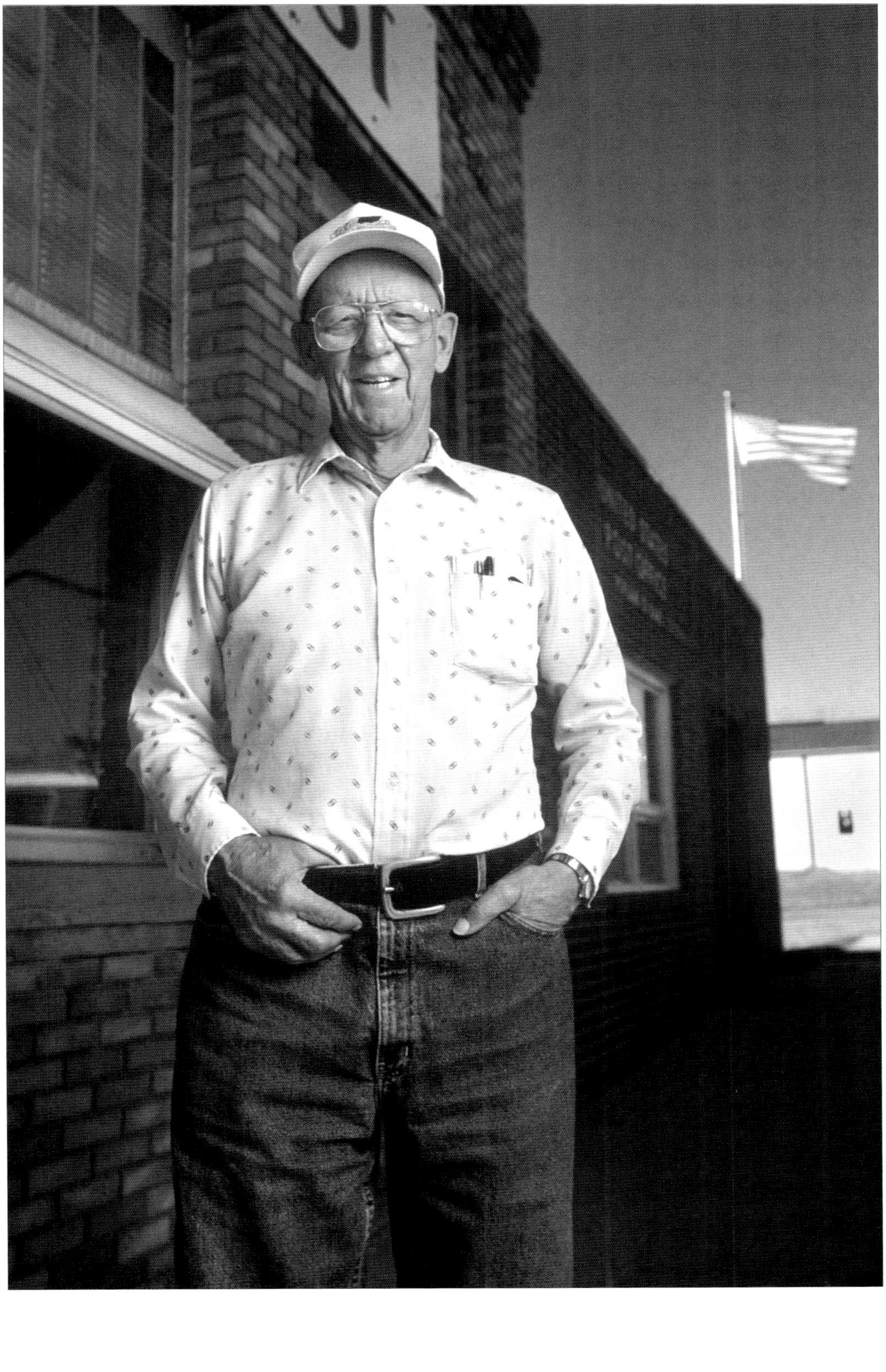

FRANK BRANAUGH ☆ *Yankton*

Joining the Army long before World War II began, Branaugh spent nearly six years in service to his country fighting with the 3rd Infantry Division. Ironically, he didn't receive his near-fatal wounds until after the war was over.

I was 18 years old when I went into the service. I left a pretty fair job at that time. I was drawing $9 a week working seven days a week at what is now known as the Sohler Stockyards east of Yankton. We built the thing from scratch about three years prior to this.

I couldn't see much to look forward to working at the stockyard, so I joined the Army on October 26, 1939. I enlisted down at Bellevue, Nebraska, and that's where Custer left from. He come to Yankton, and he didn't fare much better than I had at that time.

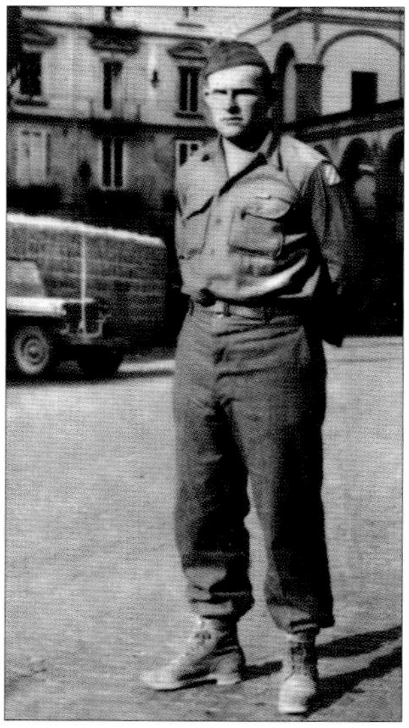

I rode a train from Omaha, Nebraska, out to Tacoma, Washington. That was the first time that I ever had $75 in my hand at one time. The Army gave it to me to buy food on that train. That's how long it took us to get out to Tacoma. It rained quite a little in that country out there. It didn't seem to make any difference to the Army. When it was time in the mornings, you went to drill — whether it was raining or not, it made no difference. That's the Army I lived in for the next several years.

We were declared an amphibious division, which is one that works from the water into land. We practiced on Puget Sound. That's probably the coldest inland water there is in the United States. It did not bother the Army much that it got cold, because there weren't many officers that ever got out in the water. But I can assure you the rest of us did.

We were told the Japs had attacked Pearl Harbor. I really wasn't overly educated — I didn't know who they were talking about. I didn't know if Pearl Harbor was a woman, or what it was. I was soon to find out it was an island situated out in the Pacific.

I believe I was a corporal at that time. I was to take a truck and get some old WWI ammunition, about 15 or 20 rounds. I believe I was given about 10 guys in the back of a truck. I was in command. Up until now, the only thing I had ever commanded was a few cattle in the stockyard. I did know how to handle those. It was just about as intelligent a job to handle those cattle as it was to handle these soldiers.

I was told to go to a town named Bandon, Oregon, which was several hundred miles south of Fort Lewis. I was to drop off these men, a couple at a time, to guard different projects on the West Coast. I remember particularly I was to put two men out when I went across the Columbia River at Vancouver, and one of them would be on each end of that bridge and guard the bridge in case the Japs blew it up. Now this may sound ridiculous — I was also told the entire West Coast would be under Martial Law. And I didn't know who he was either.

There were to be no lights on along the entire coast. We were to see to it on the way down that there were no lights, absolutely none. And the Japanese would be attacking the West Coast.

I dropped off different people at different electrical substations, and I believe there were three left — including myself — when I got down to Bandon. So that spread us out pretty thin, to guard a 500-mile stretch of the West Coast with 10 or 12 men.

We set up an artillery gun down there, wired in with our telephone communication into the old Bell system, at a gasoline station. I had a good surveillance of the ocean, but it was very, very dark when I got there. I set her up, dug it in, did the best we could to get ready to defend the United States.

We hadn't been much more than set up until we saw our first Japanese submarine. And I let it come in as close as it was going to. We were all just scared as all daylights, you can bet on that. I loaded that thing up — I bore sighted the gun, jerked that lanyard, and blew into that Japanese sub.

I didn't see anybody come out of it, and it didn't sink, so I give her another round. Bore sighted it, aimed in there and got right onto it. "Give her another one!"

One of the guys started to laugh. He said, "Branaugh, I don't think we're going to sink that. I think it's a log." And he was right, that's what it was. That was the

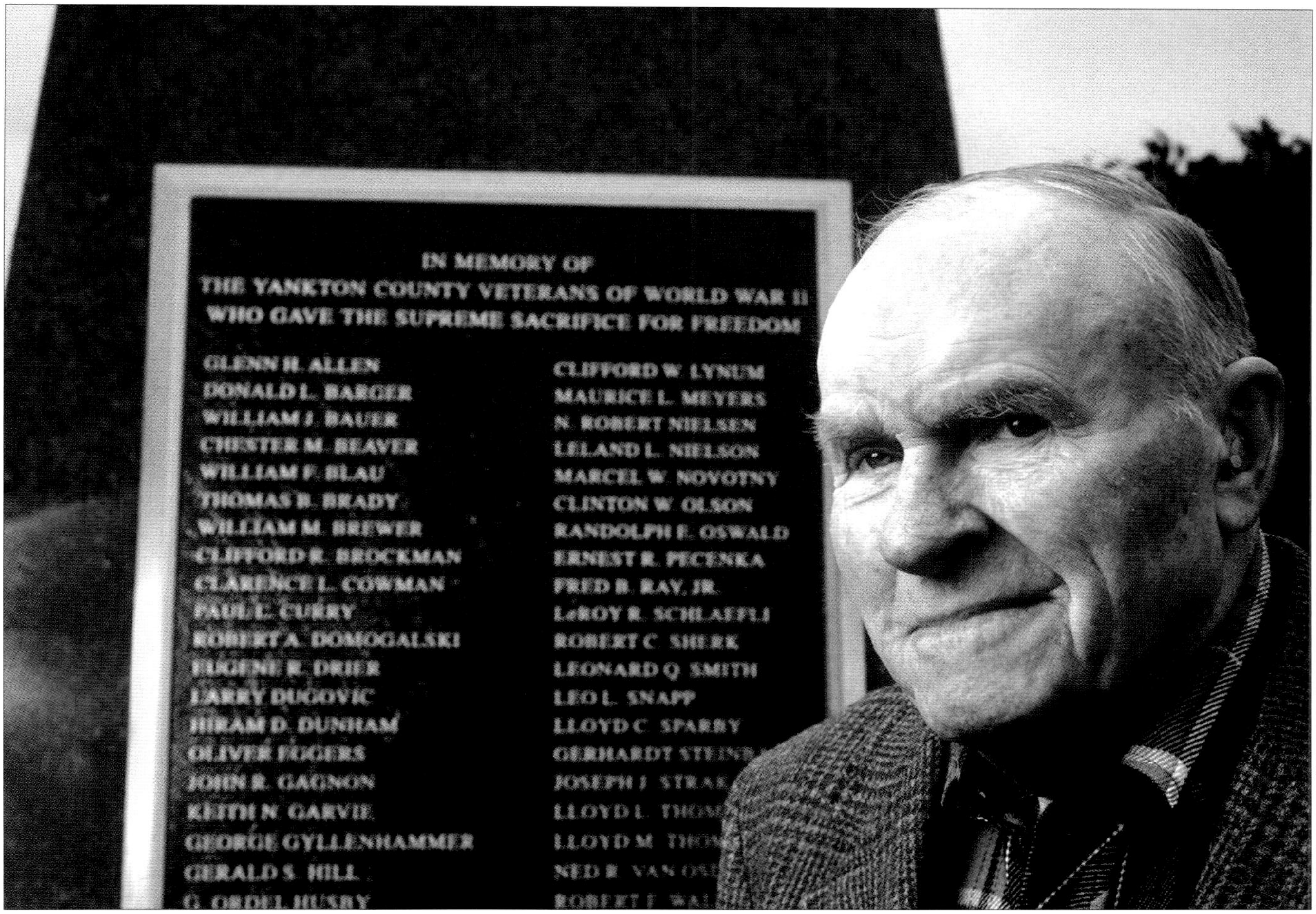
IN MEMORY OF
THE YANKTON COUNTY VETERANS OF WORLD WAR II
WHO GAVE THE SUPREME SACRIFICE FOR FREEDOM
GLENN H. ALLEN
DONALD L. BARGER
WILLIAM J. BAUER
CHESTER M. BEAVER
WILLIAM F. BLAU
THOMAS B. BRADY
WILLIAM M. BREWER
CLIFFORD R. BROCKMAN
CLARENCE L. COWMAN
PAUL L. CURRY
ROBERT A. DOMOGALSKI
EUGENE R. DRIER
LARRY DUGOVIC
HIRAM D. DUNHAM
OLIVER EGGERS
JOHN R. GAGNON
KEITH N. GARVIE
GEORGE GYLLENHAMMER
GERALD S. HILL
G. ORDEL HUSBY
CLIFFORD W. LYNUM
MAURICE L. MEYERS
N. ROBERT NIELSEN
LELAND L. NIELSON
MARCEL W. NOVOTNY
CLINTON W. OLSON
RANDOLPH E. OSWALD
ERNEST R. PECENKA
FRED B. RAY, JR.
LeROY R. SCHLAEFLI
ROBERT C. SHERK
LEONARD Q. SMITH
LEO L. SNAPP
LLOYD C. SPARBY

beginning of the war for me.

They told us that we would be going to Africa. We landed near Casablanca at Fidela on November the 2nd, 1942. Each section had a 3-inch gun. We were to go in under a coastal artillery unit, which was concrete emplaced with four big guns that would be firing as we came in. The closer we got, they could not lower the level of their barrels down. And they did fire. But we had firepower behind us.

Most of the ships that we had were WWI ships. We had two cruisers, and three or four destroyers and a couple of sub chasers plus the ships that we went over on. There was quite an armada — that's what we thought anyway. But every *(invasion)* we made after this was a little bit bigger.

We got in on the beach — that was my first landing under fire. I saw a train moving out, just a little bit over the sand hills. I got that gun emplaced and looked down through that barrel — couldn't ever get a scope on it, I don't even know if we had one there — and I fired that first shell out there. And the train stopped.

We weren't too far away from the train, maybe three or four hundred yards. And what comes out of that train but 75 or 100 German soldiers in uniform. They were getting away from us, but when this shell hit, it completely missed the train. I had it broadsided — I led it just a little bit like you would a pheasant in this country — and I hit the railroad tracks right in front of it. It was an electric train getting its power through the railroad track, and when I hit the railroad track, it was out of power. The train stopped, and out come the German soldiers. But lo and behold, they had their hands over their heads, behind their neck, wanting to give up. That was our first victory that we had in WWII.

I went from Africa to Sicily, from Sicily to Salerno in southern Italy, then I went up through the mountains that first winter, then I came back to Naples and went up to Anzio. I was in Anzio every day. One hundred and thirty days — I was there all of them. That was a horrible thing, that Anzio beachhead.

I was a little bit of everything. I was a sergeant most of the time, in command of something or other. I always figured that I had a minimum of 75 or 100 guys to keep happy and to keep them guys from wishing they were

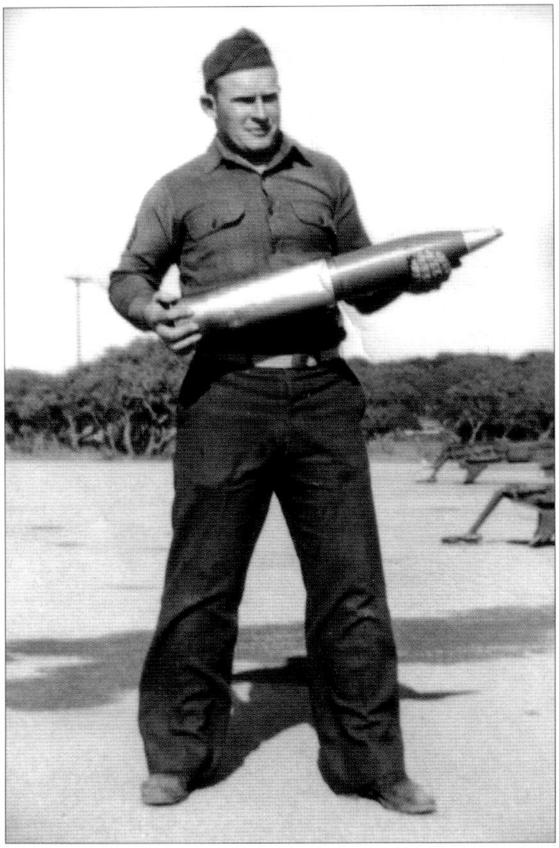

back home. I'd either tell them a lie or a story or whatever you had to; about something I'd heard — how good things were back here in the States — I'd think up something to tell them. That was part of the war. You have to have a joker in every place, see. Sometimes you have to entertain people. If you sit down to eat and you can gather a dozen of them around you, just keep talking to them.

It's just living a life very similar to the way the Indians did here. Except they got back to the igloo at night and could wrap up in a skin. You'd go for days and days and days and never have any shelter of any kind. In the wintertime, it was rough. Really rough. I feel sorry for my dog. She's never slept outside at night since we've had her. I wouldn't leave my dog out in the cold or rain, but you do that with human beings in time of war. That's the way things are in wartime.

Everybody cannot live with the lifestyle that's required of that kind of war we was in. Don't you think that just because you got lots of replacements in, that it's all going to pan out. They would come up and give me replacements. You get under heavy fire, they'd lay right down and just lose their nerve and just go nuts. They ain't no good to you. You send them back.

War is dangerous. I suppose we had as many guys get hurt from either frozen feet or malaria fever and all this kind of stuff. There's a lot of things involved in war besides getting shot at.

I left Anzio and I went into southern France. We were much better supplied after we got to France. We entered a more humane environment. You could tell a lot of difference between France and Germany. When we went from France to Germany, you might find that the French might have had more fun, but the Germans kept things far more orderly. You could see the difference when you crossed from one country to another, especially if you was walking. If you went into a German place, the fence would be fixed, with whatever they had to fix it with. Their houses were kept up better. They might have had cattle in the same house that they lived in, but the shed would be clean and they washed it every day. You have to give credit where credit is due. They might have been the enemy, but you had more respect for those people. You didn't find that in France. It was a filthy country to me. It was not well kept; the people weren't even proud to be a Frenchman.

I supposed I witnessed tens of thousands of Germans wanting to surrender *(as the war was ending)*. They had a high respect for authority. They would come out in the middle of the road and stack their arms — like only the military knows how to stack them so they wouldn't fall over — put their hands behind their heads and want to give up. As far as the eye could see, there was that many people wanting to surrender. And they'd surrender to one lonely American! All they want to do is go home. They really ain't mad at nobody. The SS troopers were mad, and they were going to kill Americans. But the regular soldiers were no different from us. They were taken out of their homes, sent overseas, and probably suffered a little abuse.

I got up in Austria, and there were some big fish ponds up there. There was thousands of potato mashers *(German grenades)* around then. You could take a carton of them and sit down by a lake, pull the pin and throw them out there. And there'd be some lake trout that would come up. I took off my clothes, went out — I have to laugh at myself — but I took one in each hand. I had two hands then, see, and I was going to swim back. You know, you cannot swim with a lake trout in your hand. It will get out of there.

So I had to go out, get one at a time and put it in my mouth like my dog used to do, and swim in with a lake trout at a time in my mouth. But we had trout to eat. That's an unusual way to fish. Don't ever try that, unless you plan on carrying them in in your mouth.

If you got 85 points at one time you were supposed to get to come home, and I think I had 138 points the day I came out. They couldn't send me home, they told me right offhand, "because you're essential to the war effort." So what the hell good did it do to have the points?

We were in an old house. There was a grenade — now, I don't know if I can remember it just right or not, because I was the receiver. A guy that lives up in Minnesota, he said, "What is this?" He tossed it toward me, threw it off on my right side. I reached for it, and I never did get ahold of it. It exploded.

It hit me full blast. It blew this arm off *(left forearm)*, but it had to have exploded over on my right side, because that's where it did all the damage, except blowing my hand off. It crippled up this right arm pretty good here, and the elbow. I pretty near bled to death out of that right bicep at the top. It busted the bones down through here, including my hand. My wrist has never worked right since. I was injured pretty badly through my chest and the like. They called it multiple injuries and fragments.

Eventually I wound up in Paris in a body cast. They never took that off until I got out to Utah. *(Branaugh recuperated from his injuries in a Utah hospital.)*

The best thing you can have is youth and health. Those are the people that are rich. ☆

Branaugh spent his post-war years working in construction and lobbied for many years on behalf of veterans. He was instrumental in creating a monument to the 53 Yankton County men killed in WWII.

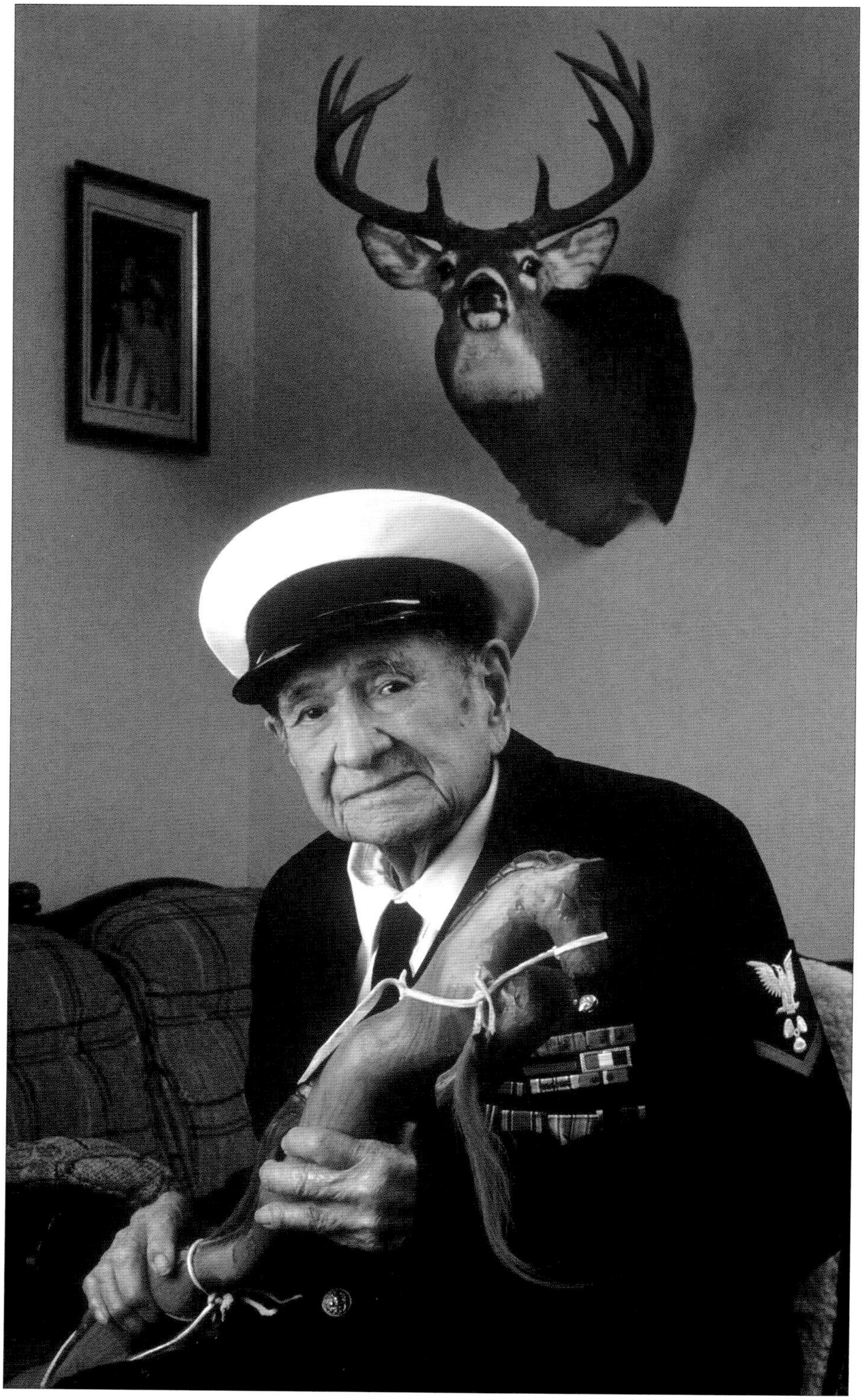

Reuben LaBatte ☆ *Peever*

The majority of LaBatte's war service was spent on the battleship New Jersey *as part of a 16-inch gun crew. Prior to that, he was stationed on the aircraft carrier* San Jacinto.

My mother and I walked — in them days Indians didn't have cars — to church. This priest we had gave the news. He said, "The United States declared war today. All the young guys 17 years on up will be drafted." A few days before Christmas we got notice to go to Bremerton, Washington *(for training)*.

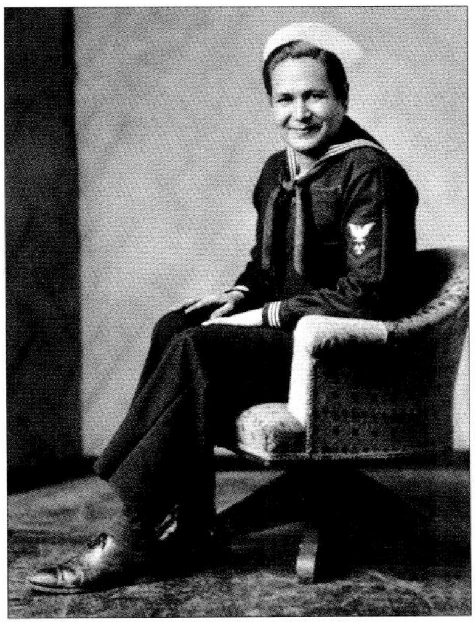

I was assigned to the carrier *U.S.S. San Jacinto*. It was named in honor of Texas. President *(George H.W.)* Bush was a pilot on that carrier at the same time I was on there. I didn't know him at all.

Then they took eight of us to the *U.S.S. New Jersey*, a battleship. I was the only Indian on that 2,900-man crew. I was surprised — where were all the Indians?

I was in an air cooling unit. I helped load the guns and I watched the cooler; that 16-inch gun has cooling *(that would bring its temperature during combat)* down to 30 degrees. There were 11 of us that manned that 16-inch gun. I was on the 40mm *(anti-aircraft gun)* too. We saw the kamikazes, and we shot them down.

One of them hit in front of us *(and exploded as the ship passed over it)*, and you could hear that big battleship like we hit a rock pile. Lot of them sailors lost their hearing. So I know what a bomb is.

That guy *(James)* Forrestal, we'd be at the church service, and he always came to sit by me. He was a big wheel on the ship. He always sat by me or he greeted me anytime I'm on the deck. He says, "Reuben, you're a Native American Indian. Don't you know you're the only Indian we have on this ship? When the war is over, and we get home okay, I will write to you." And he did! *(Navy Secretary Forrestal later became America's first Secretary of Defense under President Truman.)*

I sang a victory song in Indian after the United States conquered the Gulf of Leyte. We pulled out and the commander said, "Chief, give out a war whoop!"

So I gave out a war whoop. And then I prayed in Indian, "Lord, we thank you for your guidance, that you have brought us through this war without injury. And we won the war! You protected us. Through Jesus Christ our Lord, Amen."

So that prayer must be in the air in the South Pacific waters. I always remembered them prayers in Dakota Sioux language. I pray for the living and the dead.

Ira Hayes, he was one of the Marines who put the flag up at Iwo Jima. That's the only Indian person I ever met over there. I remember him as a brave warrior. Look how brave he was. Look how he helped raise the United States flag. Way up there, a target — like a sitting duck up there on the hill. He protected the sovereignty of the Indians.

I had a cousin, Elmer Feather, from Big Coulee. I went to school with him; we roomed together, sang, graduated high school together. We played football together. He was killed in that bloodiest battle in history at Iwo Jima.

And then Francis Bird — he was the youngest of us. We are relatives; we are cousins. He was a little bit under age, but somehow he made it through. The United States Navy pronounced him missing in action.

Three of us from this Big Coulee district, we *(risked)* our lives for all people. We want to keep our sovereignty, our democracy, our freedom, our speech. We fought for that. And those guys never came home, and I did. So it was kind of sad for me.

You know, I've got knowledge — I'll say a voice of wisdom. I'm an Indian interpreter. Just like a dictionary, you've got to know the words of the English language, then you interpret to Indian. You have to speak good English.

I've got no one to talk to now. All the ones that talked Indian are all dead now. It's sad. ☆

The Sisseton-Wahpeton tribe honored LaBatte with a war staff (pictured with him at left) upon his return from WWII. After a stint in carpentry, LaBatte spent 23 years as a Dakota Sioux interpreter, helping tribal elders communicate with hospital staff.

LeRoy Clarkson ☆ *Belle Fourche*

Although trained by the Navy, Clarkson spent most of his time on land, spotting targets for naval guns offshore. He led a team of spotters and forward observers during both the Sicily and Normandy invasions.

I'd had Citizens Military Training and ROTC at college, so I'd seen quite a bit of the Army. I decided I'd try something different. But then I spent all my time with the Army after I got in the Navy — as a naval liaison spotting naval gunfire on the landings.

I kind of just fell into it. I was raised on the range, so I had an awful good idea of distances, and my eyes were a lot better than they are now.

I was with the 45th Division in Sicily, and then in Normandy it was the 4th Division. We landed in North Africa and maneuvered there for a time or two and made a couple of fake landings, and headed for Sicily. I was in the second wave going into Sicily. The Germans were still pretty good with airplanes at that time. They were doing a lot of bombing. I was in there for about a month.

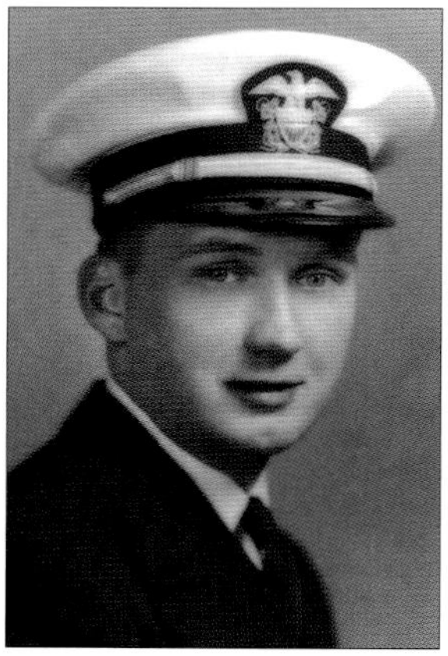

The Navy had different ships. They had mainly destroyers, but also cruisers and battleships at Normandy. They had one or two battleships at Sicily too. It was mainly the destroyers that did the work. They'd come in close and they'd move so fast that they didn't figure they'd get too much artillery. They had maps with coordinates, and all we'd do is pick a target — troops, tanks, or whatever — and return it to the ships. In Sicily we used Morse code, but in Normandy it was just voice.

When we came back from Sicily, we brought prisoners. There was a German general and several hundred prisoners on this troop ship that I was on. The other prisoners would always salute the general. They'd let them out on deck after we went on, and you could tell they didn't believe all those ships that were in that convoy.

The only thing I'd learned from Sicily is that you'd better get off the beach if you could. They did quite a bit of strafing, even in Normandy. My radioman got wounded with shrapnel in Normandy, right on the beach.

The ones that stayed on the beach were the worst off because they did lay a lot of fire on the beaches and you had to get the hell off there as fast as you could. They would strafe the beach to beat hell. Landing craft didn't get us too close; you waded in about chest deep. Those waves are just minutes apart; they started going in before daylight, and it was probably an hour or two after daylight when I went in there. We went in a ways and kind of stayed there.

There's artillery with every battalion of infantry, and that's who I stayed with and did this spotting. The first night or two we weren't too far from the beach. Every night you had to dig in. You'd get about 6 inches down and hit rock, and decide that was deep. Then when they started shelling at night, you'd think, "By God, the next night I'm going to dig deeper!"

Those towns we went through in Normandy were pretty well shot up. We'd shoot the hell out of it before we moved forward, then they'd shoot the hell out of it when we did move forward.

In Normandy — I wasn't in the jeep — my jeep driver hit a mine. He hit with the hind wheel and blew the jeep up and they gave me a new driver. That kid — he was probably about 15 or 16 — I didn't think anything bothered him but he went up in the air quite a ways and came down. It didn't really wound him any, but he didn't want any more war. He was just lucky as hell to be alive.

The spotter I had, he'd climb up trees to see better. But I think you can get shot out of those trees by your own men awful easy. He was a reckless kid. You know, 15, 16, 18 years old is the best time to go to war. You think nothing's going to happen to you. After you get older, you're not so sure. There's one thing about war — it grows you up pretty fast.

It's an experience that I wouldn't look forward to now, but I didn't mind a bit of it then. I enjoyed my time in the Navy. I enjoyed everybody I met, and got along pretty good. When you get my age, you enjoy everything *(that happened)* when you were younger. ☆

Clarkson returned to a banking career in Belle Fourche and still maintains an office downtown at Pioneer Bank & Trust.

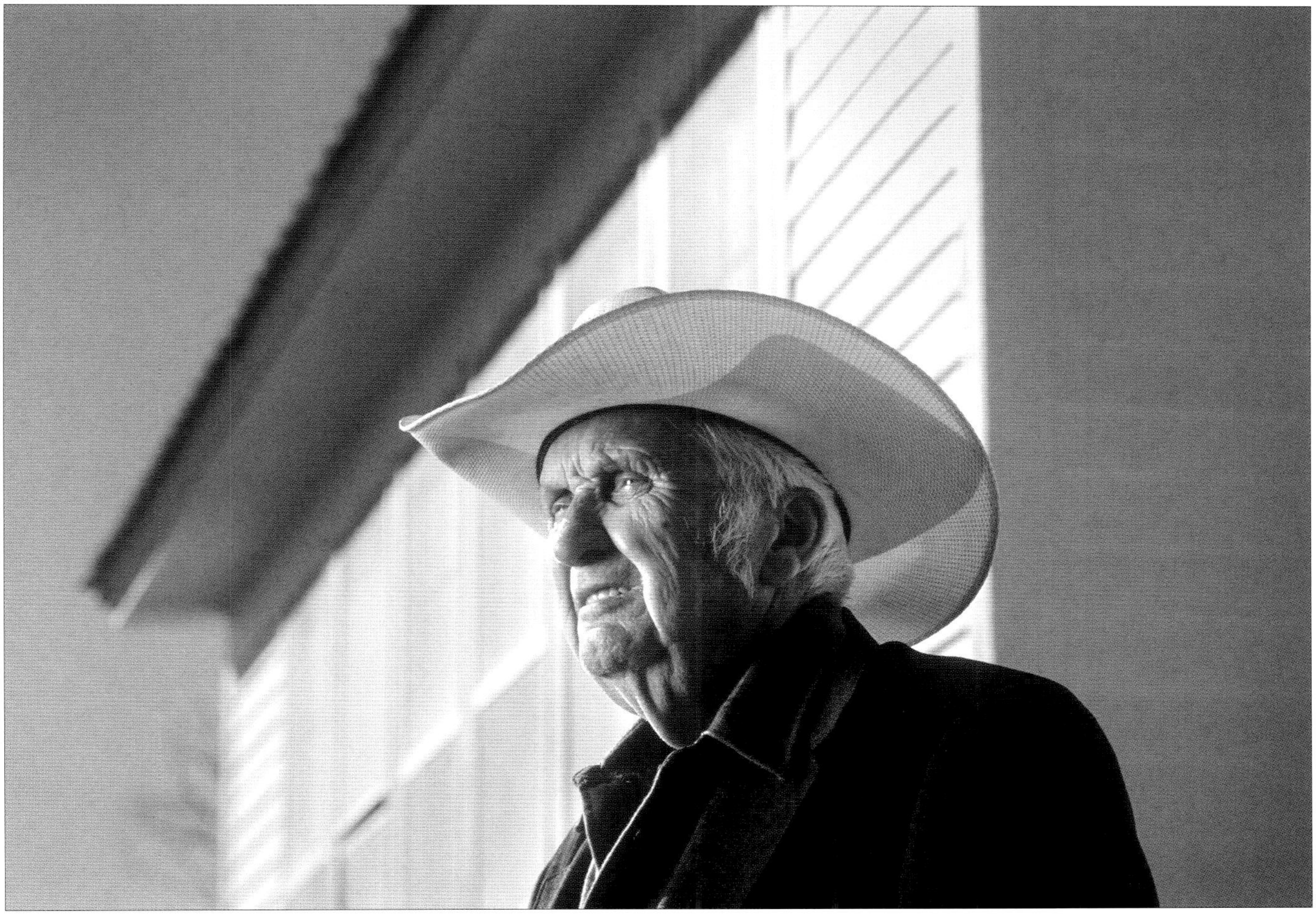

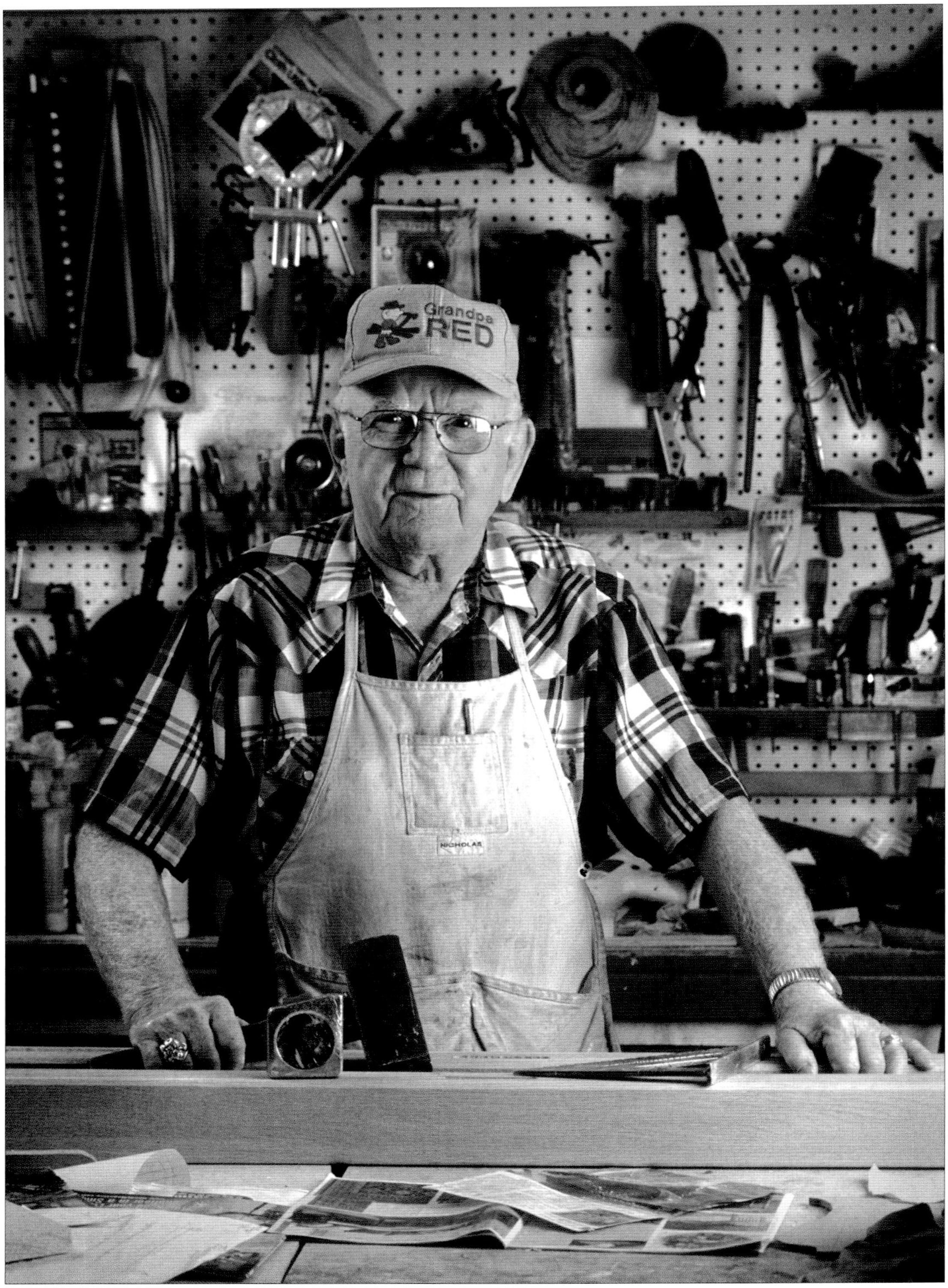
Grandpa
RED
NICHOLAS

ALBERT ZARECKY ☆ *Pierre*

While training in the Navy, Zarecky and a friend decided on a whim to become Corpsmen (medics), a duty that put them ashore with fighting Marines and utilized attributes from both branches of service. Corpsmen worked under extremely difficult conditions in all theaters of World War II, but normally the action took place on land. On November 17, 1943, Zarecky found himself in a very different type of danger en route to Bougainville with the 3rd Marine Division.

In our group, I had 17 men. We were all on the *U.S.S. McKean* — that was a converted four-stacker. It was hot, so a lot of us weren't down in the hold, we were up on the top deck trying to get some sleep. We were all kind of cuddled up into corners.

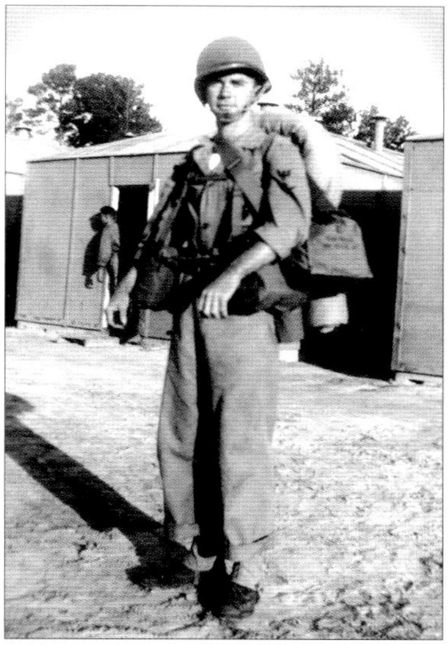

I don't know why the Japs picked that ship. They knocked at 4 o'clock in the morning, and they sunk us. The ship went down fast. I was scared as hell.

They said, "Whenever you jump off the ship, don't jump off way in the front, because that's the highest." Well, that's where I was. I jumped! Right down in the oil. We knew we had to get down in the water and get away from it so you wouldn't get sucked in. You just swim until you could grab something that was floating. You tried to swim out of that oil, for fear of catching fire. In our area, I don't think the oil did catch fire. We knew we had to get out of there. With all that oil around there, you had to get out of there as quick as you could.

(The rescue ship) wouldn't pick us up until daylight, which was around 7 o'clock. There we are, hanging onto a raft piled full of people. The raft was about halfway down in the water. They picked us up and they took us to the island.

We lost everything. We didn't have our gear, we didn't have a toothbrush, we didn't have shaving stuff, we didn't have weapons, we didn't have nothing.

They were piling stuff on a pile that was personal stuff from Marines that didn't need them anymore. We went through that and got our toothbrushes and shaving stuff, and our weapons; we got all fixed up. I didn't lose anybody out of 17. We were lucky.

We were getting baptized quick.

On Thanksgiving Day, we were supposed to get relieved by the Army. So they came and relieved us, and we moved back on the shoreline. The Japs overran the Army, and we were supposed to be there enjoying a nice Thanksgiving meal. We had to go back up there and kick the Japanese out.

After Bougainville, we went back to Guadalcanal to regroup and all this and that. When we were ready, we hit Guam. These Japs were smart; they always let the first wave get in on the island a little bit, and they always wanted another wave to come in there before they do anything. I was in the first wave, and I got on there, and I said, "Well, hell, this is a piece of pie." We dug in and when the second group came in there — bingo! They let loose. We got in there and knocked the hell out of them. We cleaned up that island pretty quick.

I was a corpsman. When you hit the island, two or three or four of the corpsmen go with Marine patrols. You'd be caring for your wounded, and if anybody looked like they were not well enough, you make sure he got out of there and got a replacement. I can understand how a lot of guys couldn't handle it, but it didn't bother me.

As far as shooting the Japs, it was just no big deal. I got a few there, but the way I look at it, if they're shooting at me, trying to kill me, I'm going to get them first. That was the whole idea.

I can see where a lot of guys, after they get back, can't handle it. It just kind of works on you.

Oh, I don't know, I loved it. It was just like a great big camp out all the time there. You sweated a lot, and you had your worries, I guess.

I wouldn't trade it for nothing, you know that? ☆

The U.S.S. McKean *slipped under the waves 28 minutes after taking an aerial torpedo. She lost 116 men. Zarecky went on to work as a pharmacist in Pierre for over 50 years. Now retired, he enjoys honing his woodworking skills.*

Charlie Johnson ☆ *Mitchell*

Sailing on missions that lasted for several weeks, submarine crews ravaged Japanese merchant and military vessels throughout the Pacific. As a pharmacist's mate on the U.S.S. Puffer, *Johnson monitored the health of the submarine's crew and administered to them as necessary.*

The *Puffer* sailed out of San Francisco in July 1944. I stayed on her for the sixth, the seventh and the eighth war patrols. *(The* Puffer *had nine patrols in WWII.)*

You're a hunter. You're an opportunist. You're looking for anything, anyplace, anytime. We fought in four-boat wolf packs. We had areas assigned, and the area was along a line. It wasn't a big square or a block, it was a line. And lines would cross, and lines would mesh. So what you'd see and you couldn't get to, the guy on down the line was alerted. If he couldn't get to it, the guy above him or below him was alerted. There was always somebody in a boat that could get it. And that's how we hunted.

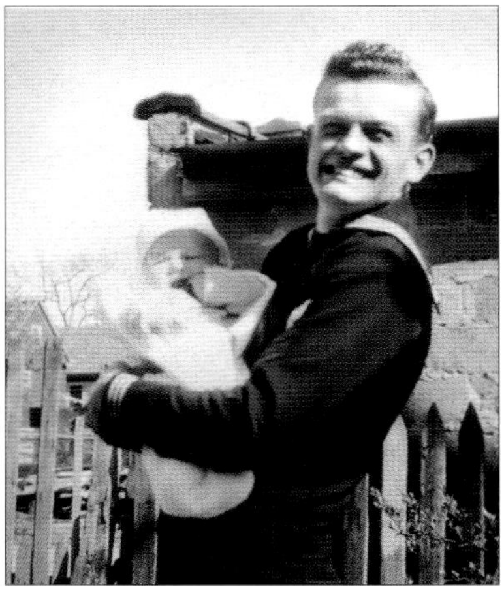

We shot the bow off a Jap destroyer. We put a torpedo into him right under his second turret. Took the bow off. And that son of a bitch laid down 136 depth charges on us. All you'd hear is a click and BOOM! And everything would just *(shudder)*. If it'd get close enough to you, it would bust all the light bulbs in the ship.

This kid was going to undog the hatch and get out of the boat — he couldn't stand the noise. I had a pair of jeans with a pocket in the bottom, and I used to keep an 18-inch crescent wrench in it. He started up for that hatch, and I reached across and grabbed him, slapped him under the ear with the butt of that crescent wrench and knocked him colder than hell.

He came to — I was sitting on him — and I said, "Tony, how you doing?" He says, "What the hell happened, Doc?" I said, "You got a little excited and blew your top. You were trying to get topside and we were 300 feet down." He said, "The hell I did. God, the side of my head feels awful sore." Then he started laughing, and he knew what I had done to him.

It was my responsibility to make sure I saw everybody every day. Not to be in their face, but just to know what they're doing and how they maneuver, how they stand their watch.

The one tragedy in my submarine career was when I lost the chief of the boat because he couldn't swim.

When I found out about it, I confronted him with it. I said, "I'm going to put you on the beach." He said, "Don't do that to me, Doc. First of all, I need the money. And second of all, my career is about done. Leave it alone." Little did I realize that before we finished the patrol, he'd be dead.

(During the patrol, a sailor had a large valve accidentally close on his forearm.) He had severed all the tendons in his wrist. I had him laid out on the mess table, trying to get those ligaments together. I finally gave up. I told the old man, "We've got to get this man to a hospital or he's going to lose his arm. There's no way that I can perform the surgery with what I have. I know what needs to be done, and I can do it, but I don't have the equipment to do it."

The skipper got on the horn. We made a rendezvous with a carrier. We put the guy in a little whaleboat, put him on the carrier, got him taken care of. But in the meantime, the seas roughened up a little bit, and we washed the chief of the boat over the side. Couldn't swim. He had a Mae West life vest on, and never pulled the cords, never popped the little gas cylinders to inflate it. Wouldn't have done any good if he had — he hadn't closed the valves. In other words, he'd never taken care of his Mae West. To him it was just a fixture. It cost him his life.

When the skipper found him face down, he'd been in the water 23 minutes. We worked on him for four hours. Got all the water out of him, tried to revive him. The captain hit him with drugs, I hit him with drugs. We couldn't get his heart started. He was gone.

Foolishness. Damn foolishness! He should never have been on the boat in the first place.

I've lived with that for the better part of my life. I knew better, but I was going to be a buddy. And it cost him his life — the only man I ever lost. ☆

Johnson worked in county government after the war.

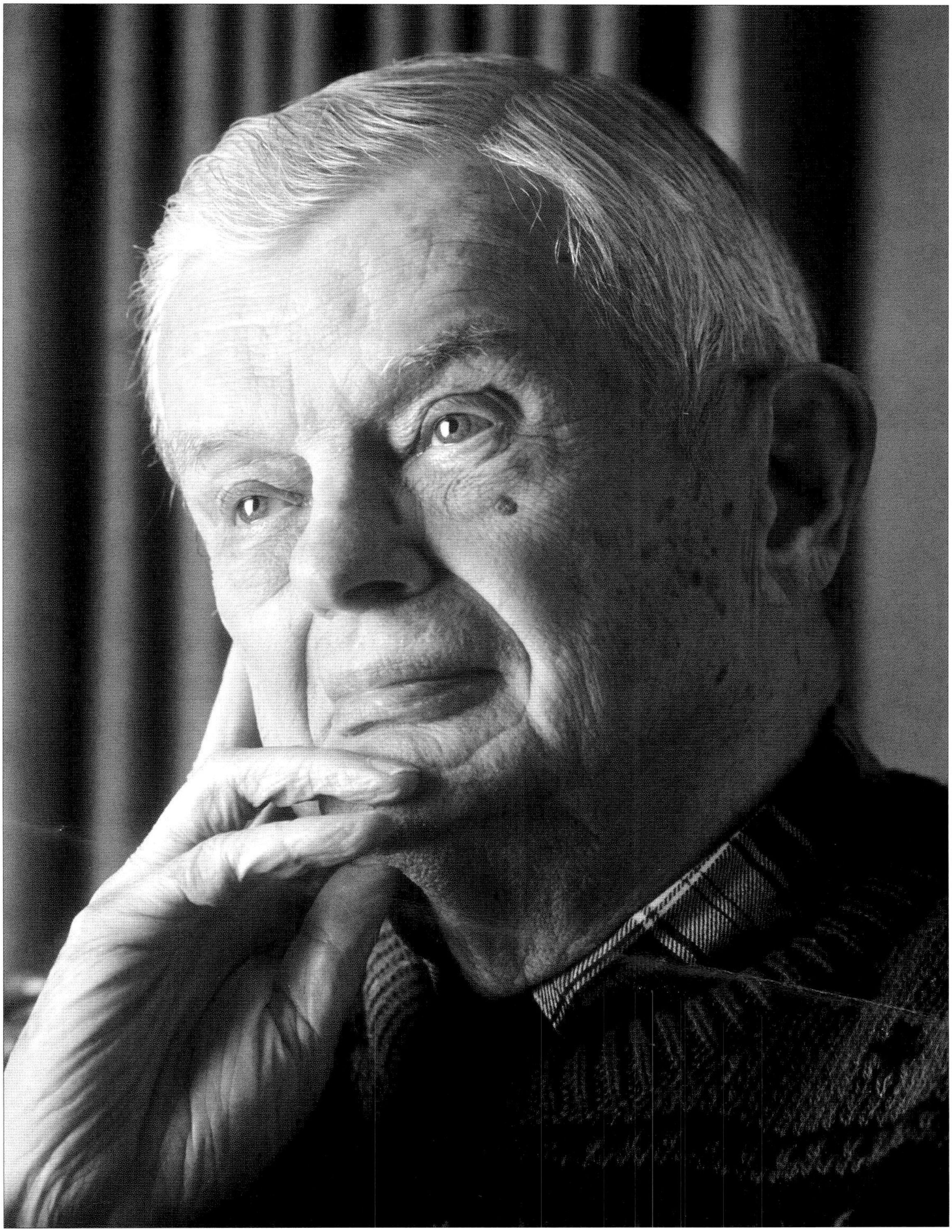

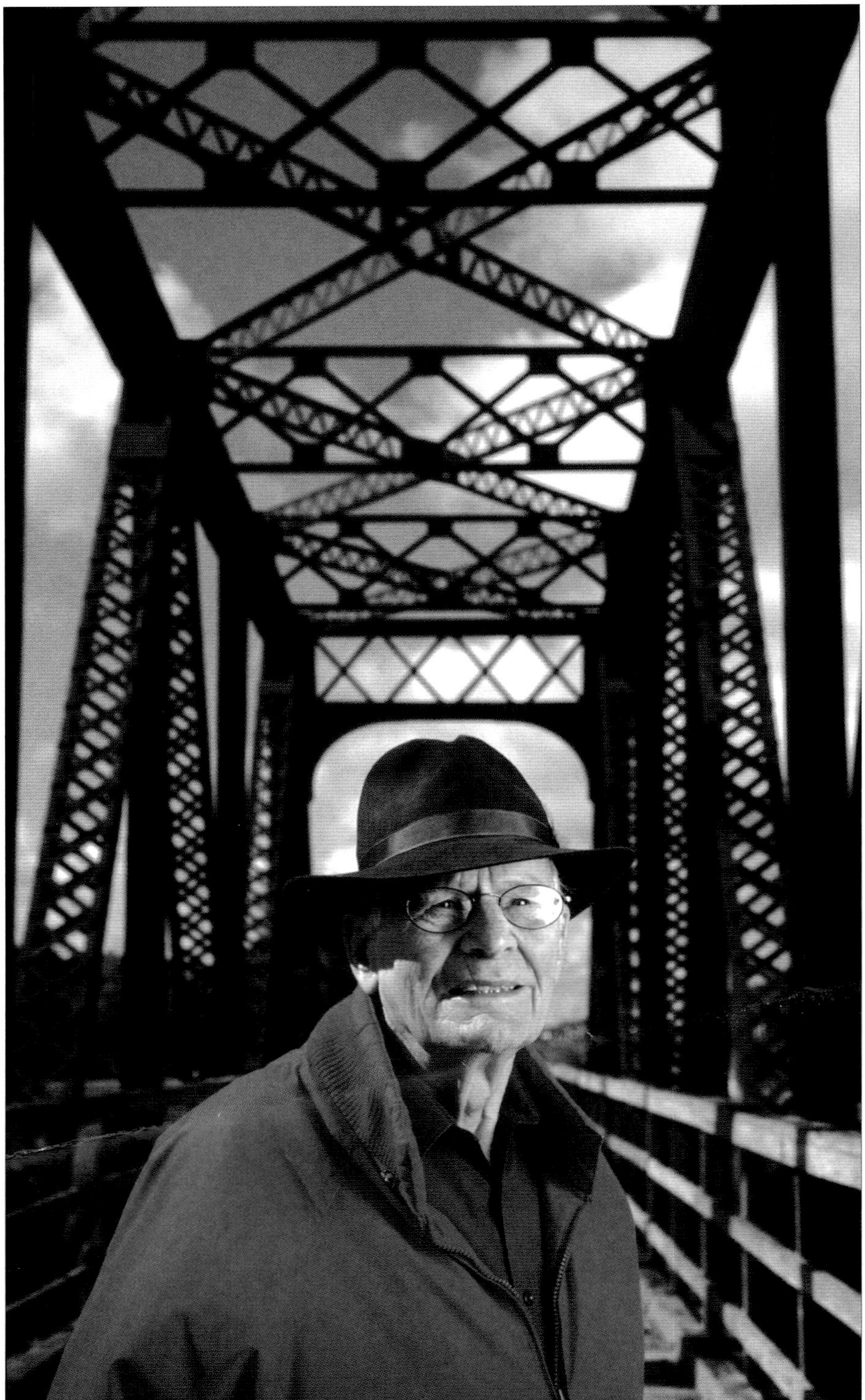

Morris Magnuson ☆ *Sioux Falls*

As a P-47 Thunderbolt pilot, Magnuson's job was to destroy any part of the German war machine he could reach with his powerful machine guns. He enjoyed great success until his luck finally ran out on his 80th and final mission.

During the Depression and the Dust Bowl years, we lived in central South Dakota where we experienced probably one of the worst areas in the state for dust and drouth. Really discouraging times for everyone — the farmers and the ranchers as well as their families and the merchants. They all were hit and shared in this. So the memories from that time are not very good.

At that time, we lived down on White River. My two brothers and I both had Shetland ponies and then horses to ride later on. We had the river there to swim in and fish in, and prairie dogs to hunt, pheasants and grouse and coyotes. I had an interesting boyhood. We rode 2 miles to a rural school with about 15 kids there. We attended church in Kennebec, which was 17 miles away from our farm/ranch, and I enjoyed friends from that part of the area too. We enjoyed it and had fun, even though we didn't have much of anything.

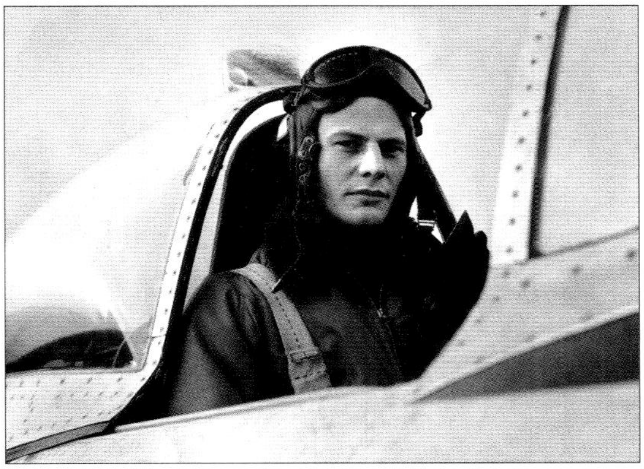

I enlisted shortly after Pearl Harbor. They had such a surge of interest in enlistments and young men who wanted to go to war, I had to wait for six months before they could fit me into a slot. I was finally called to cadets, and I remember we came in with our suitcase of clothes and in civilian suits, and they put us in a truck to haul us from the station downtown to Santa Ana *(California)*, where the cadets went.

They unloaded us out there on kind of a rainy day. They kind of lined us up in rough ranks and marched us down to the barracks. There was a big puddle there across the street — it would almost go up over your shoes — and the first fellows that came to that, they went around the side, and I started to, too. The sergeant in charge said, "Now boys, we're going to have an understanding here right now." So we got back on the other side of that puddle. He said, "Now you don't break ranks for a little thing like that." So here we were in our nice shoes — we walked right straight through that after this little lesson. When they tell you to do something, you do it. You don't question it or wonder about it, you just do it.

That day, there was a fellow there with me that was from California by the name of Don Madden. Generally it was alphabetical, and m-a-d and m-a-g were right together. We were together in all of our assignments and all of our classes and all of our flying from that day on.

We were good friends, although he was kind of an outlaw. When he went to town, I generally felt that part of my job was to look after him. He was the sort of guy that would go into a bar and have a drink and pull out his billfold *(and say)*, "Set 'em up for the house. Buy 'em all a drink!" And so I became the guardian of his billfold, and also to limit his drinking and look after him.

We finally got through the pre-flight training, which was a good refresher in math and the sciences and some military. We finished up there at Santa Ana and we were assigned to the airfield up at Visalia, California. We were assigned to the little PT-17. It was a low-wing, open-cockpit plane, a two-seater. The student was in the front cockpit and the instructor in the back. The first time I ever had been in the air was when we got in that little trainer and took a flight there around the mountains. It was exhilarating.

We were getting close to what we had been hoping for. Both Madden and I were assigned to fly P-47s — fighter planes — at Baton Rouge, Louisiana. It was in February *(1944)* when I graduated. We were sent to New York and got on the *Queen Mary*. During its passenger days, they took about 5,000 passengers. But they loaded up with 15,000 troops and took us overseas on that.

We landed in Prestwick, Scotland. I was assigned to the 36th Fighter Group, which had been over there about three months before we were assigned. We replaced some who had been killed in battle or who had been shot down and taken prisoner.

Becoming a part of that group was a little hard. They were all pretty well seasoned at that time. I suppose they had 15, 20 missions in. But they were pretty good about helping us, giving us advice and shepherding us along.

When a new plane came in, of course the ones who'd been there the longest got the new plane, and the older ones were passed on down the line. So when the new boys were assigned, they got the oldest, most obsolete plane in the bunch. They assign you, and many times you got the tent and the cot of somebody who had been killed. One thing that did: It motivated us to be such good pilots that we'd never get shot down. In the time that I was with the 36th, we lost about half of our pilots.

When we first joined, we were stationed in England at Ashford, right near the White Cliffs of Dover. We flew quite a few escort missions with B-17s, but our range was a little bit limited. Even with belly tanks, we could get hardly four hours of flight time — more like three and a half hours. We could escort bombers to targets in western Germany, but we couldn't take them to Berlin.

When we were escorting the bombers, then the flak was really the thing that bothers you — these black puffs of smoke. If it was below you or above you, you didn't worry too much about it. But when it was right out there in front of you, then you did.

As the war went on, then the P-51s kind of took over as the escort. We were assigned more to work with the troops, bombing and strafing gun emplacements, bridges, railroad cars and locomotives — a favorite target — and trucks and tanks and all sorts of targets of that kind.

The 47 had four .50-caliber machine guns in each wing, which were pinpointed and bored in at about 150 yards ahead. It was a powerful thing. The German infantry had a lot of respect for the 47s, because we could even strafe foxholes. They weren't safe, even in there.

They pretty well protected the pilot in that thing. We had a bullet-proof windshield, and we had an armor plate behind the seat. You could get it knocked up with bullets and it would still come back. It was a good, tough plane.

We flew out of England there until shortly after D-Day. It just happened that there were a number of us that were in London on June 6th of 1944. We knew that this was coming; we didn't know just when. As soon as we heard in London, we went right back out to the base, and starting on June 7th, we were all flying sometimes several missions a day. They had painted black and white stripes toward the tail of the body and the wings for identification, so they'd be easily identified during the confusion and the battles there over the Normandy beachheads.

I'll never forget that sight over the Normandy beaches where the men and the ships and the trucks were going right into the machine gun fire and the cannon fire that they had on that heavily fortified area. It was just unbelievable, and I had so much respect for them.

We were so elated when the invasion went successfully and we were able to get a toehold over there. About a month later, as soon as they had an area claimed back of the beaches and had the Germans pushed back some, they moved our airfield over there to Caen, France.

They put down a metal runway for us; it's made out of a kind of metal grid — really rough. The runways weren't any longer than they absolutely had to be. It was tough to take them off on that thing and tough to land them. They just put them in as level a pasture as they could.

We lived in tents at the base there in Ashford and at the base in Caen, and then after they had moved down toward Paris, they moved the base down to Le Mans, France, which is west of Paris. We were still living in tents. And then we made another move to the north of Paris — this is after they had taken Paris — we still lived in tents. And finally when we arrived up at Namur, Belgium, south of Brussels, we located on an old German airfield where we had a blacktop runway and they had some brick buildings which were really still uncompleted inside but at least it was an improvement. And they had a shower in there, which was wonderful. Before, we'd been just washing out of a mess kit or helmet or basin. So our living conditions improved there greatly.

The last base we were at in France, that was right up in the champagne country. One of the big problems when we moved onto the base: They didn't have any water supply there yet, so we drank champagne, and brushed our teeth with champagne, and got along all right until they got the water in a couple days later.

We were kind of a family and tried to look after each other. We were together 24 hours a day. We got to know each other real well and supported each other.

I tend to downplay a lot of the missions, because it was

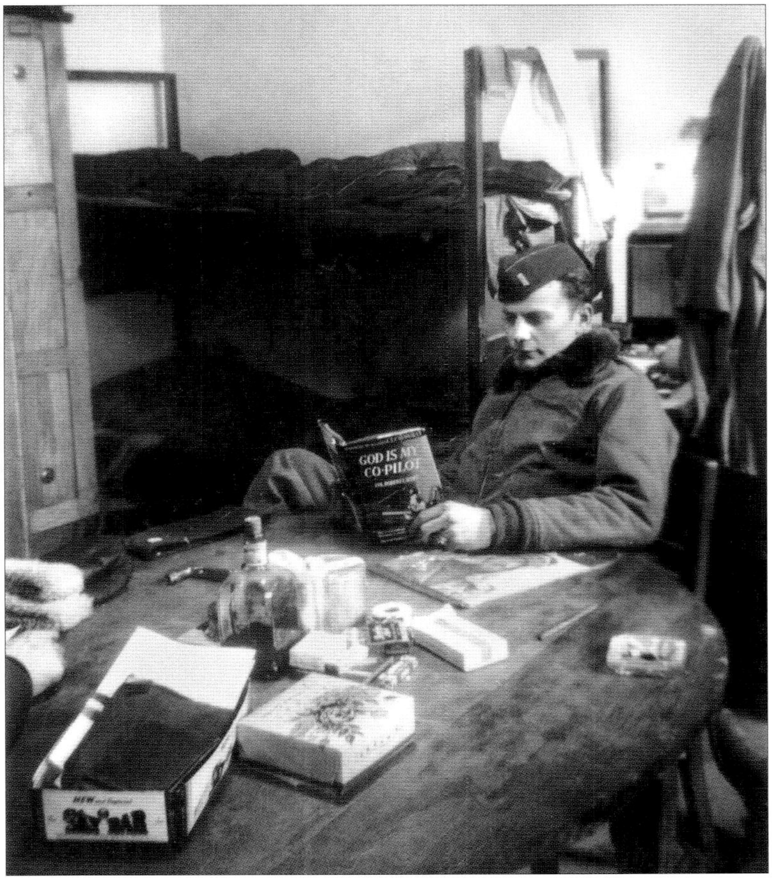

Reading God Is My Co-Pilot, *Magnuson relaxes in the unfinished and recently commandeered German barracks at Namur, Belgium. "My mother was really happy to see this picture at the time and she figured that I wasn't causing any trouble," he recalls.*

a tough job. I don't really try to think about some of those things. For instance, when we carried napalm, which is a jellied gasoline, and dropped those on troops, it's — well, it's just not nice to kill people. It's tough.

Or when you're strafing troops. I was raised in the Lutheran church, and I had always gone to church. My mother had given me a New Testament when I went over. I carried that with me all the time and prayed. But a lot of times when I was going down on those troops, I couldn't help but think that Germany is largely a Lutheran country. And I thought, "Boy, I'm knocking off these other Lutherans." That's sure not a nice thing to do. But then you think of Hitler and the SS, and you had to think of it more as that when you're looking at the mayhem and killing that you do.

Toward the end of the war, the Germans were so low on gasoline they were even using horses to pull some of their guns. When we were hitting those areas where they had the horses pulling, I found it almost harder to shoot a horse than a German soldier. It's almost like kicking a man when they're down. But on the other hand, they weren't giving up. They could have given up at any time.

We had targets that we knew of and we were briefed on: gun emplacements, where they were and what we could expect in the way of flak and fire, and whether or not there were thought to be any German planes that might be coming in there. We were briefed very well on that. If, after you got that target and you had ammunition left, then you could go after what we called "targets of opportunity." Occasionally, toward the end of the war, they would send you out on what we called a "rhubarb," where you'd go out just looking for trains or trucks or troops or whatever.

The weather was not good at all *(one day)*, so they cancelled all of the missions. But they gave us permission to fly a rhubarb if we wanted to. Doug Lane and I went out together. I was kind of a devil-may-care sort of a guy and kind of adventuresome, and the same way with Lane, so we took off and flew right along the Rhine River, which was really protected with guns. With the way the weather was — overcast and kind of drizzling and raining and foggy — *(the Germans)* didn't expect us at all.

We came down there, and there were all sorts of barges and boats on the Rhine as well as trucks and tanks and everything. This was not too far from the lines. We really had a heyday until we ran out of ammunition.

I was flying Lane's wing, and when we got all through down there — they were firing at us all the time — Lane said, "Let's get the hell out of here." And I said, "Okay!"

And the dumb-head, instead of flying right on the treetops, he started pulling up and they just really *(shot us up)*. We both got holes in our planes. We did make it back to the base, but we should have stayed right on the deck where they can't depress their guns down quite low enough to get a person. I suppose it was kind of foolhardy, but it was kind of a game with us too. Maybe it was a little conceit on our part, but we had a reputation after that mission to uphold.

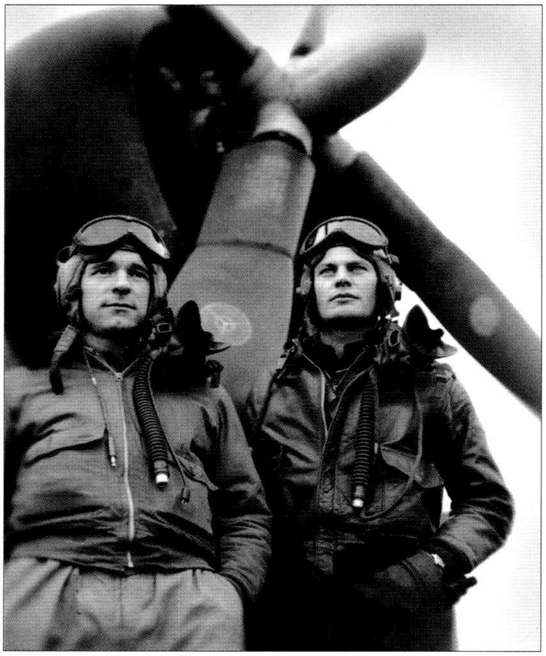

Doug Lane, left, and Magnuson after their dangerous but fruitful "rhubarb" mission.

When we were in Le Mans, France, in August, this friend Madden took off on a mission and his engine quit. He bellied in; the plane caught fire and burned him quite badly. He spent about two or three weeks in the hospital there, getting behind on missions and being away from us. He did recover and came back and started flying again. You normally could get a trip back home after 60 missions. As I neared my 60th mission, he said, "You really should volunteer for a few more missions so that I can get up to my 60 and then we can go home together." I volunteered for 20 more missions to fly, and they all went pretty good until the 80th one.

Here again, fate is kind of fickle and you can't tell what's going to happen. I wasn't scheduled to fly at all that day, but I went down to the flight line. We were always interested in what was going on and where they were going. The flight leader became ill that morning and couldn't lead the flight. They asked me if I'd take it, and I said sure, it didn't make any difference to me. I volunteered to fill in for him on my last mission.

We were briefed on hitting an airfield 100 miles east of the Remagen bridge, which had just been taken maybe a week before. This was on March 14th of 1945.

There were 16 planes. We took off and headed over for that airfield there. Usually we'd fly over at fairly high altitude — I suppose we were at probably 15,000 or 20,000 feet. When we spotted the target, I told the squadron to circle up there, and my wingman and I went down to kind of look it over and see what was there.

That day they really weren't expecting us. There was hardly any ground fire. I made a pass. I dropped my bombs on some planes and then I strafed a couple more, and my wingman did the same. We pulled on up and I called the squadron and told them to follow me on in and we would work over this airfield in good shape.

The second time I came down on the field, they were kind of expecting me, and I came down going pretty fast — we did quite a little work like that at 250 to 300 miles an hour. I sprayed a bunch of planes there with my machine guns and as I came across the runway, they got pretty much a direct hit into my plane.

It got smoky in the cockpit. I had to throw back the canopy and tried to lean out to see where I was going, and I immediately started pulling up and going west toward the American lines and the Remagen bridge.

I flew for perhaps a couple of minutes or so and had gained some altitude when the engine quit. I knew that I had to bail out. They really didn't encourage us to try and crash-land them because even if you bellied it in, *(the Germans)* would use it in some other way.

I unhooked my oxygen mask and my microphone and the harness and the belts that were holding me in.

We'd always been told that when you bail out of the P-47, you should kind of roll down onto the wing and go under the horizontal stabilizer so it didn't break your legs. I managed to get all this unhooked and ready to go and I almost kind of stood up in the seat there and I evidently was going faster than I thought I was — I was probably hitting 300. I got up there and WHOOSH! the air just took me right out. The first thing I knew, I was out away from the plane and hadn't hit the stabilizer or anything. I pulled the rip cord and I didn't swing very many times before I hit the ground.

I hit in kind of an open little pasture there. It was a pretty fair landing; I didn't get hurt or anything. I gathered my chute up and ran into some woods that were right close there. I don't know just why, but they'd always told us when you bail out, you should hide your chute in case they're looking for you. Then they wouldn't be able to find that and know right where you started from. So I hid that under some leaves and some junk.

There was still some snow at that time, and quite a little water running in some of those streams. I started to cross this little open area there, just got out of the trees, and here were some German soldiers who were already starting to look for me. They hollered at me and shot. I don't know if they were shooting at me or over my head or what. I turned around and ran back into the woods.

I started running in kind of a northerly direction, because they were west of where I bailed out. And I ran as long and as fast and as hard as I could until I just was completely exhausted. I probably went several miles, I'm sure. I crawled into some brush there and I thought, "Boy, I'm going to have to just sit it out here for a while."

They beat the brush around there all afternoon. I could hear them off a little bit in the distance. They didn't get real close to me there that day, but then along in the latter part of the afternoon I heard the bloodhounds baying. Luckily it was wet enough and I had crossed a couple of little streams, so they never did pick up my scent at all. They worked around there with those bloodhounds for a couple hours until it got dusk. Finally it got quiet and they left.

I had painted "P-47" on the back of my leather flying jacket. I'd have much rather been caught with them thinking I was a bomber pilot rather than a fighter pilot, so I took my knife and one of the first things I did when I was evading was to scrape that paint off there so I was no longer a fighter pilot.

I started my trek west. I knew I had about 100 miles to go, and we had an escape kit which contained a compass, a rubber map of the area — water didn't damage it at all — and we had a water bottle in there and halizone tablets for purifying water. You could fill it out of a cow track and put a tablet in there and in 30 minutes it was safe to drink. There was first aid equipment and a peanut bar, which was about the size of a big bar you would get now.

I divided that into eight parts and I thought that I'd be able to get back in eight days, and just ate one little piece a day. I traveled just at night, and probably one of the worst parts about that was spending the days there — from daylight until dark — just sitting. In all cases, I had to be in fairly heavy brush so there was nothing to watch or nothing to do but read the Testament that my mother had given me, and I did a good job of reading that.

The 23rd Psalm was the thing that really kind of gave me strength at that time to get through there, even though I was all alone and felt there was no help for me. That did kind of buoy me up and gave me hope for the way it was going to come out. "The Lord is my shepherd, I shall not want...Yea, though I walk through the valley of the shadow of death..." That was really meaningful to me.

I had a .45-caliber pistol and I found a good stout club about 2 feet long. I carried that .45 in one hand, all cocked and ready to go, and that club in the other. I started out and I didn't use a compass that first night. I thought, "I know where I'm going," so I headed west.

First I had to cross a highway and it took quite a long time. I was so cautious. I didn't want to get caught. I was going down a little forest trail, and I thought I was going straight west. And all at once I walked right up to a German jeep, and then I saw where there was a little camp there. So I backed off very quietly and went way out around it. Pretty soon I came to a little stream, and I had to wade across that. I went and went and went, and pretty soon I crossed another little stream, and pretty soon I came to a little path through the forest and

I started on that. I came down to that same darn jeep — I had made a great big circle out there! After that I used that compass, and I used it about every five minutes to make sure I was headed in the right direction.

I just had on my flying suit with the leather jacket and it was cold. It would be frosty in the mornings. Many times I wouldn't sleep very long; I would wake up and I would be shivering so much it would wake me. It was kind of hard to get that rest, although there were a few sunny days where I managed to get a location where the sun would hit me and warm me up.

I tried to walk at a pretty fast pace, and occasionally I would run. Most of the time I would move a little cautiously. A lot of the area I went through was wooded. In fact, I tried to avoid the open areas so it made walking more difficult. It was sometimes kind of noisy coming through those things, too. So I'd walk a ways and then stop and listen to see if I would detect anyone around.

It was a Sunday morning; I think that was probably the sixth day. I was getting fairly close. I could hear the battle ahead of me. I thought, "I'd like to get a mile further so I could cross the lines tonight." So I started out in the daylight, going through kind of a sparsely treed area. I was being real careful, and all at once here was a German soldier probably 50 feet ahead of me, an older man. He had a rifle.

He got behind a tree about 10 inches or so *(in diameter)* and started shooting at me. I got behind one that was about *(7 to 8 inches in diameter)*. I tried to make myself as thin as I could. I started blazing away at him with my .45, and I suppose it was about our last shots and *(his bullet)* hit the tree and glanced off and just went through the fleshy part of my *(thigh)*. And then I hit him in the shoulder, and it knocked him down.

He got up and he went in one direction, and I went in the other direction, running. Here again, I went for quite a ways and then crawled in the brush. I didn't hear a single thing. I thought with all that gunfire that they would zero in on me. I don't know what happened to him. I'm just not sure what the deal was. I don't know if he wasn't able to travel very far to turn in the alarm or what it might have been.

That evening I waited until it got good and dark, and then I thought, "This will be the time. Tomorrow I'll be eating pancakes with the Americans."

I hadn't gone very far, and I thought I was being so cautious. I walked right into some German soldiers. There was probably five or six of them. I just didn't have a chance to do anything; I was just a few feet from them. There were so many of them, so I had to just throw down my pistol and my club, and surrendered there to them.

They didn't hit me or beat me there, but they all kind of pushed me around a little bit, and then took everything I had: my watch, all of my escape kit and my pistol. They took me down to a shoe shop, which was also used for building coffins. They kept me there that night and the next day, and then there were two of them that took me up to the prison camp at Wetzlar, Germany, which was used for interrogation of prisoners that they had captured. I was there for a couple of days, and then on down to Nuremberg. They were so full of prisoners that they didn't have room for us, so they put me in with 150 other prisoners and started our march down to Stalag 7A, which was near Munich. I don't remember how many days we spent on the road there.

Occasionally we would ride a train, but the railroad tracks were so cut up you couldn't go more than 10 miles. When we were out on a target of opportunity, if we didn't find anything else to shoot, we got good enough so that you'd come down on a railroad track and give it a burst, and it would move the rails enough to derail the trains. We just tore those things up.

The train rides we got there would maybe be 10 miles or so, and then here we'd come to a spot and have to stop again. If we were working on fixing the tracks, we were always free to flee during an American attack as long as we pledged to come back, and we did that. They had a lot of Jewish slave laborers working with us on the track, but they were made to stay there and couldn't run.

One day they put us on a train to go down the line a ways. We were riding in open box cars. We got into this little town, and the P-47s were hitting a marshalling yard right where we were parked. After the attack, one of the Jewish slave laborers had been hit in the stomach very badly. The German in charge handed his rifle to another Jewish laborer, and made him shoot the man in the head. I was standing right there. It was kind of a tough thing to go through. It was toward the end of the war, and I think the German in charge must have felt that he may get in trouble if he was the one pulling the trigger.

Shortly after that, they put us to work fighting fires there, and several of us were manning a water pump that was hooked into a tank wagon — it would pressurize the water for firefighting. Let me tell you, we were really motivated to pump hard after what had just happened.

We walked most of the way — about 150 miles — down to 7A at Moosburg. When the barbed wire gates swung open down there, the first guy I saw was Phil Wright. I had been leading the squadron the day he was shot down, four days before myself. He said, "You son of a gun, you got me shot down. I'm glad to see that they got you shot down!" It was in a joking way, but that's been going on between us over the many, many years, until he died.

I didn't know how many prisoners were in this camp. I knew there were a lot of them. I've been reading up on this and I came across an article *(that said)* there was 77,249 prisoners there at Stalag 7A at the end of the war — all different nationalities and all different branches of the service, infantry and artillery and signal corps.

We didn't have much to eat in the prison camp. The Germans didn't have much to eat either, as a people. We had thin soup and sauerkraut and black bread. We got one batch of sauerkraut that was kind of spoiled. I don't know how old it was, but it had little white worms in it about so long. Most of us, we just picked the worms out and ate the sauerkraut; we didn't see anything wrong with that.

We did get a few Red Cross packages which were really welcome, and they included some crackers and little canned meats and a Hershey bar and cigarettes. But a lot of that the Germans intercepted and kept for themselves. They did try to go by the Geneva Convention, but they were a little bit leery about stealing too much of the Red Cross stuff. They had to treat us with some kindness.

It was quite an experience to be there. I think there were probably 40 to 60 men in the barracks, with three bunks *(stacked atop each other)* and straw mattresses. Probably one of the worst things about it were the lice and the fleas that we all had. It was hard to sleep — you were always scratching. The food that they gave us was cold, so we rigged up little stoves from the tin cans that we got in the Red Cross packages.

We were there in prison camp until April 29th of 1945, when we were liberated by General Patton's troops. That was probably one of the most emotional times that I've experienced in my whole life.

They had kind of a brief skirmish. We were all laying on our stomachs in the barracks there with the bullets zinging around. The guards put up a half-hearted fight with the troops that were storming it.

When it got a little quiet, and about the time we looked up, the Americans pulled down the Nazi flag and raised the American flag up above the camp.

Bedlam broke loose. There was crying and hollering, and tears would run down my face. We were happy, and we were slapping each other on the back.

Some of those fellows had been there for years instead of months like me, some of them for four or five years. I think there were some there even from Dunkirk, when the British had that invasion there *(in 1940)*.

Shortly after I was shot down, my parents received a telegram telling them that I was missing in action. Some time later they got another telegram that there was no word on what had happened to me. None of the fellows that I was flying with that day saw me get hit. It's kind of understandable; there's a lot of confusion. In the smoke and the fires on the ground and the confusion, they just didn't notice me go down at all.

When I had been in London *(prior to being shot down)*, I had ordered an Easter lily for my mother to be delivered on Easter Sunday — and my folks received that Easter lily and the telegram at about the same time. It was within a day or two. My mother kind of took that Easter lily as an omen of faith that I would make it.

When we got into New York, I was able to get to a phone and call the folks. They didn't know if I was alive or dead.

I said, "Hi mom. I made it." ☆

After finishing college at South Dakota State University, Magnuson entered the education field, serving as principal and superintendent at Brandon Valley schools for several years. He then worked for the state as the executive director of school administrators in South Dakota.

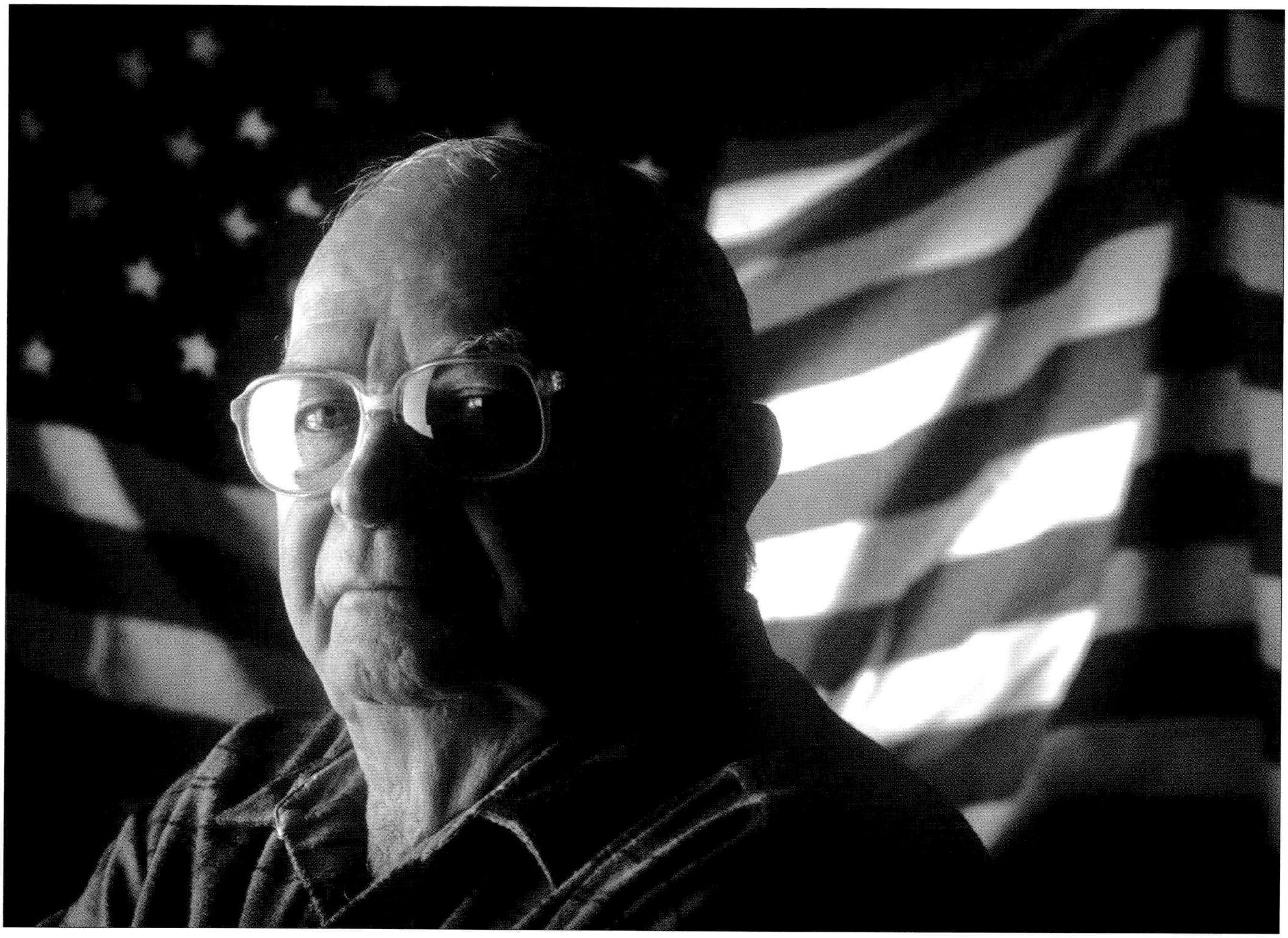

Don Fuhrmann ☆ *Spearfish*

While the legendary flag-raising at Iwo Jima became the image defining the war against Japan, a similar but less conspicuous event occurred when 1st Division Marines raised the American flag at Shuri Castle on Okinawa. Fuhrmann accompanied the flag-raising party as a scout and sniper.

I did good in boot camp. I was the second highest *(marksman)* in the platoon; therefore, I ended up going to scout/sniper school. The training put me in good stead when I was in combat, because you learned how to take care of yourself, and you learned to be observant, and you didn't necessarily go by the book. Of the 120 of us *(scouts)* that went over, five came back to the States. Out of the five, I was the only one who hadn't been hit in some manner. Luck of the draw, I guess.

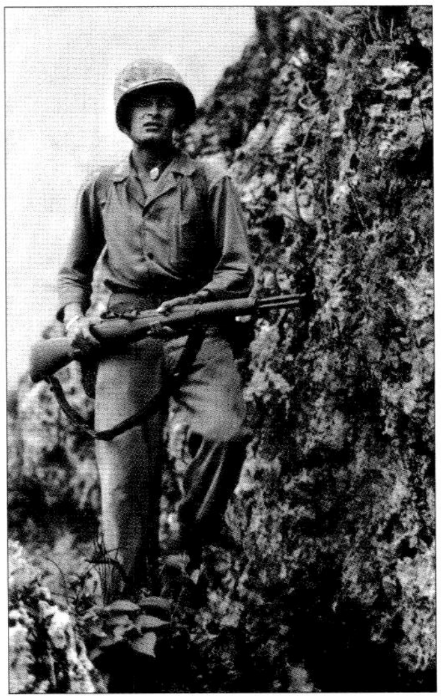

Prior to going into Okinawa, it was probably the most beautiful sight you'd ever want to see on an island up there. The sea was just blue — that bright blue. The skies were blue and had all that white smoke coming up from the naval bombardment. It was quite a sight.

When we went in, we were a little teed off. Generally, on an invasion, your breakfast that day was supposed to be steak and eggs. Well, we were looking forward to that and we got down to the mess hall — it was like 3 o'clock in the morning — and it was hard-boiled eggs and dry toast. What happened to that steak!

In combat, I spent an awful lot of my time behind enemy lines. I was G2 *(intelligence)*, and I was primarily there for scout work. We used to go through and scout for artillery or mortar positions.

It was miserable there. It rained for about 30 days. The seams on my boots rotted out. You'd have given $100 for a clean pair of socks. Another thing that used to really get to me was when they'd run you through the delousing bath. We got into body lice in these caves where the Japs had been. You'd take your clothes off, and they'd run those through the laundry, and they'd spray you. After it was all done, you'd itch like the devil.

I can't stand flies to this day. Just bugs me, because I can remember them crawling in and out of the nostrils and the eye sockets and the mouths of dead Japs, even dead Marines Flies just put me on edge, I tell you.

During that rain, they couldn't get the bodies out for graves registration, so they were stacking them along the road. You've seen cordwood stacked up? That's the way the bodies were. They kept them sprayed down with DDT and kerosene until they got to the point that the rains finally stopped and they could properly bury them. I'm glad I wasn't with graves registration at that point.

I was called into the colonel's tent and he showed me on the maps where the castle was located. He said, "We've got orders to send a patrol up to raise the flag on Shuri." Shuri was not entirely secured at that point. And he says, 'You're going to be chief scout. You'll be the one leading the thing." I think there were about 15 of us all told — with the people who had the flag — and we had some officers with us, lieutenants.

We figured the best way was to go through the lines and come up from behind, because it wasn't entirely secured, and the Japs were holed up on what they called Wana Draw, which sort of surrounded the castle.

So we came up from behind and took over the top part fairly easily and dug in. There wasn't much left of the castle. There was some underground stuff, tunnels. It had been used by the Japanese high command as a command post for a long time. We got there and we held there for two days.

It was like a turkey shoot while we were up there. We were dug in, and these Japs in Wana Draw were deserting. They didn't realize we were holding the top of the hill, and we took turns picking them off. The flag had been raised, and the pictures had been taken. We had everything that they wanted out of it, but we couldn't get out at that point and started running out of ammo.

Until that draw was secured, there was no way for us to get out. It was a great day when it was secured. We all made it out. ☆

Fuhrmann also served in the Korean War, and spent his post-war years as a baker.

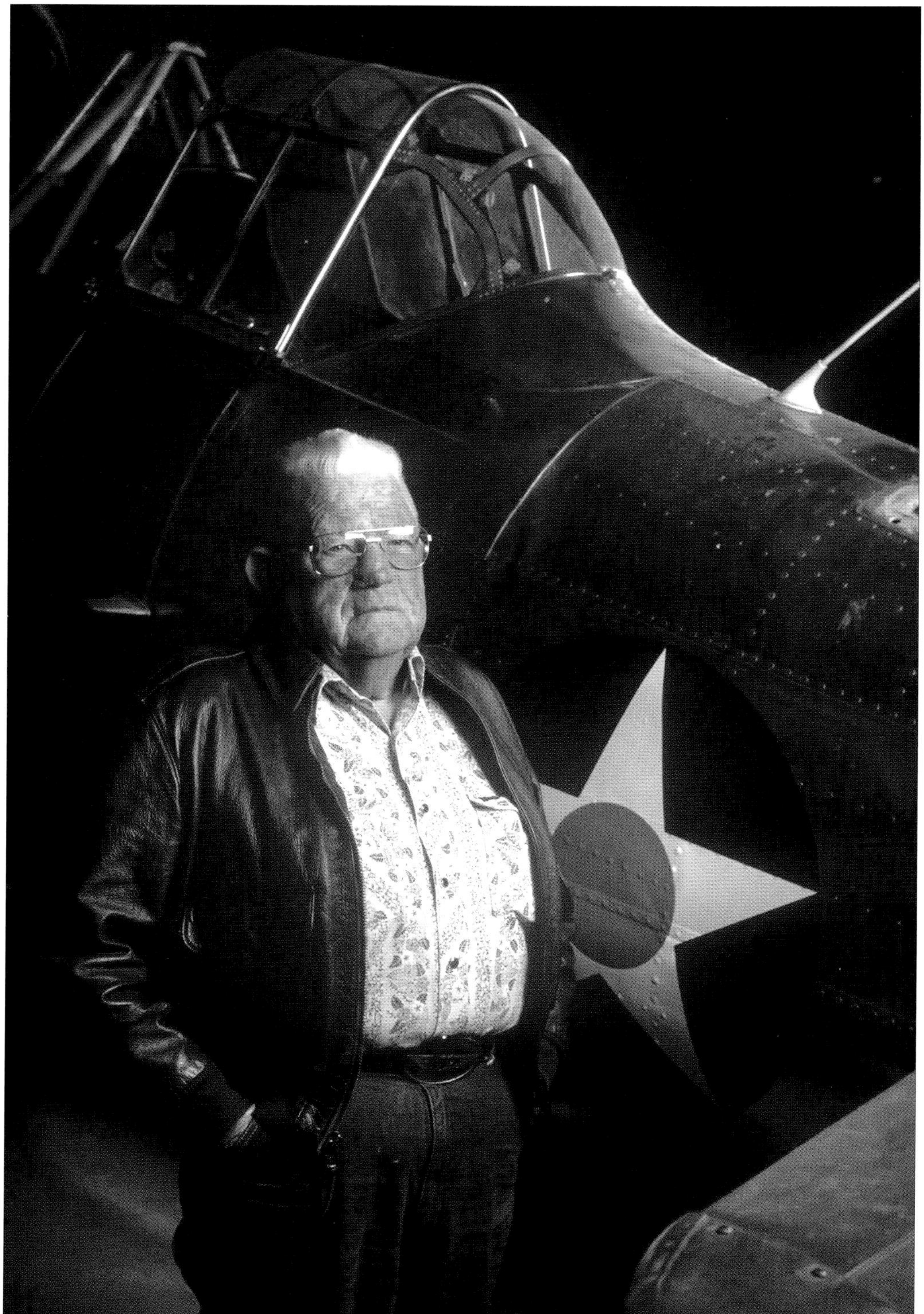

JOE HABEGER ☆ *Madison*

Habeger served the war effort as a B-24 pilot and 415th Bomb Squadron leader, flying missions out of Italy and causing great damage to Germany's war production.

I went over in October of '44. My orders assigned me to the 415th Bomb Squadron. I went over on a Liberty ship — 31 days — and then we went by truck right down in the very heel of Italy where the 98th Bomb Group was. It turned out to be a real good tour of duty. I finished with 37 missions.

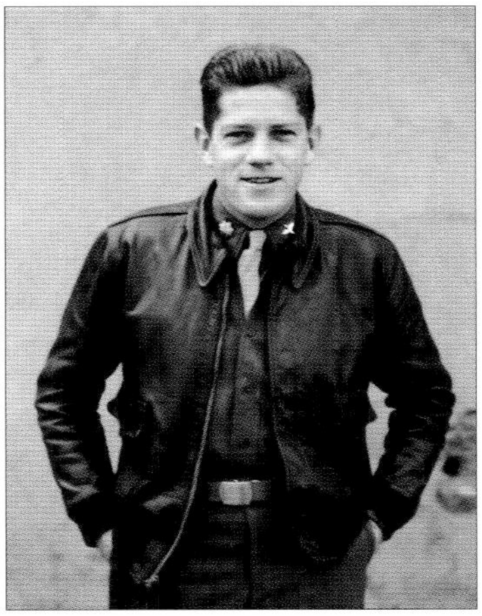

I think it was the 11th or 12th sortie that I went on that I was squadron lead. A squadron commander could make up a crew of his own out of remnants of other crews. I had a crew by then, and this new airplane comes in, so that was the squadron commander's airplane.

My wife was a petite blonde, so I named it *Lil' Blon-Dee* — her name was Deloris *(Dee)*. Well, *Lil' Blon-Dee* had some accidents along the way. One time, we had a tire shot out. We had a lot of flak damage, and we were assessing it. *(The co-pilot)* looked out, and he said, "The right gear is coming down." Well, the chances of that were just about absolutely zero, but the likely thing was that the tire had been shot out and it was drooping down. But before I could say anything to him, he reached over and he kicked the gear handle to the UP position, which if the gear had been drooping, it would have brought it up. The problem really was that we had all our hydraulic system shot out except our reserve supply for braking on landing. And when he hit that gear handle, he dumped that pressure.

So here we were, a flat tire on the right and no brakes. We got it down okay and just landed on one wheel until we lost enough airspeed and eventually that wing drooped. We were slow enough — we could just turn power on/off, used the engine to keep it from turning too fast — and we came to a stop out in the grass. The damage to the airplane really was enough that we could have scrapped it out, but we elected to replace the wing and so forth. So it flew again.

As the lines collapsed, and as the length of the front the Germans were defending decreased, the concentration of anti-aircraft guns increased. That increased in intensity as we hit targets that were closer to Berlin.

A few missions later, I was deputy group lead, and the other squadron was designated as group lead. I had two engines running on *Lil' Blon-Dee (waiting for takeoff)*, and the group commander stuck his head up and said, "Joe, we're going to have to change officers on the crew. *(Group leader)* Colonel Nelson's aircraft has gone out of commission. So we're going to have to put him in this aircraft, and it'll be in the group lead position." I'd take a spare. I said, "Colonel, I think it would be better if we switch the entire crew." I just knew that either crew wouldn't like it if they got a new set of officers. We just left the engines running, got out of *Lil' Blon-Dee* and got in the spare aircraft. This went on with no radio conversation, so they didn't know any switching was going on.

We take off, and as it turned out, the group lead had one bridge in the Brenner Pass, and deputy group lead — which was my squadron and the one behind me — another bridge.

I called "Bombs away!" and started evasive action, and looked over at Nelson and his lead position, and just then — BOOM! — they took a direct hit, and just disintegrated. There wasn't a parachute or anything left. And that was *Lil' Blon-Dee*.

That lead aircraft was down. Well, now I'm in command of the group. Because I had assumed group lead, I had to go to a special briefing that delayed me 20 minutes or so getting back to my squadron. I was walking in — saying hello to the guys and nodding — and as I approached some of the men, one of them said, "You know, he was a pretty good squadron commander."

They were talking about *Lil' Blon-Dee* going down, and knew it was my squadron aircraft. So they thought my crew and I went down on *Lil' Blon-Dee*. ☆

After retiring from the Air Force in 1962, Habeger returned to Madison to teach math and physics at Dakota State University. He was instrumental in creating the annual Prairie Village Threshing Bee, which was first held on his farm.

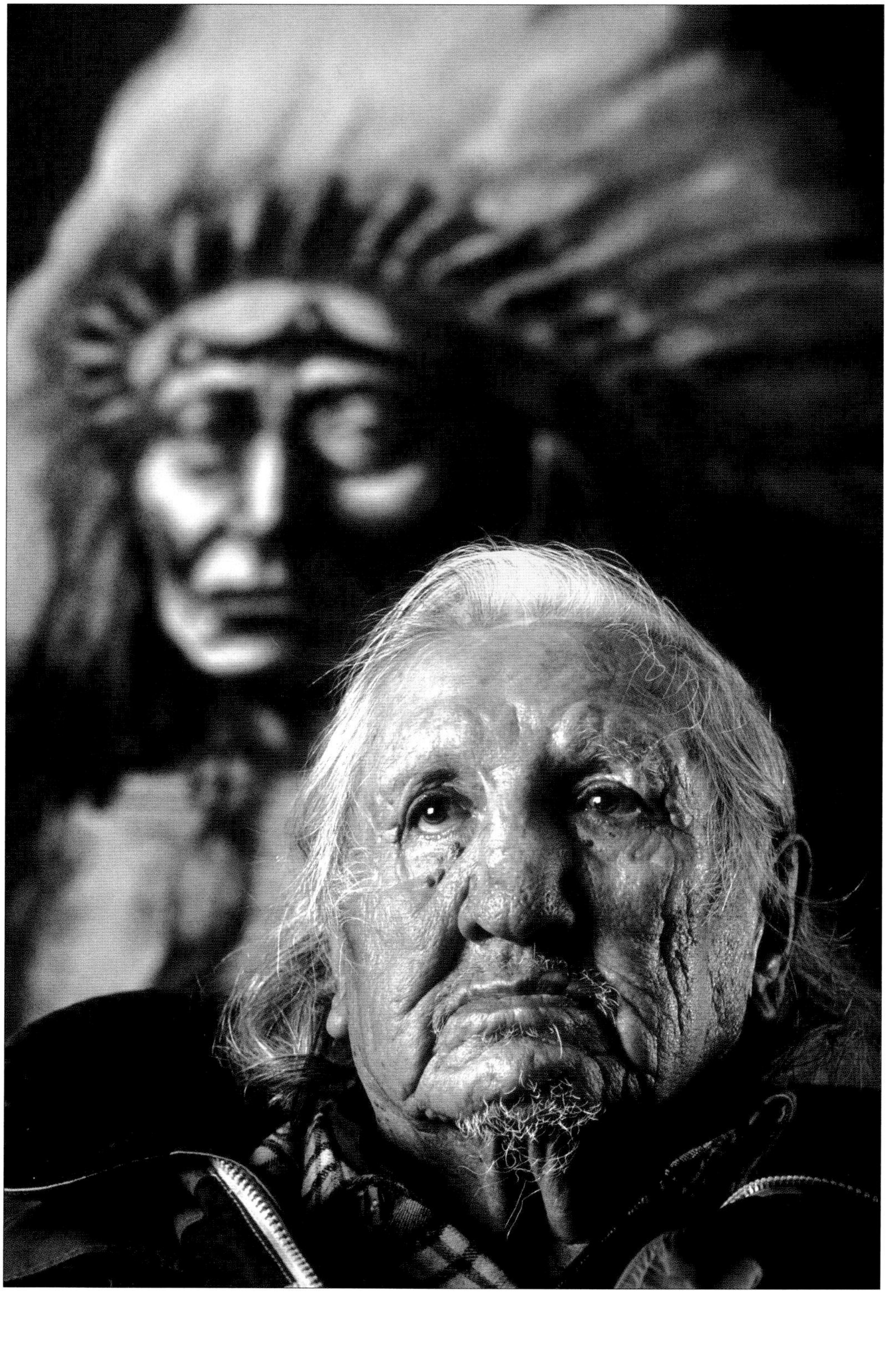

Clarence Wolf Guts ☆ *Wanblee*

At least 15 Native American tribes lent their languages to the war effort, with the Navajo code-talkers garnering most of the attention. However, South Dakota provided its fair share; at least a dozen Lakota code-talkers served in the Pacific and European theaters.

When I was a little boy, I learned the Lakota language. I could read and write it. I wanted to be a teacher, but I never got around to it.

I went to school at St. Francis Mission, and I was in the 11th grade — just turning 18 — when they started attacking Pearl Harbor. Some of the boys I went to school with died over there.

I thought I might as well join up and see what I could do for America. I signed up and went to train.

I had one more day to go until graduating Ranger training. At that time a general's jeep drove in. They walked over and said, "Clarence, the general wants to talk to you." What the heck did I do now?

I thought back and wondered if maybe I said something to offend somebody.

They taught me everything — stand two feet in front of him, salute, state your name, rank and serial number and say, "Reporting as directed." We spent almost half a day learning that.

All these were high-ranking officers, and they called me in by my first name. The general had two stars. "Sit down, Clarence, sit down." At that time he pulled out from the drawer a quart of whiskey. He poured a shot. "I want to talk to you man to man, none of this 'sir' or 'general.' Just talk to me like a man."

"I like your spunk," he said, whatever that means. He said, "You're Indian?" I said, "Yes I am. I'm a full blood Lakota Indian." I didn't say Sioux, because another tribe gave us that name. *(The general asked)*, "You can talk Indian?" I said I can read and write it. He said, "Oh, I hit the jackpot! I want you for my radio operator. Could you get some other of your clan *(to join you)*?"

Radio operator? I never had anything offered to me like that before. There were four of us. Iver Crow Eagle was one of them, and Roy Bad Hand, he's from around here. And Benny Red Bear Sr., he was from Oglala.

All the time, two guys learned how to crank the radio and operate it. *(Code-talkers worked in teams of two.)* There were two boys in the artillery that understood the Lakota language. *(The officers)* would tell me to "get your boys to zero in" on a certain point. We'd tell that in Lakota to them, and they'd do it.

We got bodyguards, too. Nobody could come within 10 feet of us. That's how important we were.

Whenever I talked in my language, it was my own thinking and my own actions. Mostly we used everyday words to describe military things. One word has a lot of meaning to it. You have to be specific with what you want to say. The Japanese couldn't understand it. Well, nobody could understand it.

We tried to get the Japanese to get out of this island and go back to their country. I prayed to God when I was in there. Bullets were flying over, shrapnel whizzing by. None of them landed with a direct hit or nothing, and I thank the good Lord for that. I didn't make any promises of any kind — all I said was, "Dear Lord, take me back to my country and my people and I will lead the way with your name at the top of the list." That's the only promise I made. I came back with no wounds or nothing — the only wound I ever had was not being able to be with my people. I always thought about home and my people.

I was from Rosebud at that time, and I always wondered if they had food on the table, if they're dancing, if they're remembering us. I used to write to my uncle in Lakota language, and he answered me in Lakota language, back and forth. I often wonder how it passed the censors. We never talked about the war or the enemy. We just talked about how things were at home.

Sometimes it's really hard to understand what I've seen and what I went through. Sometimes when I lay down, then I remember and I clench my fists.

I thank the good Lord to this day for bringing me back alive. It's really hard to think that we survived. We all came back, all four of us. They honored us when we came back. Iver was dancing, and I was singing.

Now they're all gone. Dead and gone. I'm the only one left alive. I always say, "Rest in peace, brothers. You did more for your country than anybody ever could." ☆

Wolf Guts returned to the Pine Ridge Reservation after World War II. He and Charlie White Pipe of Rosebud are the only two surviving Lakota code-talkers.

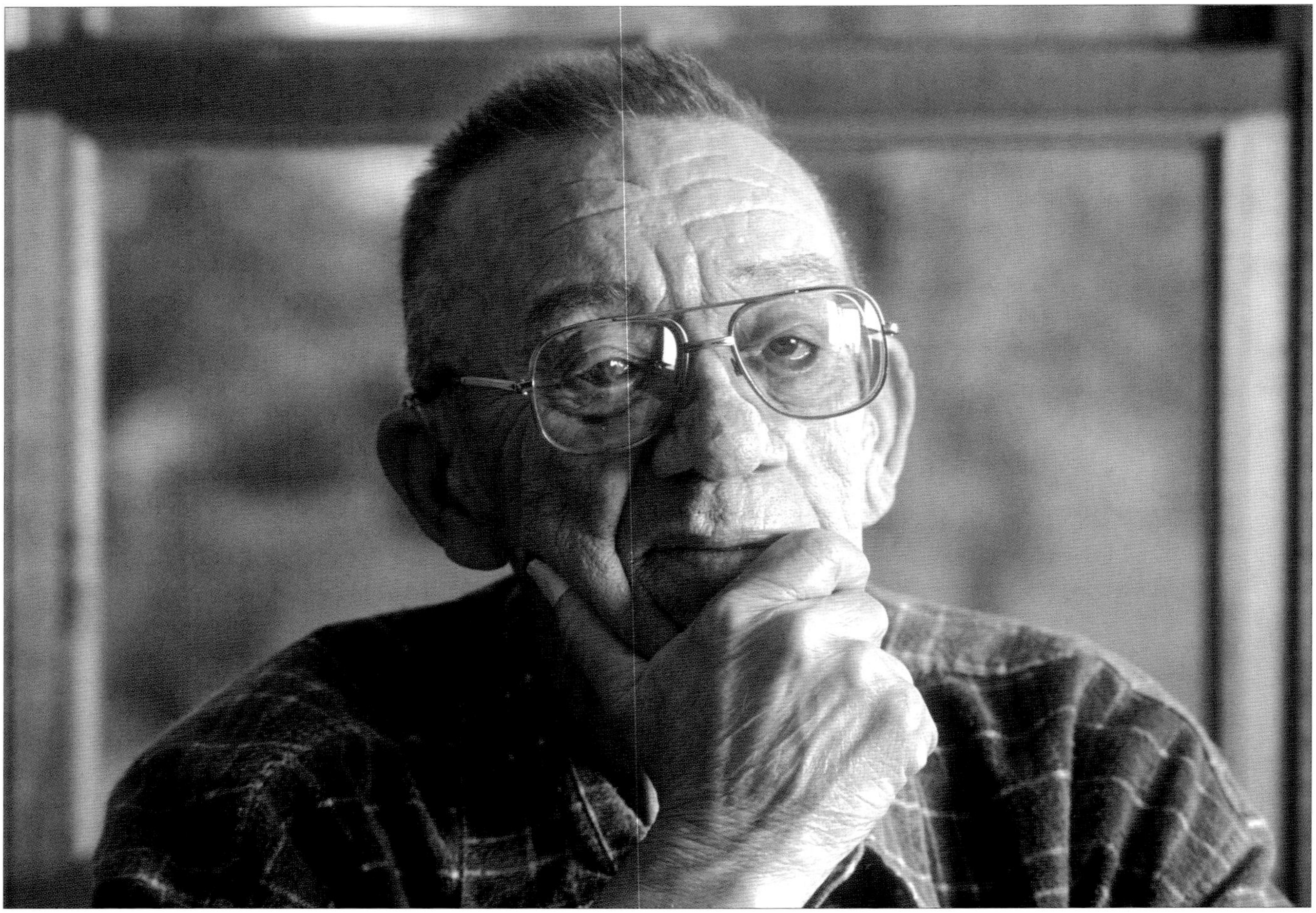

Monte LaBarge ☆ *Lemmon*

Stationed in one of World War II's lesser-known theaters of action, Wakonda native LaBarge spent much of the war in Alaska, maintaining anti-aircraft batteries, radar installations and an assortment of other equipment. The troops there prepared for a potential Japanese invasion after the attack on Pearl Harbor. In June 1942, the threat became reality.

I was stationed there at Dutch Harbor for the better part of two and a half years. We had a sub base with about 30 submarines based there.

We knew eventually that the Japanese would go north, whether they wanted the Aleutian Islands or just a diversion. We knew that we were going to be attacked.

Around the Battle of Midway, we were briefed constantly on where the Japanese navy was and what was going on, what we should expect. We knew the weather was favorable for them. They were about 300 or 400 miles out. We had expected that they would cut us off and move into Kodiak and into the mainland. There was information available to us to confirm that idea. I don't think everybody knew it, but there were many of us that did.

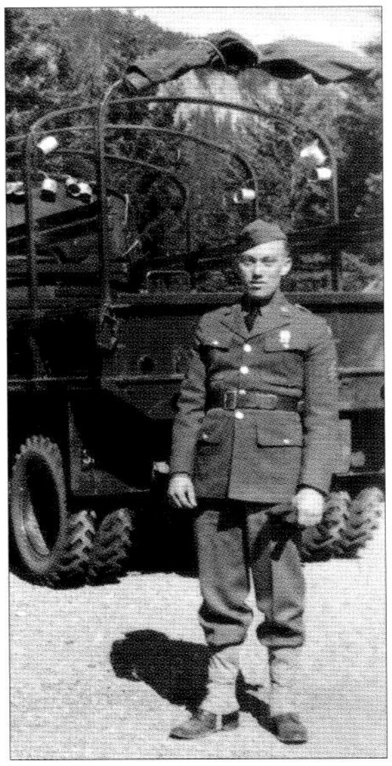

Well, you get ready for those things. You stash a few extra cans of goodies away, and instead of 100 rounds of ammunition a day, you put two or three hundred away. We were very practical people.

Three days before the Japanese attacked, we were ready. We knew there were aircraft carriers. We didn't have any idea how many, but we knew they were there. The sub boys had filled us in on this. We knew that the battle of Midway was on — we were aware of that.

Our air support was very limited. We had a few fighters. We had a couple P-38s and some P-40s. Very few. We knew it'd be damn hard to get reinforcements to us. But we also knew that if the Japanese navy came in, they wouldn't get any reinforcements either.

The weather was atrocious up our way. You could have cut the clouds with a knife. I've seen 30-foot waves that were just unbelievable. And most of our traveling up there was not by air. Most of it was by small craft, 60- to 80-foot vessels. When the Japanese did come in, they came in under the cover of a storm.

We got hit with a hundred Betty bombers, and they came off of carriers. They were either stupid and didn't know what they were doing, or intelligence had given them information that misled them. They hit one of the Marine barracks, which was dug in the ground — we never were told how many were killed, but it was a limited number — they hit two oil tanks, these were for refueling ships. The only thing they damaged as far as we were concerned was a warehouse with paper in it.

We shot up some fighter planes that were strafing. They really poured it on. They weren't as accurate as our bombers, but boy they were persistent. We poured up a stream of fire out of that place that was just like the Fourth of July.

(After their initial attack, Japanese troops controlled the islands of Attu and Kiska for nearly a year until the 7th Infantry Division invaded in May 1943.)

In the first American re-invasion of Attu, we went in behind the infantry, and that was tough. I had seen combat before I went out there, but not on a big scale. Those guys went in there with what I call fall equipment, not winter. I don't know how many guys we hauled off to the field hospital. They kept us down there for the major part of the conflict. It wasn't pleasant.

On one bombing run I went down with this commander from the Navy. I was his .50-caliber gunner because they were short of gunners. We dropped a torpedo on a base installation, and we hit a mess hall. And of course we had machine-gunned the hell out of them.

The Japanese were having dinner, so they figured they must have had her won. They didn't. ☆

The islands of Attu and Kiska were recaptured by the Americans in May 1943. That July, eight B-25 bombers flew from an Attu airfield and attacked the Japanese homeland for the first time since the famous Doolittle raid in April 1942. LaBarge worked in various capacities after the war. He spent 25 years with the BIA, and served as an administrator and teacher in Lemmon-area schools.

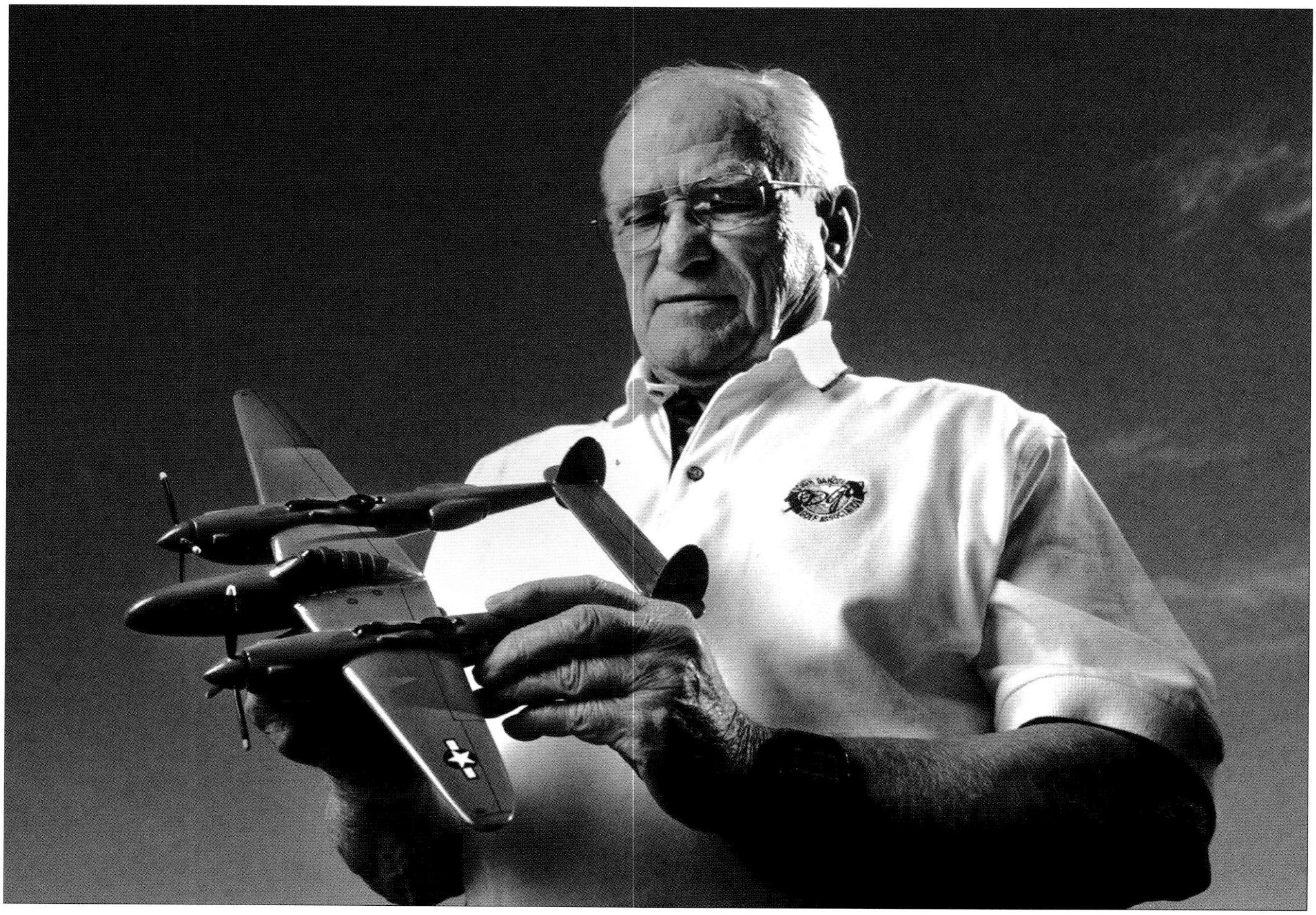

Hod Nielsen ☆ *Yankton*

Dubbed the "Fork-tailed Devil" by the German Luftwaffe, the P-38 Lightning was a powerful aircraft. Nielsen flew one as part of a photo reconnaissance squadron and played a vital part in the preparations for the Normandy invasion.

When I was a junior in college, the war situation was such that our age group knew that we were going to be involved. I wanted to be a pilot, so I investigated that and went in *(the service)* prior to getting my degree.

Joe Foss was one of the people who had some bearing on it. He and I got headed off good together right away before anybody ever knew Joe Foss. He was just a farm boy from around Sioux Falls. When you got to know him, he was really a great personality.

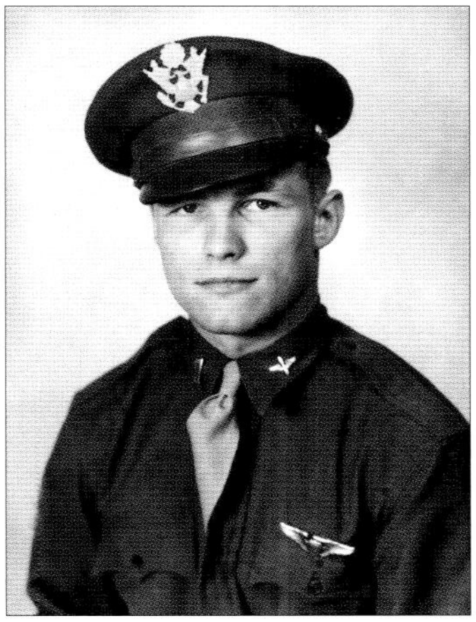

He graduated in 1940, and he went right into the Marine Corps. In '41 he was coming back, and I'd already signed up for the *(Army Air Corps)*. He came back to Vermillion after he got his Marine Corps wings, and boy, he really went to work on me, trying to get me to join the Marines. That was in 1941, in the spring. I got my wings in May of 1942.

We were sent to a "PR" unit that was being formed in Colorado Springs. PR? What's that, public relations? No, it was photo reconnaissance! And there was no photo reconnaissance in the Air Force at that time. There was in the RAF, and they were making good use of it.

We were in the first unit to be formed. They didn't have the air base done yet when they sent us there, so we were flying Piper Cubs and everything to get our flying time in. The training in those days was not as adequate as it was later.

Our training took to navigating as much as anything. Where we were going, we were going to do our flying by ourselves — we weren't going to have anybody with us — and we found out pretty quick that one of the best things was to learn what things looked like at 30,000 feet. So we used to go to that altitude and then pick out targets in the country to go to. We'd go to Chicago, for example. Sounds like an easy trip, but when you're traveling at 300 to 350 miles an hour, if you make a little bit of a mistake it magnifies itself in a big hurry. We got pretty good at picking out things on maps and knowing how to read maps, and that was important to us.

Later when we flew combat, we flew normally around 33,000 feet, which was pretty high in those days. I have flown over 40,000 when we were in combat — we'd get jumped by some *(German)* ME-109s or something — and they didn't go that high. There wasn't much of the war fought at that altitude.

When we went overseas, there were 27 pilots in our squadron. We were the 13th Squadron; that was our number. There was one squadron that had gone over to the 8th Air Force before us. When we were starting to be on our way, they were assigned to the North African invasion. So they flew from England down to North Africa, and there weren't any PR units then until we got there, and that was the 1st of November, 1942.

We didn't have a base of operations because they weren't that well organized, and the 8th Air Force had just got going. It was February before we got onto our base and then we started operations in March.

We got a base right near the British photo reconnaissance unit. Our place was called Mount Farm; it was a little base just 9 miles south and east of Oxford, in the Thames Valley. Beautiful part of England — and really an interesting part — so that helped. I was over there for 14 months. That was at the time when we did not have air superiority over Europe. The Germans did, and we had a lot of losses. But that got better as our numbers got better and we got more experienced.

Our job was to go over there and get pictures and get them back, which precluded having any combat. There were no guns and no armament on our aircraft at all. Just get in and get out. Our mission was to bring back photos of the target, and that was drilled into us all the time. With some of the goofball pilots that we had, if they'd had guns they'd have wanted to use them. They'd have gone looking for trouble.

We had several primary things. One of them was bomb damage assessment. When the bombers went over and bombed Essen or the Ruhr Valley, on their way back they'd see us going over. We were over there when the smoke was still coming up to take pictures of the damage that they had managed.

The advantage that we had was timing. For example, when the B-17s went over on a mission, I knew where they were and what they were doing and everything. If I was assigned to go there and cover that particular thing, I would take off and be going over *(the target)* when they came out. The *(German)* fighters were all up with the bombers or hopefully down on the ground.

We also kept track of the shipping in the English Channel. Every day that we could, we had planes flying over the ports and taking pictures of the ports and seeing what was going on over there. We used to do test hops in our planes after they'd been overhauled. I was up over England one day and I ran into a *(German)* JU-88 that was obviously another photo plane. He ran away from me; I didn't run away from him.

We had one bit of publicity while I was there. *Colliers* magazine sent some people over to do an article, and they did a cover article in the summer of '43 about the Focus Cats — that's what they called us.

You can't see much detail from that distance. We're talking about five miles or better. We were looking down at it, but we were also looking around, trying to keep anybody away from us. We had four cameras. We had one 24-inch focal length camera, and that took some great detail. We had three 6-inch focal length; two of them went out to the side and the other one was straight down, and they all worked together. No sights or anything, we just had a button that was all set for us.

That wasn't always perfect. I remember a couple times when I made long trips and didn't get anything, mainly because of the temperature where we were and it froze up on us. They gave us big, big rolls of film — rarely did we have all of the film used *(on a mission)*.

We didn't do any low-altitude stuff very much. Any of that that came along, the British did with their Spitfires. We got so that we were losing planes so fast, they started sending fighters with our photo planes on important missions. They started doing that because nobody was getting the film back.

There were 27 pilots that went over. There were seven that came back. That ought to answer your question *(about the danger involved)*. In addition to that, we had replacements; we had 103 or 104 percent *(turnover due to casualties)*. There was anti-aircraft whenever you'd go over any of those places. *(The Germans)* and the British both had the rudiments of radar at that time. They could keep track of you.

They took five of our squadron and gave us an additional assignment, and that was very interesting.

They were just starting to figure out where they were going to make the invasion in early '43. They found that the maps they had available of Normandy and Brittany in France were made by Napoleon's armies, and that was quite some time before then.

So we mapped those two provinces. I'd go down to St. Nazaire for bomb damage assessment or something down in the Bay of Biscay area, and on the way down and the way back we'd do some mapping.

Each time we went on a mission, we were briefed by our intelligence people on where we were to go and what they wanted. The five of us were given areas that they needed. When we came back from a mission, we'd be briefed three times. First and second stage briefings, and then for the third stage, we'd get in a jeep and we'd take this film and we'd go down about 30 or 40 miles east of us on the Thames River. It was an old British castle called Madnaham. Movies were made at the castle; it had a moat and the whole deal. We'd go in there and the thing was an intelligence headquarters, not only for us but the British too. They had some of the sharpest people I ever met. They'd take those films and they could tell you anything that you wanted to know about what we took pictures of. They wanted to talk to you about anything you might have seen or might have run into. They made the maps — they were engineers and intelligence people.

A couple months before the invasion, the colonel called us in and he said, "Goodbye. We've got orders for you to go back." We said, "What for?" He said, "They don't want you to do any more flying over there, you've got some information that we don't want the Germans to have." In other words, we knew pretty much where the invasion was going to be, but we didn't know we knew it. They didn't want us shot down over there. ☆

Nielsen enjoyed a long career as a radio sportscaster, and is still a sportswriter for the Yankton Daily Press & Dakotan.

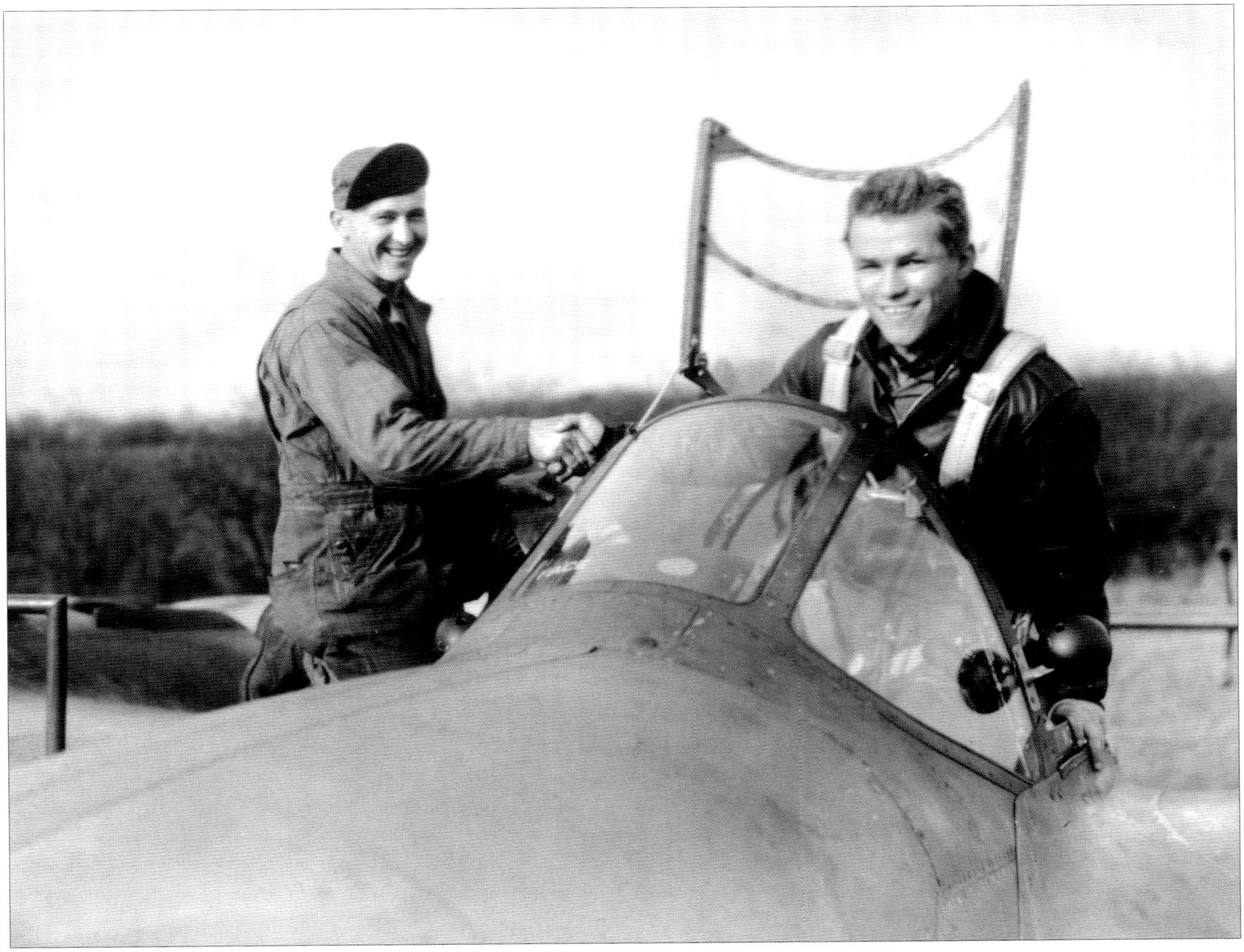

Nielsen gets a warm greeting upon his return from a successful mission in his P-38 Lightning.

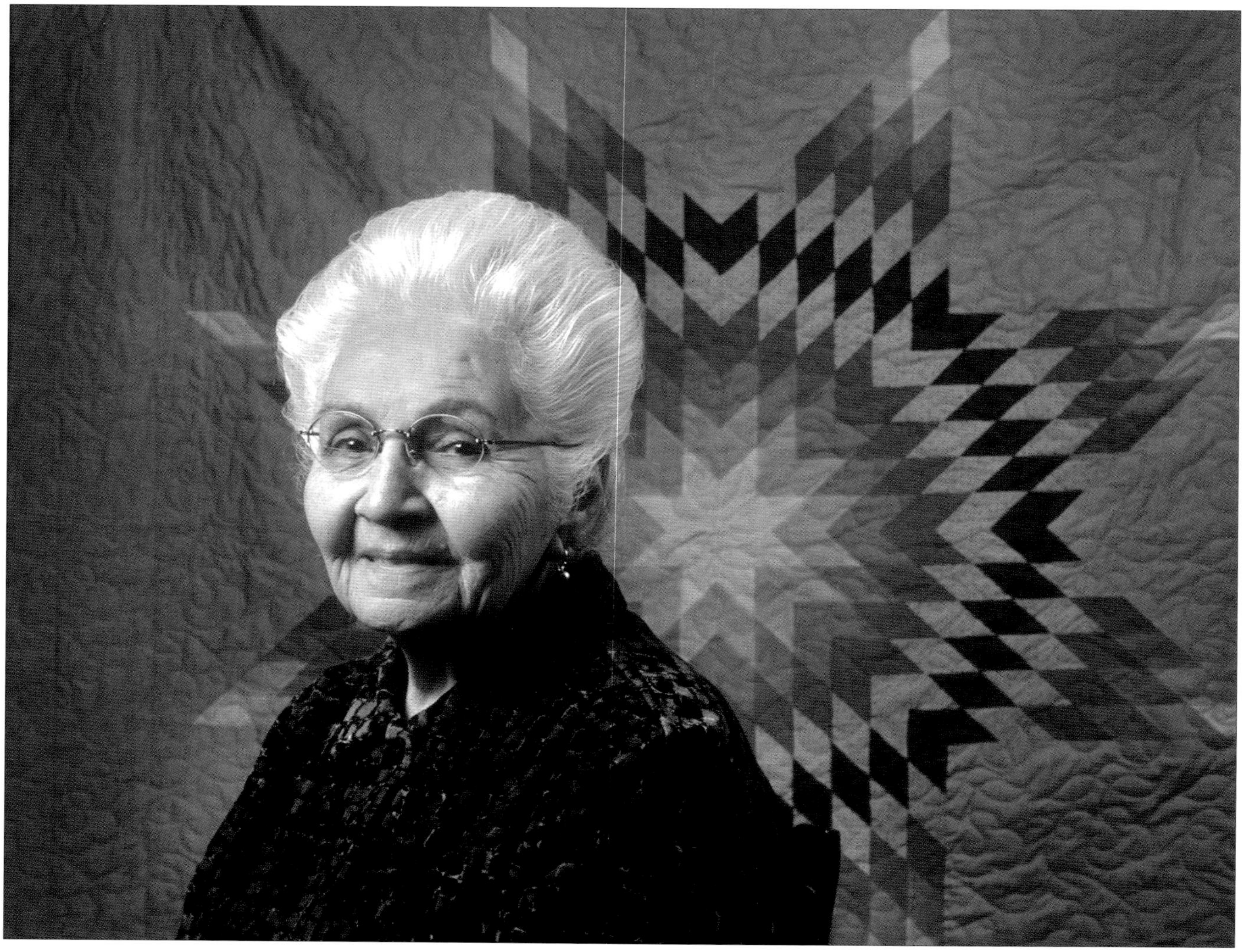

MARCELLA LEBEAU ☆ *Eagle Butte*

Serving with the Army Nurse Corps, Marcella Ryan helped to heal soldiers from England to Belgium during nearly two years in Europe. Her work began at an England hospital as soldiers began arriving on D-Day.

I was born at Promise, South Dakota, and have lived on the reservation all my life — except to go to school and the military.

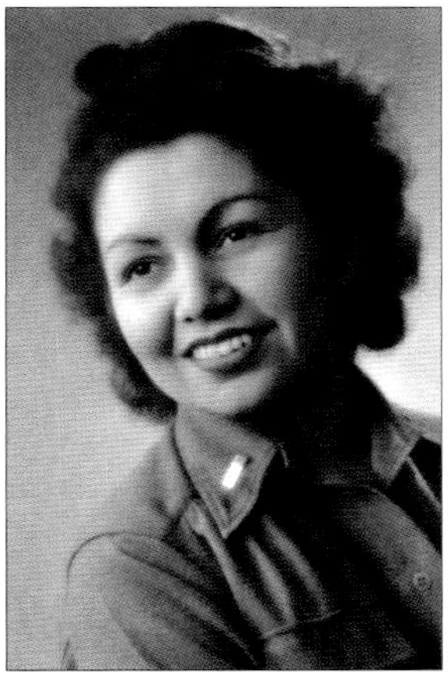

I was young at the time, and I didn't know what war was. And so everything was new to me. We got our first convoy of patients from D-Day at 2:30 in the morning, and they kept coming after that.

It was around the middle of August, as I recall, when it was safe enough for us to cross the channel. We landed in Normandy in the Utah Beach area. When we landed at Utah Beach, we didn't have an actual hospital — we stayed in a cow pasture there for several days. We just camped there, waiting for transportation to Paris, France. They took us by open truck to Paris, and we went through St. Lo, which was pretty well demolished. We stayed *(in Paris)* and worked a few days before we went on our way to Liege, Belgium.

We moved into this tent hospital, and my ward was A1, which was the first ward on the unit. It was a surgical ward, a soft tissue wound ward. We were very busy with patients coming and going all the time. As soon as they were stable, they were sent on, either back to the front lines or to other hospitals on their way back to the United States.

We had a small chapel on our compound. We had a Christmas service *(1944)*. The minister was praying, and there was so much noise from the buzz bombs *(German V-1 rockets)* and from the ack-ack *(anti-aircraft fire)* in the distance that there were times when you couldn't hear him pray. But he kept right on praying.

We took our turn working the night shift on other wards, and I worked on a shock ward. I was working night duty there one time, and this nurse asked me if I would go see this Native American soldier. I went to see him, and his name was Eugene Roubideaux from Rosebud. She told me that he lost both legs up high, and that they were afraid that he might try to commit suicide. They were afraid to allow him to have a razor for that reason. He wouldn't talk to them.

So I went to visit him, and he was quiet like Native Americans are. But he talked. He told me about D-Day, about going out every day, and they never knew when D-Day was going to be. It would be a dry run and they'd go back again, until finally D-Day happened. I offered to write letters home for him if he wanted to, and he didn't want to write home. I would take him papers from South Dakota that I got, and just go and visit him.

One day he was gone, and so I lost track of him. For many years after I got back to South Dakota, I would ask about him. I was a nurse, so I went to a lot of nurse's meetings. If there was someone from Rosebud, I would ask about Eugene Roubideaux. I never caught up with him, and that was about 40 years.

One day, we had a young lady who came to our hospital to explain about using a different form. She had her inservice, and she left. The next morning, I received this call *(from a different woman)*, and she said, "My name is Ann Lafferty. Do you know Eugene Roubideaux?"

I said, "Yes!" I got so emotional I couldn't talk.

And she said, "He's my father."

I couldn't answer her, so finally she said, "Are you okay? Are you all right?" And so I said yes, finally. We visited, and she said he lived in Yankton, and that she was *(his)* oldest daughter. He moved to Yankton, was divorced, and remarried and had a big family.

She gave me his phone number and his address in Yankton. I didn't think I could call him right away. I waited. Then finally I called him a day later, and I said, "Do you remember the nurse that stood at your bed in Liege, Belgium?" He said, "I'll never forget."

I get all choked up when I think about it. What I think about is the sacrifice he made. And he did it for us. ☆

LeBeau returned to help the Lakota after the war, working as a nurse in Eagle Butte. With assistance from local veterans' organizations and auxiliaries, she honored Roubideaux at Eagle Butte on November 11, 1984. She and her granddaughter now sew quilts in their Eagle Butte workshop.

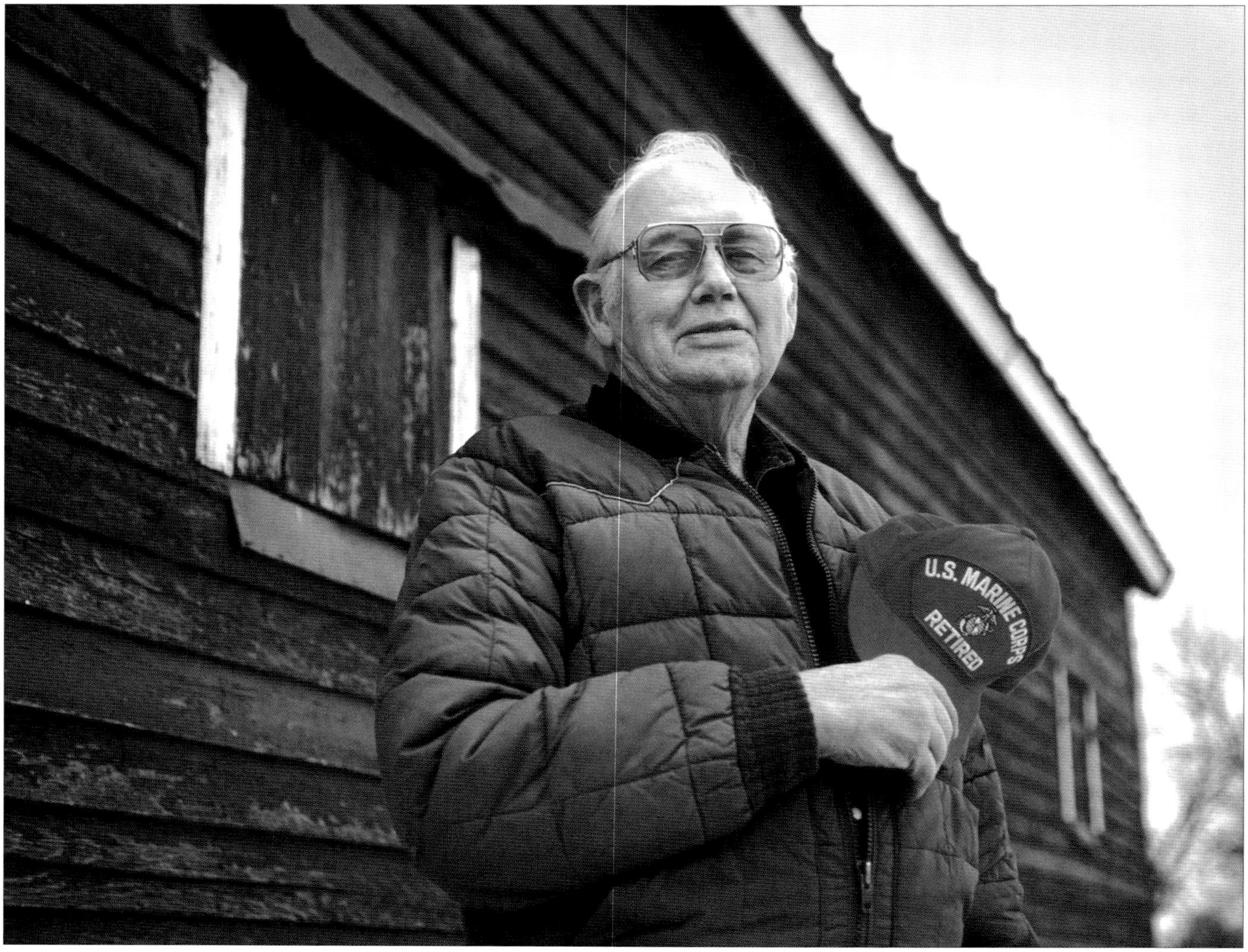
U.S. MARINE CORPS
RETIRED

ALBERT SCHAMENS ☆ *Hazel*

Schamens was a runner in the 3rd Marine Division, hauling ammunition, food and messages to and from the front lines. He grew up quickly on the sands of Iwo Jima.

In the '30s, it was terrible. The dust was blowing, and a lot of times we didn't even go to school. There were nine of us kids, and we didn't have that much food to eat except what we raised. My time was coming up, so I enlisted in January '44. I was one of the last ones to sign up for the Marines at that time.

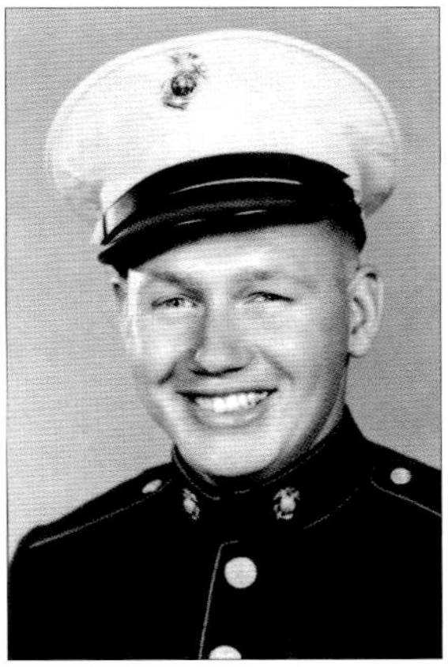

I was a rifleman and a barber and a runner. When I got over there, they needed someone to cut hair, and I had been cutting hair on the ship, so I was the company barber. It got me out of a few work details. I cut a lot of hair over there.

We had one day of combat on Guam, and then we were out mopping up the island. We went for chow one morning, and three Japs fell in line with us — they were getting hungry. They didn't even try and dress like us. Of course, we took them as prisoners. They just walked right in.

It was December when we left Guam. We got about three or four days out on the ocean, and they put us through the maps and stuff *(detailing)* where we were going to hit and what we were going to do. And then it was Iwo Jima.

We'd never hit a beach before, so we had no idea what it was like. I wasn't one of the first ones in, but I was in the second wave about a day later. We crawled down into the Higgins boats, and then when they got close to shore, they dropped the end and we went to shore. There were dead guys laying all over. You don't realize how many people were killed — there were over 7,000 *(Americans)* killed on that island.

It didn't look like there was anything on Iwo Jima, really. There was no vegetation whatsoever. It was so much different than Guam. It was just a bare island.

They were dug in so bad, you couldn't see them at all. They'd stick their head out and start shooting at you. You never knew where they were at. One day we were just sitting there and a Jap stuck his head out of a hole out there just a little ways from us. We took a TNT satchel charge and dropped it down in there with him.

That's the day that a kid stepped on a land mine and blew his legs off. When he stepped on the land mine, it blew him up pretty well and he says, "Cover my feet." He said his feet were cold. Well, he didn't have no feet — his shoe was laying out there with his foot in it.

The Japs knew how to yell "Corpsman!" *(to trick medics into thinking Marines were wounded)*. One of them kept hollering, "Corpsman! Corpsman!" Our corpsman came around the corner, and they shot him with a machine gun right across his chest. That was kind of tough on us.

I was always on the front lines. The only time I was gone was when I'd go back to get something or deliver a message. The guy that shot me, he was behind the line about a mile, and I had another mile to go to get back to the company commander. I was going back with a message that day. We walked that track I don't know how many times, carrying up stuff. We'd carry up chow. One day we took up doughnuts and coffee. I was just walking when I went by him. I'm sure he had a hole with a lid, just like a gopher. The bullet went under my helmet on this side, and through the back of my neck and out my helmet on *(the other)* side. It was a clean bullet: "Zing!" and it was through there. It just barely missed my spine. Felt like somebody stuck a red-hot poker through *(my neck)*.

It just knocked me out. I came to, and my legs were paralyzed. "Oh brother," I thought. But then I got to wiggling them, and the feeling came back when I was still on the ground. I was scared, and prayed a little bit.

They stuck me on the stretcher — blood was running down the back of my neck — and put me on the ship. The doctor said, "Boy, you are lucky."

I'd like to have a picture of the things that go through my mind and show people what it looked like. When I came home, I didn't talk about it — my dad always used to bawl me out because I wouldn't talk about it.

It's gotten easier since I've gotten older, but there's still things I can't talk about. ☆

Schamens has farmed and cut hair since the war's end. He was awarded two Purple Hearts for injuries sustained in the war.

ALVIN ANDERSON ☆ *Aberdeen*

Anderson spent the war probing the enemy's strengths and conducting reconnaissance patrols in advance of the quick-moving 2nd Armored Division. His tour of duty brought him through North Africa, Sicily, England, France, Belgium and Germany.

After Pearl Harbor, we all wanted to get in and go. I went in when I was 20. They took us down to basic training in Spartanburg, South Carolina, at Camp Croft. From Camp Croft we went to Fort Bragg, North Carolina, where I joined the 2nd Armored Division.

It was at that time when I volunteered to go in the I&R; Intelligence and Reconnaissance. We had specialized training. We trained as a platoon, rather than a battalion. There were 22 of us. We had a very close-knit group.

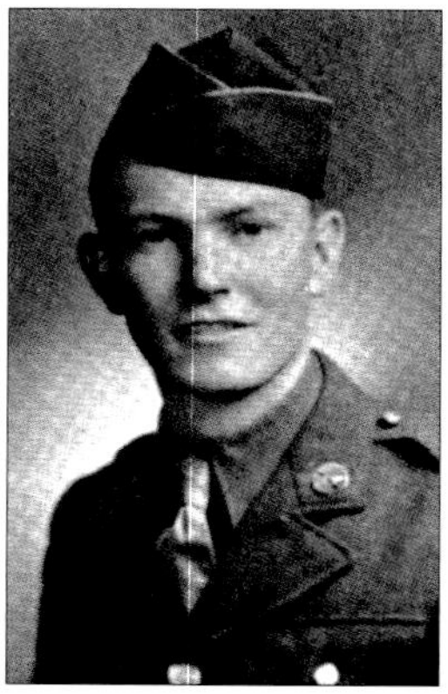

We did a lot of patrols. We'd try and go out and contact the Germans and kind of feel our way up there and see what they've got, see how strong they are. We had radios, and there were four jeeps in our platoon, a halftrack that carried two .30-calibers on the sides and a .50-caliber on the front, and we pulled an anti-tank gun.

If we couldn't clear a roadblock, then they would call up the infantry companies to come in. A lot of them we took care of. We were trained for it. *(The Germans)* were very determined that we weren't going on — and we were determined that we were.

We were at Ubach, between the Siegfried Line and the Roer River. We heard of this push that the Germans were making, and so we moved down to Celles, France. We went and attacked on Christmas Eve morning, and it was 20 below zero. It was cold and miserable. It was just like any other combat day. They didn't give us much time to think of home.

It was rough in there. Snow was deep; it was cold. There was a lot of frostbite and things like that. We didn't have any overshoes, we just had our combat boots. We'd put oil on them to make them waterproof.

We were in the forest, and we'd make two-man foxholes. You'd let your buddy rest a little bit, and then you'd try to get a little sleep in. We'd be there for maybe two or three days and then move on. The moon was bright — it was a full moon.

There were dead Germans laying around. I had to step over them on our recon patrols. Those patrols were hard. You know how the snow creaks in the wintertime in South Dakota? You could hear the Germans coming for a mile, and they could hear us coming.

Some of the funnier things: we were in Ubach, Germany, and there was an air raid shelter, and that was where our battalion headquarters were at that time. Jerry *(the Germans)* started shelling it, and we were all in the courtyard. We started running to get in the basement, and this one shell landed and the concussion from that shell blew me up in the air, and my weapons belt got hung over the knob of this door. They had to come up and lift me off of that. It was all kind of funny in the end. After it's all over, it's funny.

I don't remember the name of the little town where we got the halftrack blown out from under us. I had picked up some shrapnel. We got out of the halftrack and ran into a building, and we were cut off. We had German civilians in the basement, and we told them to be damn quiet. They were scared. The rest of the forces had pulled back to the outer edge of the city. My halftrack driver and myself spent the night behind the lines. The next morning our troops came in and cleaned out the city.

We moved on to Magdeburg, which was on the Elbe River. The engineers were getting pontoon bridges in, so we could get our tanks across. The infantry went over in DUKWs *(amphibious tanks)*, and we made a beachhead there. The Germans started opening fire about 5 o'clock in the morning. They knocked out the pontoon bridge, so we didn't get our tanks across. A couple of battalions of us were across the river, and they just shelled the hell out of us. It came in like popcorn all day long. There were days when I felt that, "Well, if I make it through today, I'll have it made." And you went from day to day.

I thought it was an honor to serve under the American flag. We were fighting for freedom. Just think of what the world would be like today if Japan would have won, and Germany. What would this world be? ☆

Anderson returned to Aberdeen and worked as a livestock auctioneer until the early 1990s.

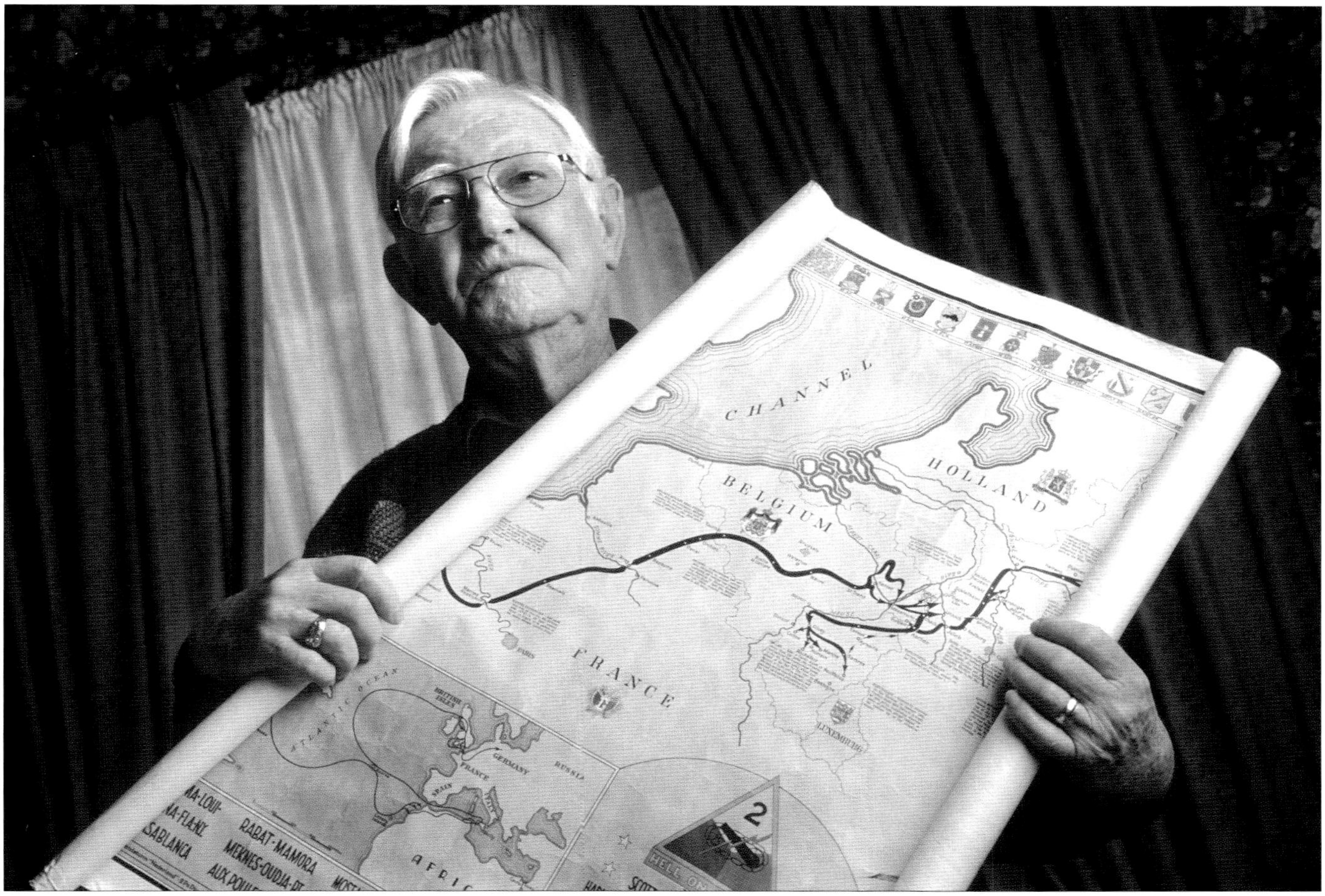
CHANNEL
HOLLAND
BELGIUM
FRANCE
RABAT-MAMORA
2

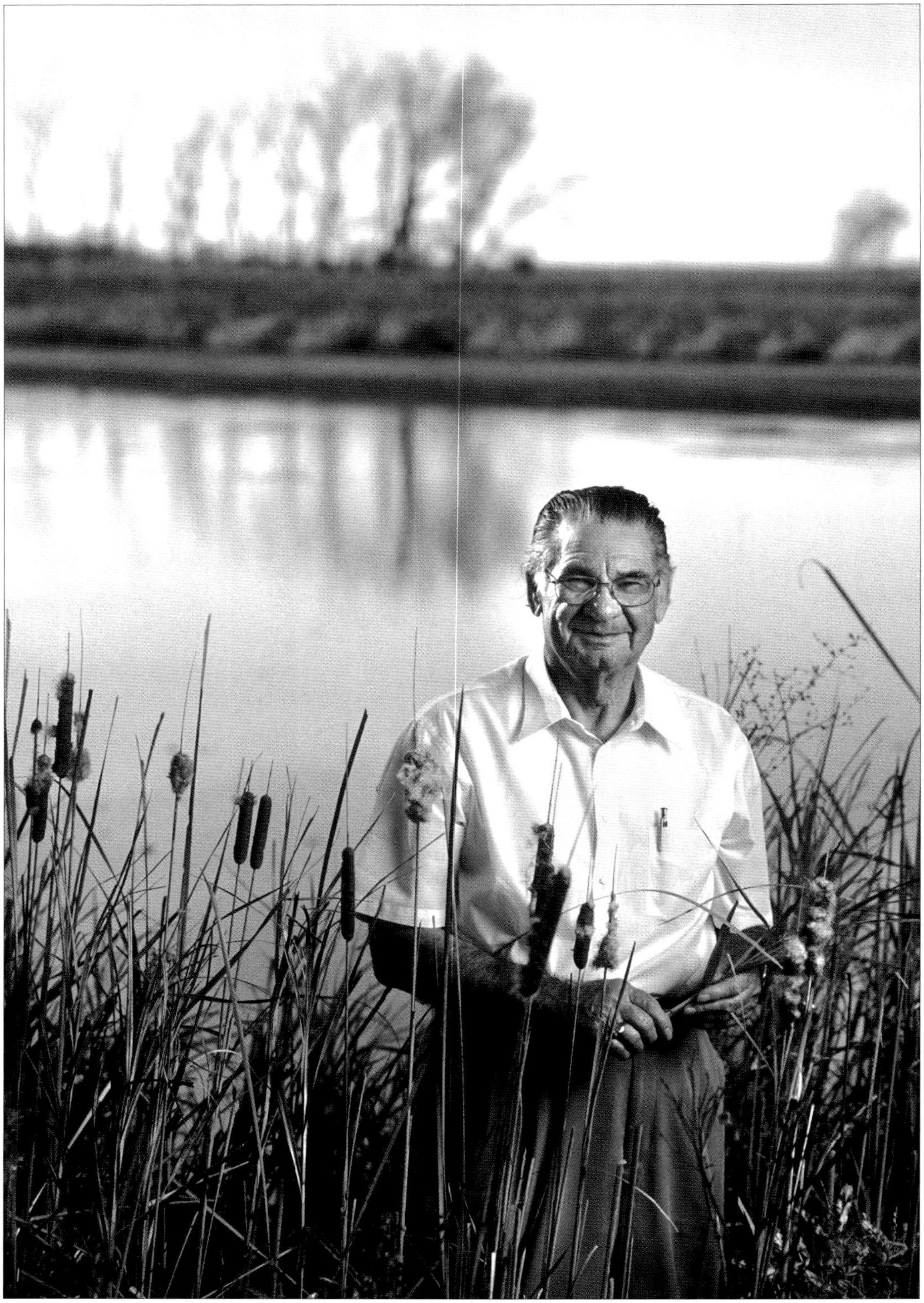

JOHN MAHER ☆ *Mitchell*

As a crew member on LST 864 (Landing Ship Tank), Maher was one of the Navy's utility players — men responsible in all theaters for getting equipment to soldiers on the ground. His first hot landing was on Ie Shima, an island near Okinawa.

I was the oldest of nine boys in my family, and when it came to World War II, I thought it was my place to volunteer when I was 17. I had an older cousin that was kind of my hero — he was in the Navy first, and I kind of followed in his footsteps.

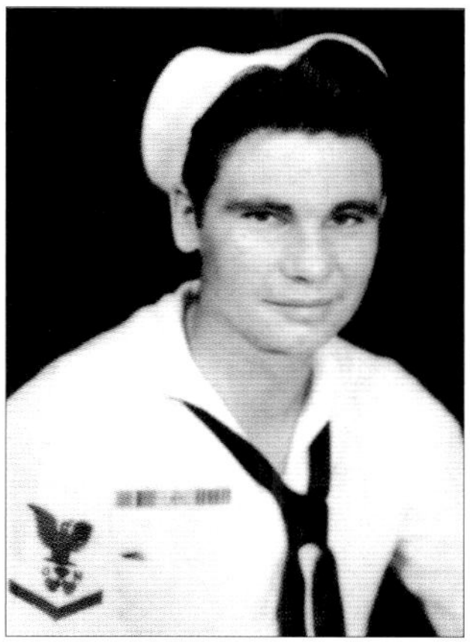

I went through boot training, and I was picked for engineering school at Great Lakes *(Naval Training Station in Illinois)*. From there, I was sent on to Richmond, Virginia, where I took diesel school.

We boarded the LST at Seattle, Washington. LST was good duty. You had four hours on and eight hours off. You had plenty of time for rest, and your chow was good. When you didn't have Army on there, your chow was REAL good — you could even order how you wanted your eggs for breakfast.

We worked on 225-horsepower diesels in the auxiliary engine room, and then we had the big engines — the 1,000-horsepower diesels — in the main engine room.

There was a battalion of combat engineers *(on board)*, and their job was to build the airstrip when we got there; Okinawa was the last jump-off to bomb Japan. It was all their construction equipment: maintainers and graders and trucks. They had trouble building those airstrips because the Japs kept coming in and bombing them.

You had the battleships in there; they shot over your head for a day to soften up the beaches. Our captain announced when we were going in. There was a lot of coral in that area; a special officer had to come aboard ship to direct the ship in. The trick is to get in there and get out. You pumped your water to the bow of the boat and opened your engines at full speed. You headed for the beach, and you drug your anchor as you went in. When you got in, then your bow doors opened and your equipment would be taken off the ship. They didn't waste any time at that. To get off the beach again, you use your anchor to pull you off and you pumped the water from the bow of your boat back to your stern.

Sometimes that was very successful, and sometimes it wasn't. Some of them didn't make it. Some of them had engine trouble. A few of them were sunk. We called our ship the *Lady Luck*, because we were lucky. Those suicide planes came in three or four a night. There was a high peak in the middle of Ie Shima, and they could come in behind that peak and they could cut their engines, and you couldn't hear them come in. But they were usually after the larger ships; they didn't bother much with an LST. So we were lucky there.

My general quarters station was a 20mm gun with another fellow from South Dakota. He was from Irene. It was kind of nice to have a fellow from South Dakota with you when you were on a gun. One was a loader and the other one was doing the shooting. The 20mm had tracer bullets, so you could tell where you were shooting.

One time a Jap Betty *(bomber)* flew over, and we were all shooting at that, and she stayed just out of range. While we were shooting at her, another bomber came in and bombed the airstrip. She was a decoy up there.

A ship alongside of us got a big Jap Betty with a 40mm, and it crashed just off our bow. Makes quite an explosion in the water when they go down. There's so many people shooting, it's like hunting geese; you don't know whether you're the one that hit it or not. We shot a few down.

Ernie Pyle was killed on the 17th *(April '45)*, right near our ship. He was one of the most famous war correspondents at that time. It was sad to see that happen.

A few days after we landed there, we went inland on Ie Shima and saw a lot of the dead enemy. That was probably the worst sight I ever saw. On Ie Shima, the women fought right with the men and carried hand grenades. There were mothers with babies on their back that were killed with flamethrowers. I have all the respect and praise for the Marines and Army that went in and made the first landings. They're the ones that softened up the beaches and made it easy for us. ☆

Maher served as a county extension agent for several years in Sanborn and Davison counties.

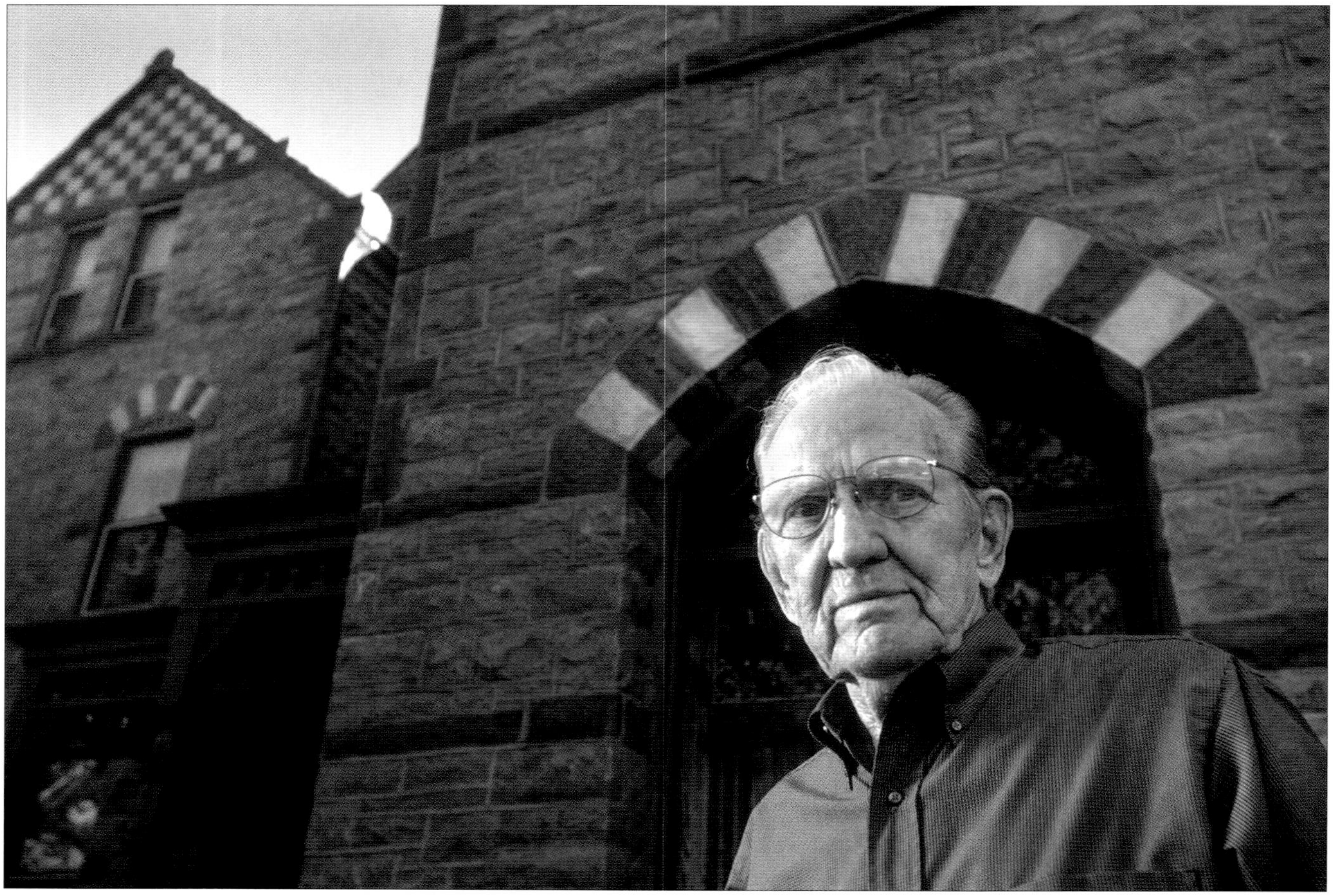

Bob Swift ☆ *Sioux Falls*

Stationed in Texas, Swift spent the first months of the war teaching bombardiers how to use the top secret Norden bomb sight. In 1943, he started flying combat missions in Africa and Italy while training B-17 crews to use the sight. He was the group bombardier on all of his missions, flying in the 301st Bomb Group's lead plane.

The Norden bomb sight was very high secret, top secret stuff. You couldn't take a bomb sight out of the vault without a .45 strapped onto your side, and you had to have at least two people to carry it out to the airplane.

I wound up with 56 missions. I was anxious to get home, because six weeks after I left the States, our son was born, and I wanted to see him. It was almost six weeks from the time my boy was born before I even knew I had a child. After I got *(Richard's photograph)*, then I took it on every mission.

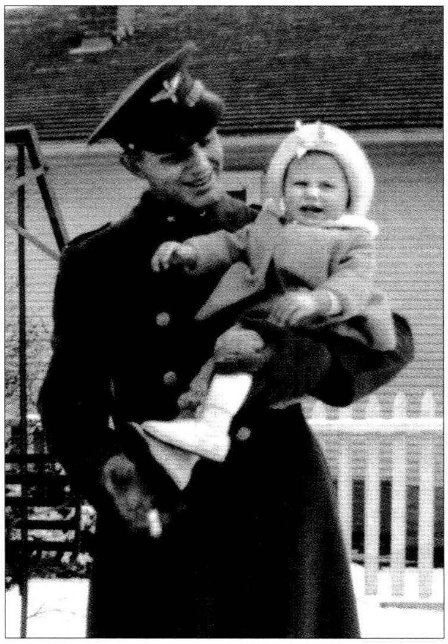

The most harrowing experience I had, we had a brand new co-pilot; it was his first mission. We started down the runway, and one engine started running away. Instead of throttling back on that engine, this co-pilot throttled back on all four of them.

Well, we were going too fast to stop and too slow to fly, so the pilot shoved them all wide open. Then they all started just running wild. At the end of the runway there was a wheat field, and this Arab was out there with a binder, a few oxen and mules on it, and they'd already started to plow around the perimeter of the field.

We were getting closer and closer to that plowed ground. I knew if we ever got into that, it'd probably nose us over. The pilot pulled back and slammed it into the ground and we bounced over that. And then we started going up this long incline, and I'm sitting there with wheat stubble under me. You're sitting up there in the nose, nothing out in front of you, all you've got is down, you know. I've got four 2,000-pound bombs right behind me, and here's this damn binder up there and we're headed right for it. These animals got wild, and they took off. We finally reached the crest of the hill, and then we were going down the other side until we picked up enough speed 'til we could get up in the air and go. And we went over and finished that mission.

They'd find your altitude, then they'd throw *(flak)* up in a checkerboard pattern. The only way you could have any accuracy with your bombing was to fly straight and level, at a constant speed. Once they got your range, why, then you wanted to get rid of those bombs in a hurry and get the hell out of there! If you had real strong headwind, you might be on the run for two or three minutes. It seemed like a day. That B-17 was quite an airplane. That airplane could come back just beat to hell.

Fighters didn't bother you quite as much as the darn flak, because with fighters, you're so busy with the machine gun. You're trying to shoot them down — it's kind of like hunting ducks — you don't think much about it.

We had a mission over Viterbo *(Italy)*, and there was an anti-aircraft shell that went off under the plane, and the fragments came up through it. I had a backpack parachute on, which kept me from getting real seriously hurt. It wasn't enough to disable me for any period of time. It scared the hell out of me. I had to readjust *(the sight)*, because we hadn't released our bombs yet. Some of the data that you prepare en route to the target, it would take you a while to get that all on that little computer and slide rule and then set these various items into the sight. Right or wrong, it's there and that's going to determine where the bombs go.

That stuff was bumped out of position. I had to hurry up and get that back in, then synchronize it on the target. I suppose it took 30 seconds, maybe. That seems like a day when you're doing it.

Yes, it was an experience. I'm glad I had it, but I wouldn't do it again if I had any choice. ☆

Since Swift was the lead bombardier on the Viterbo mission, success depended on his quick action to restore the knocked-out Norden sight. He was awarded the Distinguished Flying Cross and the Purple Heart for his actions that day. A co-founder of Swift Construction, he started the business by helping build homes for GIs returning from the war.

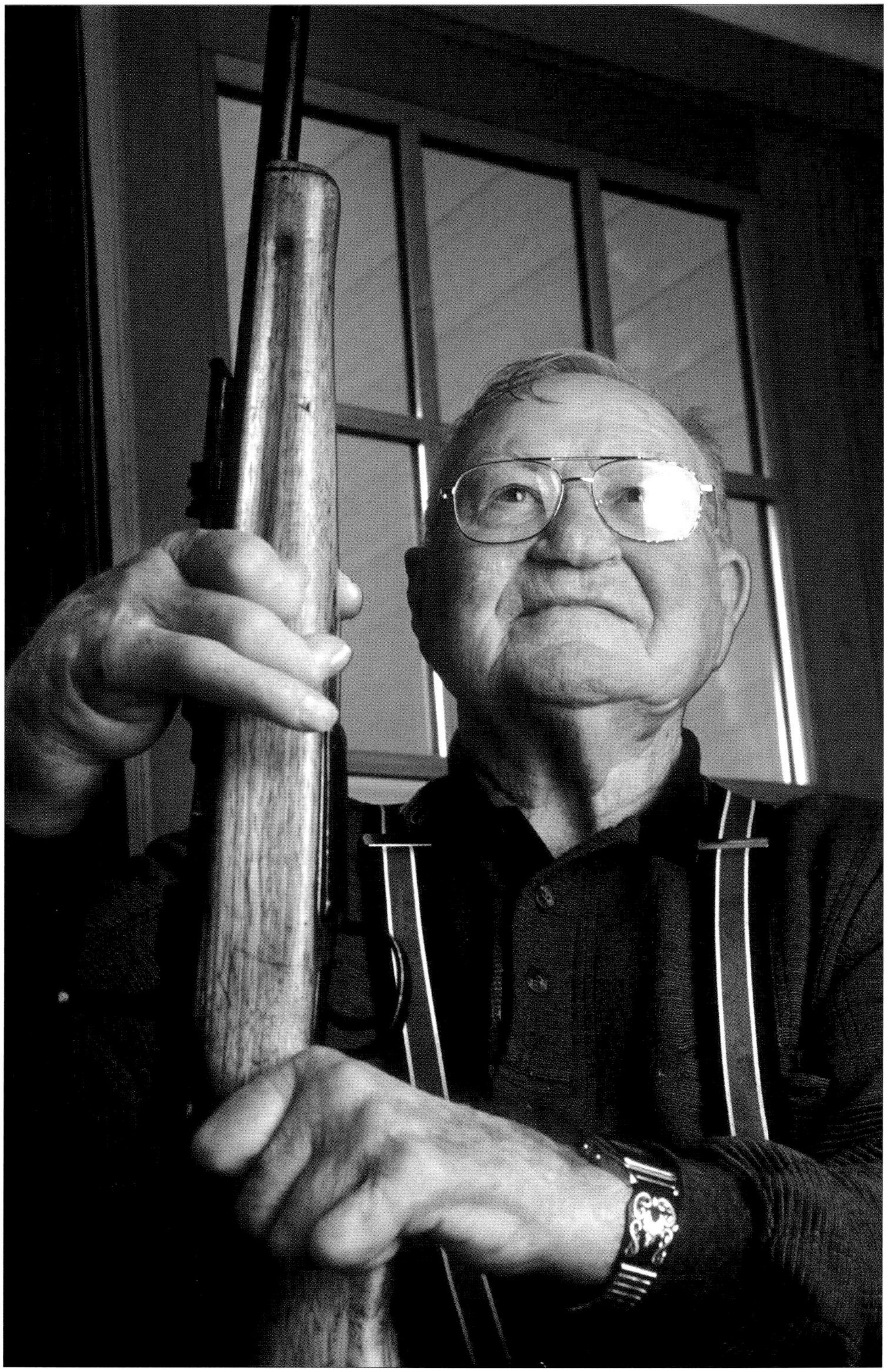

Steve Vetter ☆ *Bison*

Vetter was working in a strip coal mine in Perkins County when he joined the Army in June 1944. He and the 77th Infantry found themselves landing on Okinawa on April Fool's Day 1945. Nineteen days later, a sniper's bullet changed Vetter's life forever.

Day and night we loaded ships. Twelve hundred ships left the Philippines to go to Okinawa in one bunch. Once we loaded, they laid maps out and we studied the maps. They told us which position we were going to be in. I knew exactly where I was going to be walking.

The BAR *(Browning Automatic Rifle)* is an automatic rifle. Shoots 20 rounds just real fast. It had tripods on it where you could set it down, but we'd fire it from our hip or from our shoulder, either one. It was 15 pounds, but it was well worth it. It had firepower, I tell you. Of course the Japs liked to get rid of them kind of guys too, if they could.

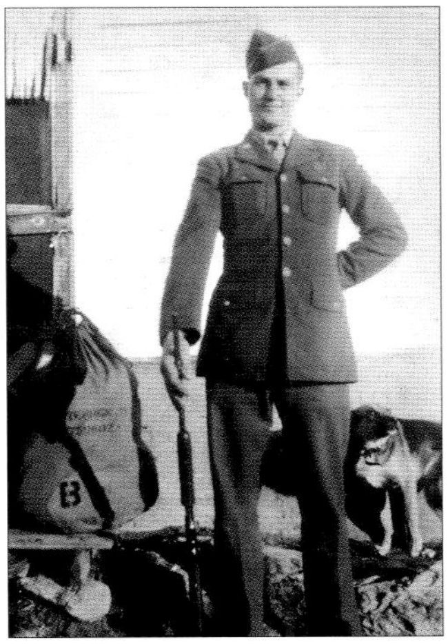

I had an assistant. That's what he carried was ammunition. He carried plenty of ammunition too, never did run out. He was real good, I mean he really was on the ball. He got killed about two minutes before I got hit. That's when I knew I was getting in trouble.

We were in a foxhole at the time, checking *(the Japanese)* out up ahead there. They were picking off everybody down the line they could get to. They got him, he was right alongside, probably 4 or 5 feet from me, and I knew I was going to be next. I happened to see two of them take off from the brush up ahead, and of course I gave them all 20 rounds. I went down and put another clip in. Just as I got up — I was going to make sure they didn't get up again — there was another one sitting there waiting for me.

He took a shot at me — he hit me on the arm here — and it went through the rifle stock and into my hand here while I was shooting. (*The bullet passed through Vetter's left upper bicep, severing the nerves, and then shattered the stock of his BAR, mangling his right hand.*) Of course that put an end to that, the rifle just fell down then. Have you ever shot a rabbit with a shotgun? Well that's kind of the way it looked. Every bone in there was broken. Knuckles were all blowed off and everything. Fingers hung in all directions. It was just completely gone. There was nothing there. And this arm here, it was just plumb dead, it just cut the nerves all off and went through the muscle there.

Well, it just went so fast, it just — pshwit! — and I jumped up and run right away, run to the rear. There was a dead furrow, and I dropped into that. When I dropped in there, there was another guy laying in the same ditch.

I hollered at him, because the blood was really shooting out of me. He crawled back up to me and he touched my feet. That's as close as he could get. He couldn't turn around. If he tried to raise up, why, there was a machine gun sitting over there shooting at us then. He had a phosphorus grenade on him but he didn't have no smoke grenade. And I had a smoke grenade, but I couldn't get it loose — no hands.

He says, "I'll throw the phosphorus grenade if you don't care. Then we'll run back." And so he threw that. It could have killed us both, but it didn't. We lucked out there again. And we took off running, and I can remember running and I finally just passed out. I run out of blood.

When I woke up, I was laying up against a cut bank. One of the medics was there giving me blood again already. They took me back to what they call their hospital; it was a schoolhouse. They laid us out there on the prairie — there was about 100 of us laying there at one time, wrapped in blankets. That's all they did, because they didn't have no room in there or nothing. They'd come and take the worst ones first, and take them in and operate or work on them.

I got hit about 10 o'clock in the morning, and I never got in until about midnight that night, because there were so many of them worse. ☆

Doctors saved three fingers and the thumb on Vetter's right hand, and reattached the nerves in his left arm. He can perform most tasks, including driving and writing, and was twice named South Dakota's Disabled Veteran of the Year. He is pictured with the same type of Japanese rifle that wounded him.

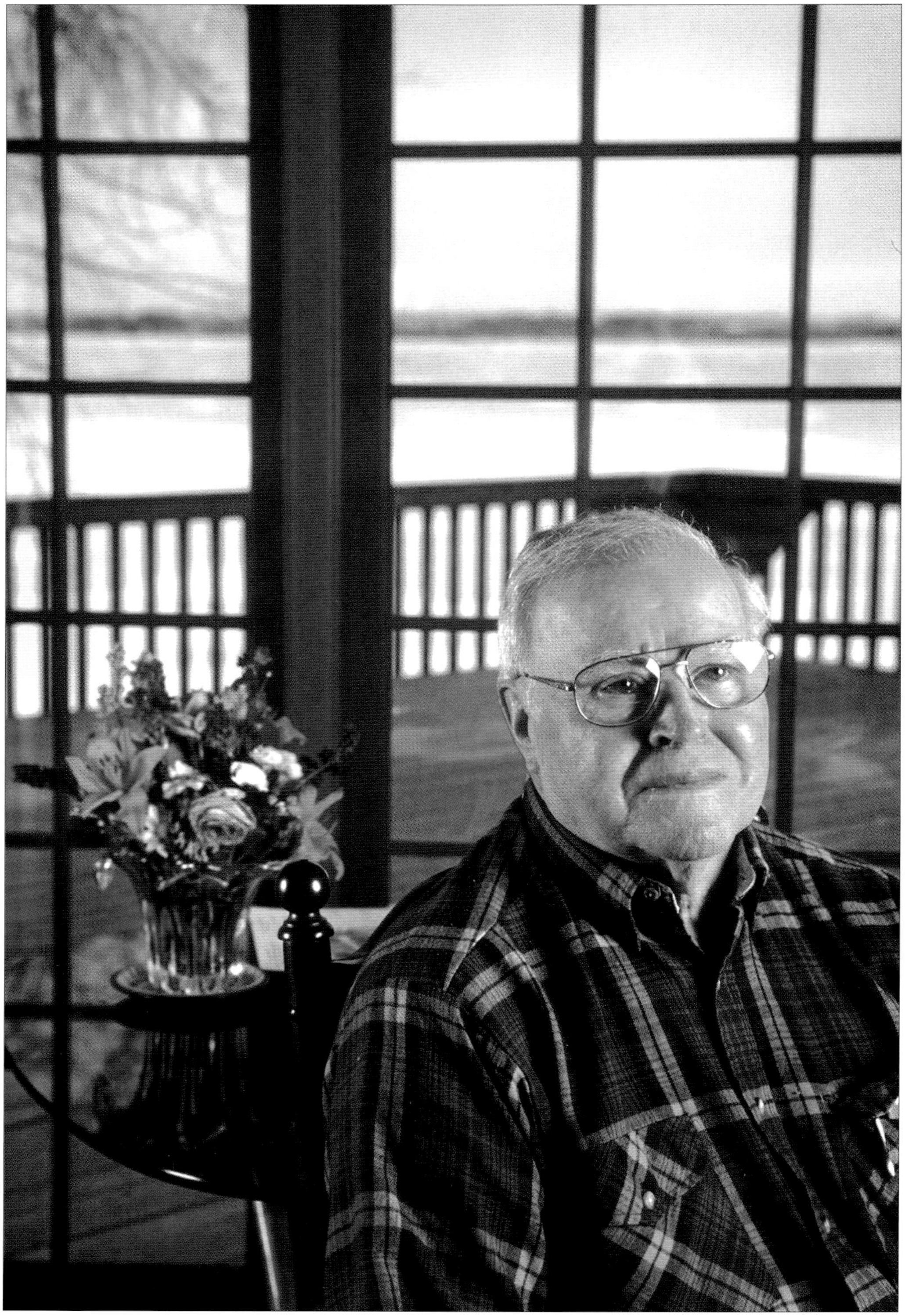

DALE COUGHLIN ☆ *Estelline*

Patrolling South Pacific islands in a small and agile 80-foot PT (Patrol Torpedo) boat, Coughlin was often in the heat of battle. He served as a radio operator on the 16-man crew.

When I was a junior at De Smet, the Japanese bombed Pearl Harbor. We didn't know where Pearl Harbor was at that time, and we had to look it up on the map. I graduated when I was 17, and then I volunteered for the Navy.

I was sworn into the Navy in Omaha, and I took six weeks of training out at Farragut, Idaho. We got aboard this troop ship, and we zigged and zagged all the way across, and we played poker on the way over. Of course, nobody had hardly any money. I think I was probably one of the richest guys on board, and I had $21.

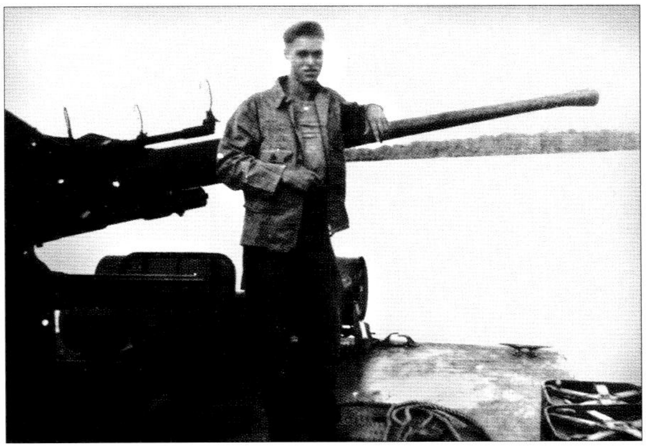

We landed in Milne Bay in New Guinea. There was no shade or nothing; it was about 135 degrees. I just fell on that cot and thought to myself, "Here I am, 18 years old, and 8,000 miles away from home." I was just a little bit lonesome then.

They assigned me to PT-344. I had to go to radio school. I took radio and semaphore — the flags. I had to learn Morse code and everything. On our boat we had 10 5-inch rockets, a 37mm, a 20mm, two twin .50-calibers, one .30-caliber, one .40-caliber, two depth charges and four torpedoes. They always said that we had more armament per square inch than a battleship did. Our boat was 80 feet long, and probably 20 feet wide at the widest point. We had 16 in our crew.

We got orders to go to the Philippines — they were assembling a convoy to go to Mindora. We had destroyers on the outside, then us, then the supply ships were in the middle. That was when we got into the kamikaze planes. They were just coming over all the time. It seems like no matter how many shells you put in the air, there's always one that gets through. It's just like when you're out hunting pheasants — one pheasant will go clear across a dozen people and everyone will miss it. And that's how those suicide planes came in.

We lost our ammunition ship. When that blew up, we weren't very far from it. Big hunks of the ship were falling all over. When the smoke cleared, there wasn't a piece of that ship left or no survivors at all. All those sailors — it just blew them to smithereens.

We got to Mindora, and we were in the harbor there. They had a smoke screen to camouflage the ships so the Japanese couldn't see them. Tokyo Rose came over *(the radio)* and said, "We dedicate this song to the ships in Mindora Harbor: *Smoke Gets in Your Eyes*."

Every squadron of PT boats would have one tender. That tender was the supply ship for the PTs. Two guys usually go to it and get the food for the meal. It was my turn to go, but this Monte Frudenfeld from Omaha, he was a good friend of mine. I was asleep, and instead of waking me up, he went in my place. He and another fella went to the tender, and while they were there, a kamikaze plane came in and he was killed. That was a terrible thing. It was my turn, and I guess the good Lord didn't figure it was my turn to go. My time wasn't up, and his was.

When you're in the war and you lose somebody, it takes a toll on you. Especially Monte, because he was a pretty good friend, and he took my place on the ship. You still think about it — you have flashbacks and stuff.

They sent us down to the Dutch East Indies. Our job was to patrol around the island of Halmahera. There were 10,000 Japanese on that island, and we were trying to keep them from getting supplies. We were just like guinea pigs. We would patrol along the shore and try and draw fire. We knew they were there, but we never saw any. If we did get quite a few bullets coming at us, we'd call the Air Force in and they'd strafe the area or bomb it. That was our job until the war ended.

It was quite an experience, but I'd never want to go through it again. I have no desire to go back. ☆

Coughlin worked in advertising at the De Smet News *for 25 years before entering the insurance field. He and wife Bev now live on the shores of Lake Poinsett near Estelline.*

VICTOR PETERSON ☆ *Clear Lake*

Peterson initially worked at the Martin B-26 factory in Omaha, and became a crew chief in the 394th Bomb Group in England as D-Day neared. Gremlin's Delight, *the B-26 Marauder that he supervised, completed 114 combat missions.*

I was sent down to Omaha where the B-26s were built. They were building the Marauders two years before the war started. When war broke out, they set Martin at full production.

I was just a buck sergeant. All the ratings and good stuff was going overseas, so I decided I had to get to one of these overseas groups going over. We came in to Baer Field in Fort Wayne, Indiana, with these new G models, the latest model of the B-26. Bigger engines, the longer wings, the bigger bomb load, and a lot of safety factors built into them. We landed there at the field, and it was the first one they'd ever seen. We were surrounded with flight people. I was talking up the plane, showing all the advantages and everything, and I met Colonel Hall; he was the commander of the 394th. He said, "I can use a guy like you."

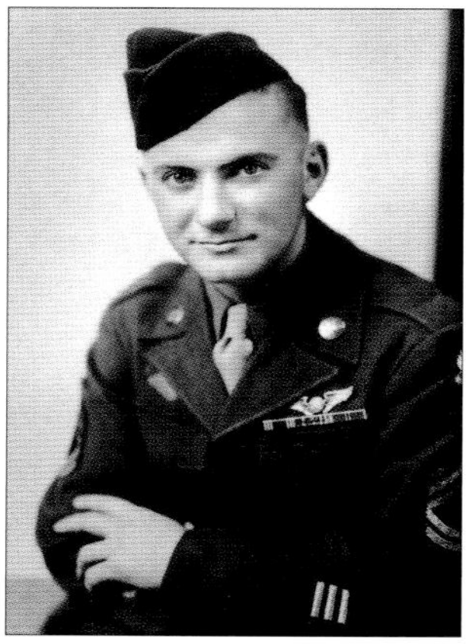

I trained a lot of crews. We started taking these older B-26s from Baer Field down to MacDill, Florida, for training. On the first trip, we started engines, built up hydraulic power, and this assistant ground crewman was supposed to pull the chocks — a three-cornered wedge that sat in front of the wheels. He pulled the one on the pilot side and came around my side, and I'm watching him out the window. He pulled that chock, and he went straight forward into the prop. That prop caught him, and he was just hashed up, so there weren't even body parts left.

The Marauders were based south of London. We couldn't go on the long flights, so we had to follow the front line. D-Day plus 10, we moved into Normandy. You could hear the big guns going off down the road. The engineers laid steel mat for us to land on, and we were in the mud. They just dozed a path through the hedgerows, because we had to have 4,000 feet of runway to get those suckers up and down.

We got nicknamed the "Bridgebusters." Marshalling yards, railroad yards, fuel dumps. We did all daylight raids, and the RAF flew all nighttime raids. We made use of the sky 24 hours a day. We were "crazy Yanks," and they were "dumb Limeys."

I had a ground crew of five. They were engineers, mechanics, and basically responsible for the aircraft. At about 3 o'clock in the morning, your crews would load the bombs, arm the guns, fuel the planes. The flight crew would be in a briefing room, where they're getting all the charts down, and all the routes in, what to look for and where the anti-aircraft is the heaviest. I would be out on the lines, supervising.

We had camouflage tape, the same color as the aircraft. The shells would come up and explode, and this flak would fly out and just tear stuff up. We'd take this tape and just cover over that hole, so them guys wouldn't have to look at that damn hole every time they came out to get in the thing. It was more psychological than anything.

That plane that we put all those missions on, I had red-tagged it. The compression was bad on most of the cylinders, and I sent it down to base for salvage. We had all these replacement crews coming over. The war was over with — nothing to do — but all these crews wanted something to fly, to go up and look around the country. I saw that plane taxiing down to the runway. I scooted around over to operations, and I said, "Who authorized the flight of that plane?"

It took off, and we watched it. I saw it was climbing too steep. "Whoa!" I said. "That ain't gonna make it." They got up there about 1,000 feet and tailed in. Seven men killed, and they wrecked that plane.

I was home once *(during the war)*, just over a weekend. The children hadn't seen me. After the war, when I came back to Milbank on the train, I got out and Gerrie and the two kids were there to meet me. She was holding our little girl. Our little boy, he had cowboy boots on and he was dressed up. I met Gerrie, and we embraced.

The little guy came up and kicked me right in the shins. "Leave my mom alone!" He didn't know me. ☆

Peterson bought a farm north of Clear Lake after the war and flew occasionally throughout the following years.

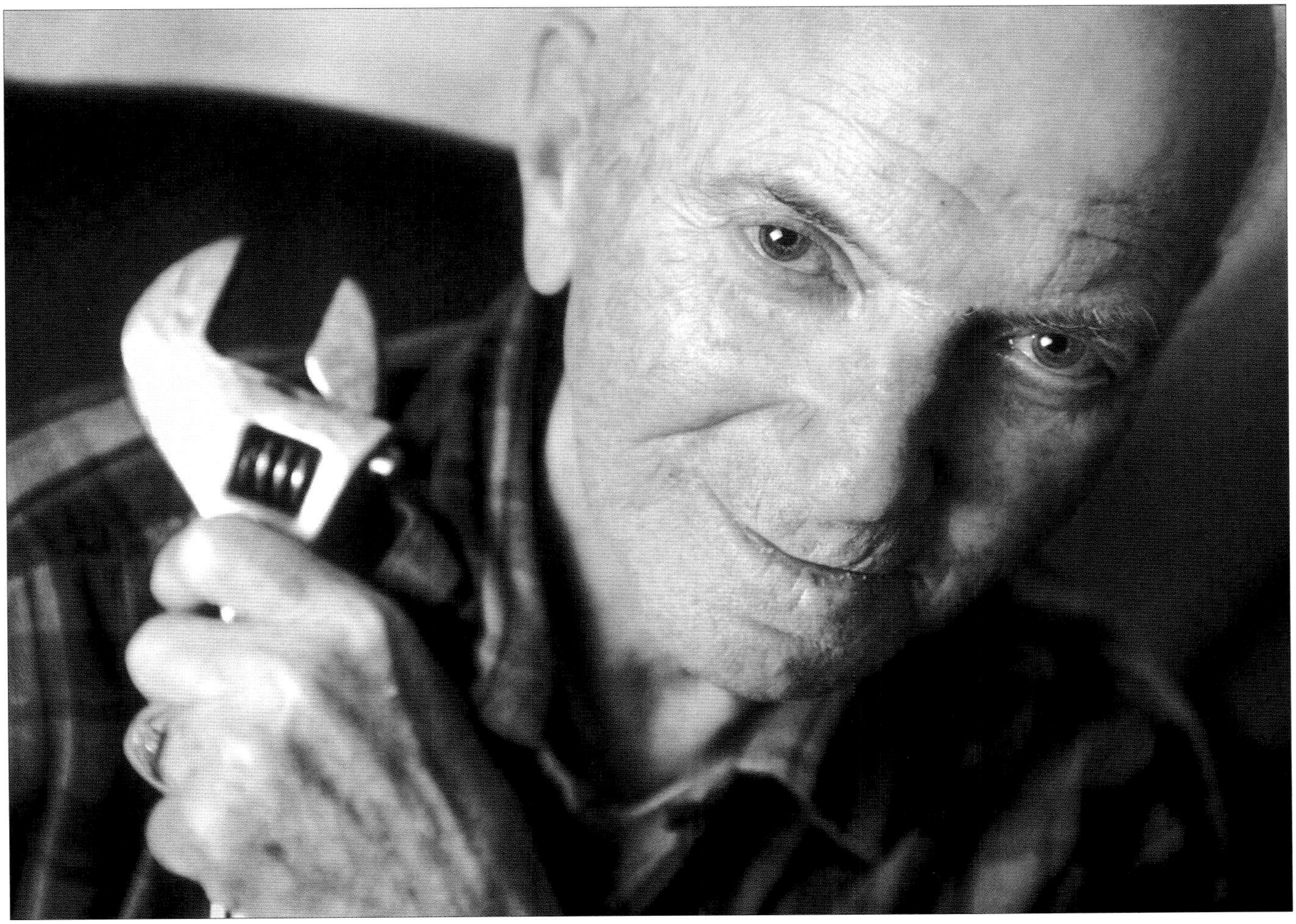

Elmer Olson ☆ *Bristol*

Joining the 91st Infantry Division after age 30, Olson fought to gain ground against the Germans in mountainous Italy.

Me and my dad were farming, and we had three years of drought when we didn't get any crops. We kept our cattle and our horses and scraped up just enough feed for them. About the time that I had to go to the Army, it just changed. The year after I was in the Army, then we really started getting bumper crops. It seems like the good Lord worked it out so we could supply our Army with food. It's still a miracle how the country got supplied and built the ships so fast to win that war.

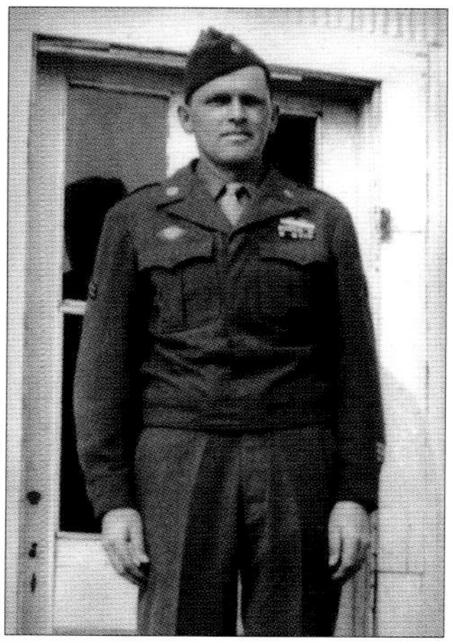

I was the oldest one in the outfit, and they called me Pappy. I always had my Bible in my shirt pocket and would be reading that. They all kind of depended on me for things. They'd always come and say, "Pappy, can you do this?" I was just kind of an example for the rest of them. We'd get to a farm place, and I'd get something from *(the farmer)* to mix some pancakes, something to eat besides the rations.

Some of us split and went to England, and some of us went to North Africa, to Oran. There were a lot of Arabs. We had a little trouble; where our camp was, you could look out *(into the desert)* and you didn't see anything. But if you started walking out there, they started jumping up, just waiting for a chance to get in there. At night, it got so bad we had to put our jeeps around the camp to keep them out. They could sneak in there and take things right from our sleeping tents. I still can't figure out how they could do it. They were pretty clever.

We went from there to below Rome. That's where I started fighting. There we got into the war. We lost a lot of men over there. Sometimes a whole unit got shot up. *(The Germans)* were dug in, with pillboxes. They dug big holes in the ground so the tanks would go down. We couldn't get those tanks out.

We just took place after place until we got up in the mountains in Italy. We stayed up there in the winter and camped. Stayed and held out there until the spring, held our line. We used to go out with our machine guns and fire all night over to their lines. The airplanes were the most scary. They were flying over, dropping bombs. That was hard. In fact, I never did get over it for years after I got home. My wife said *(during storms)* I used to turn white from the noise when the thundering was bad.

You didn't stay up at the *(front)* line too long. There were three lines. They'd bring you back one line, then they'd bring you back to the third line. Then when you get back there far enough, they'd give you leave. That's when we went to Rome and looked it all over, and some other towns like Florence. So that worked out nice; you weren't in combat all the time. And when we got further back in the line, they brought us fresh bread and things like that so we didn't have to eat rations all the time.

One thing you had to do when you were in combat: You had to look out for yourself. What I remember the most — our unit got fired on and I had to get in a ditch. I was separated for quite a while, probably half a day or so. That scared me more than anything in the Army; I couldn't find my outfit.

You didn't dare take a chance. I think that's the reason a lot of them didn't get back — they got too brave. It was pretty dangerous for us, too, going up to the front and carrying the wounded back. The medics had so many wounded up there that they couldn't keep at them. You'd carry them back. It was in some mountain range that was really rough to get them out.

Until this Pierre deal *(the 2001 WWII Memorial dedication)*, you never heard anybody around here talking about the war much. I never even talked about it to my kids. You just didn't want to do it, that's all.

I asked *(an Army friend)*, "Why is it that we didn't talk about it for so many years?" And he said he figured it's because of the people that got killed. You figure you didn't want to talk about them and combat, that you got out and got home.

I wonder if that's got anything to do with it — that you just kind of felt guilty. ☆

After the war, Olson returned to Bristol and worked as a carpenter. He built the Westside Wesleyan Church where he is pictured, and eventually worked on or in nearly every house in town.

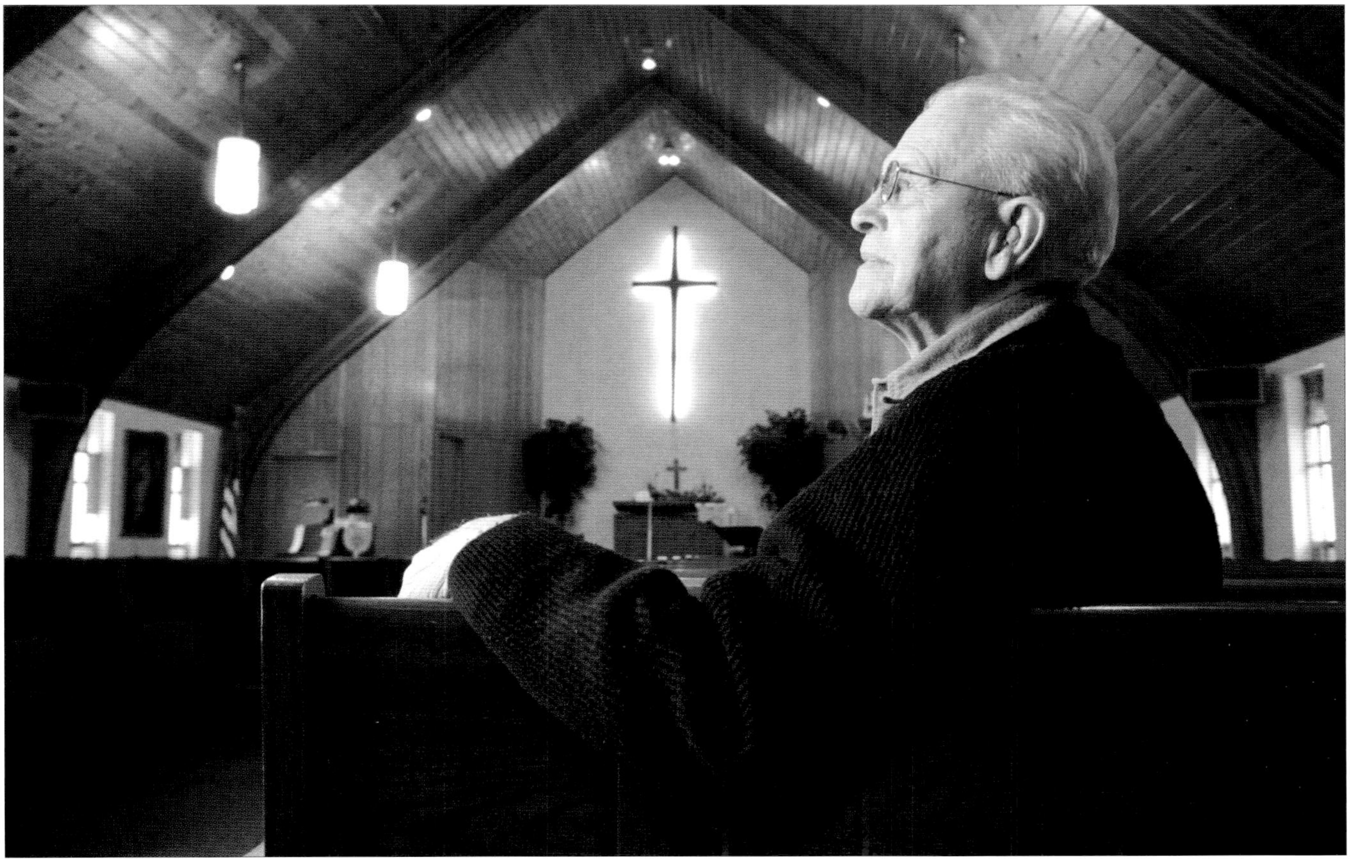

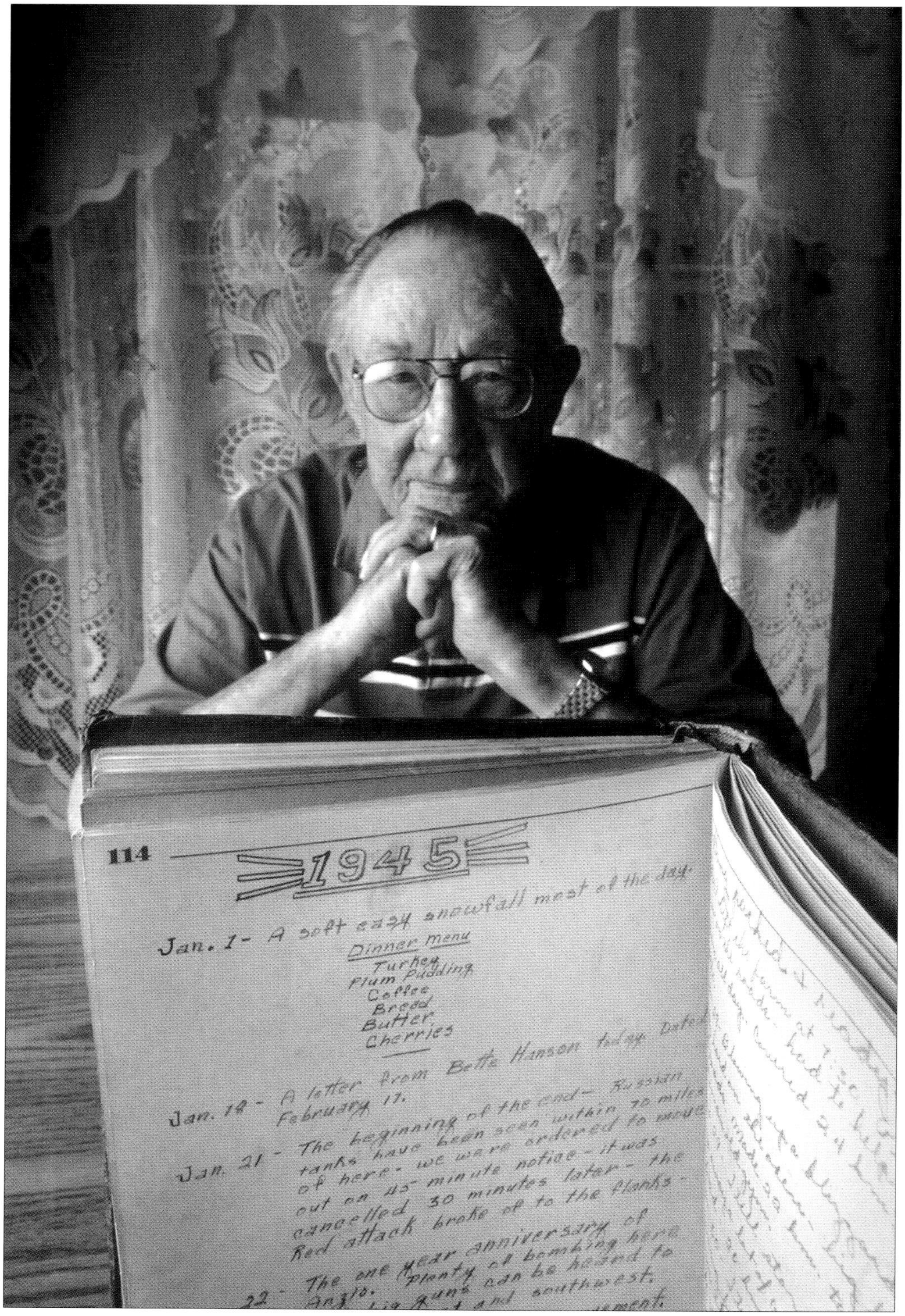
114
1945
A soft easy snowfall most of the day.
Jan. 1 -
Dinner menu
Turkey
Plum Pudding
Coffee
Bread
Butter
Cherries
A letter from Bette Hanson today. Dated
February 17.
Jan. 21 - The beginning of the end - Russian tanks have been seen within 70 miles of here - we were ordered to move out on 45 minute notice - it was cancelled 30 minutes later - the Red attack broke of to the flanks -
22 - The one year anniversary of
Anzio. Plenty of bombing here

LYLE DAVIS ☆ *Brookings*

Known as one of the most lethal units of World War II, the U.S. Army Rangers nonetheless encountered tragedy in early 1944, soon after landing at Anzio on Italy's west coast. Davis fought with the 1st Ranger Battalion.

I took basic training as a tank driver, and I went overseas as an assistant tank driver. We were in North Africa for a few weeks and then loaded in the ship again and went across and landed in Naples, Italy. I was in a big replacement depot there.

I didn't think much of the tanks. I think Bill Mauldin, in one of his cartoons, said it best: "A moving foxhole attracts the eye." I talked to a few people that I had known that had been in the tanks and gotten hit. It's not fun. Of course none of it is, but then I wanted a little better chance than that.

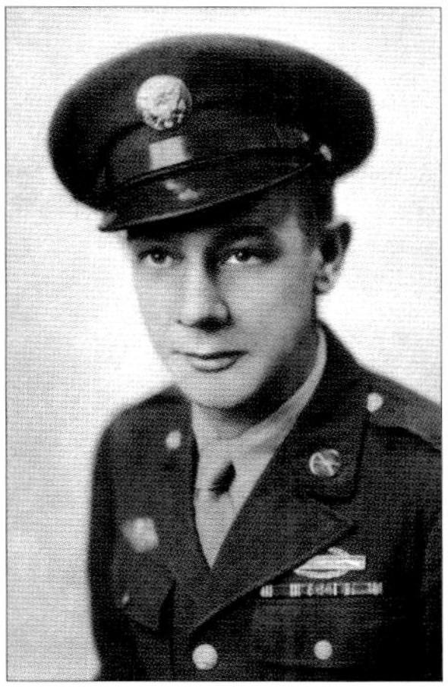

I got a chance to get out and joined the 1st Ranger Battalion. They had just come down after quite a few weeks in combat on Venafro Mountain there in Italy. They needed replacements, so I signed up for that and joined them in time to train to go to Anzio and make that invasion. This was the first opportunity I had to get out of the tanks, so I took it.

I knew they had trained under the British commandos to start with, then they expanded to three battalions. It was quite a little more intense. Physical conditioning was a big thing with them. You had to move fast. We trained in amphibious landings — we knew it was going to be something like that — night tactics, moving at night.

We were on the ship, way out at sea, ready to come in before they told us where we were going to land. We were there a couple of days on that ship getting into position, then over the side again into landing craft and onto the beach at Anzio. We had gone around the end of what was the fighting line to try and cut it off.

It was one of those middle-of-the-night things. They run these little landing craft right up on the beach as far as they can drive them, drop the front end, you get out, and that lightens the boat enough to where they can back it off. We finally cleared the town out by morning and stayed right on the beach.

The Germans had pulled back, and they were in the high ground above us, and we got all their artillery fire. They were trying to run us off the beach with that.

After about a week of that, they took the Rangers and decided we were going to go through the lines, back to a little town there on this main highway, and see if we could disrupt the German supply line going further south to the front. We moved out on my 20th birthday.

We started through around midnight, and started toward this little town — Cisterna, I think the name was — and we'd bypassed the German artillery. Their dogs would bark at us, and we could hear the German commanders giving firing orders for the artillery. We were just trucking down the road, minding our own business.

We got back there quite a ways, a half or three quarters of a mile from the town where we wanted to be, and we ran into this German bivouac area. The guys in the front of the line started through there and took the guards out with knives, and finally one of them didn't get hit just right and he started screaming, and that woke the rest of them. We were half a mile short of the town with a fight on our hands.

It's what you've been trained for. You knew that all this training you've been going through was for the purpose to survive yourself, and if somebody had to die, make sure it was the other guy — the guy in the different colored uniform.

We held out 'til around noon. I laid next to a hedgerow on the edge of a vineyard, and bullets were coming through that hedge. They knew people were in there. They were dropping leaves and branches on me. They weren't shooting low enough — they were just going through the hedge. A buddy right in front of me started to move a little too quick and he got shot through the leg. He was right in front of me.

Our commanding officer there had been killed or badly wounded, and the second in command was wounded. He finally gave the order for us to surrender. They had captured a bunch of *(Rangers)* and marched them down the road and said they were going to shoot them if the rest of us didn't give up.

I really didn't like the idea of surrendering, but that was

the order that came down. They made it obvious that if we didn't, a lot of our friends were going to get shot. And they would have, I think. It wasn't something we looked forward to, but that's what the man said, so that's what you do. One thing you learn in the Army: You don't have to agree with the orders, you just obey them.

When we finally realized what the situation was, it was, "Bide your time, do the best you can with the situation and let's survive this thing until it's over."

We broke up our equipment as much as we could, and they marched us back away from the front and dumped us in a big old house. We called it kind of a castle. Spent a couple of days there, got bombed. It was a British Spitfire that dropped a couple of bombs on that place, took a lot of the glass out of the house and a lot of the plaster. There was two battalions, 1st and 3rd Rangers. I can't really tell you how many *(men)* — there were several hundred.

I wasn't ever really interviewed by the Germans or anything. We'd been told, "Name, rank and serial number" and all of that. For the most part, the Germans honored that. They were pretty good about the Geneva Convention stuff. There were always exceptions, but there always are.

They trucked us into Rome, unloaded us right in front of the Coliseum, then lined us up and marched us through part of the town just to show us off. Most of *(the Italians)* kind of jeered and laughed at us. We got a lot of rocks and sticks and stuff thrown at us. But you'd see a few of them *(flash the "V for Victory" sign)*. Then back in the trucks again and headed north again.

I think they told us we were going to Germany. They issued us a chunk of bread and a piece of processed meat probably a little bigger than a baseball — it was just kind of a round blob of meat, minced ham or something — and told us that was for three days. Well, everybody was hungry, so it didn't last for three days.

They loaded us in these little "40 and 8" boxcars *(designed in WWI, they could carry 40 men and 8 horses)*. Of course the doors were locked after we got in there. I think we had around 50 men in that car. There was straw on the floor, and your latrine was a nail keg sitting in the center of the place.

We were on there the best part of two days before they pulled into a big railroad station. They opened the doors and let us get out in a certain area to move around a little. The German Red Cross was there and gave us each a cup of coffee. It was ersatz *(imitation)* coffee, they called it. It was made with parts barley and acorn shells instead of coffee grounds, but it was something hot and something to drink, so we drank it.

For over a month, we remained in Italian prison camps. Suffering was intense due to the cold and lack of food. We had only the clothes in which we had been captured. Our only subsistence was one bowl of watery soup and a quarter loaf of black bread per day. The bread that they fed the prisoners was a joke. That old bread was something that would stay with you if you could eat it. There was a lot of sawdust in it, chopped straw. It was "tree flour." That's what they called it. On this diet I managed to lose 30 pounds in one month.

After that, we got to where we were going: Stalag 7A at Moosburg. It was a big camp, lots of people. You couldn't get too close to the fences. There were guard towers and so on. So many feet from the fence, they had a single wire, and that was the death wire. If you crossed that, they figured you were trying to escape and you could be shot from these guard towers. People would ride that line as close as they could, just to see what would happen, and wound up counting the barbs on the wires and so on. We weren't there very long, and it was back in the boxcar.

We wound up in 2B in Hammerstein. This was a work camp. There was about 32 of us that went out on this big farm. They had an old house converted to put a lot of bunks in, and bars on the windows where we slept.

We were farm laborers. We went out there in the spring and planted trees and planted potatoes and planted rye — took care of it, cultivated it, fertilized it, harvested it again in the fall.

On this farm, we would see our bombers going over. Germans there got pretty excited about that. They'd run for an air raid shelter. We didn't figure they were going to bomb us out there in the country, so we'd stand there and watch them. There's something about watching them — maybe 100, 150 of those big old B-17s going over — it's quite a sight. There were times as the front gradually moved closer to us that we could hear the bombs explode and feel it in the ground. When that many planes start

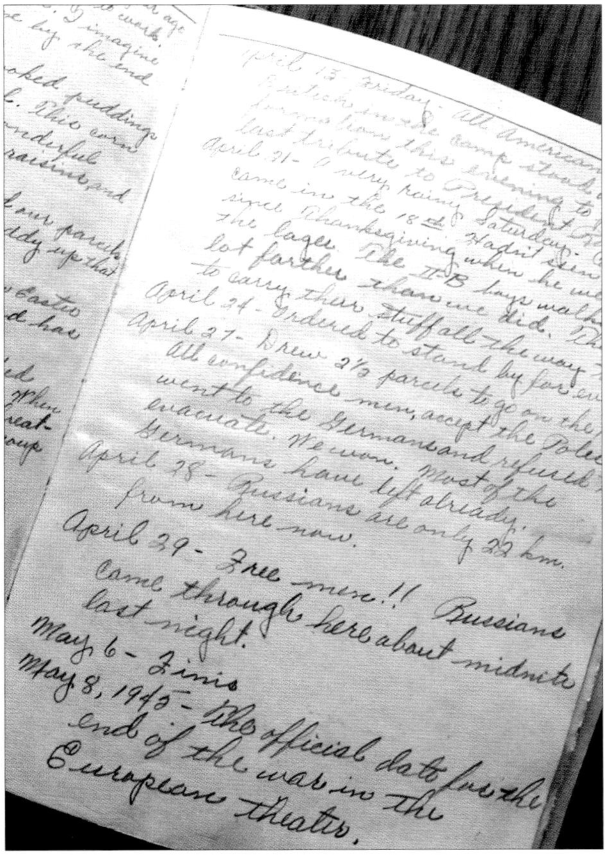
April 28 - Russians are only 22 km. from here now.
April 29 - Free men!! Russians came through here about midnite last night.
May 6 - Finis
May 8, 1945 - the official date for the end of the war in the European theatre.

dropping bombs, there's a lot of concussion and a lot of noise going on. We could hear it.

Captivity is not the greatest thing in the world. You've got to make adjustments. If you can't adjust, you're in trouble. For the most part, the treatment was more or less humane. We were never really badly abused — threatened a few times, but never really abused.

I took this book *(from a Red Cross parcel)* and I thought maybe I should just keep a few records. We'd get little newspapers — they were published in one of the prison camps — they'd send it out to us. There would be poetry in there, and stories. I thought I could keep track of some of this stuff. So I started writing in it and kept track of a lot of the things we did. Just odds and ends of things that I ran across that I wanted to write down and remember. I created a crossword puzzle one time and a calendar for '45. Various dates that I wanted to remember. Addresses of people that were on the farm with me.

When the Russians started getting closer, we were forced to march west to Rostock. It was a rather unpleasant thing. The weather turned bad, and we left during a raging blizzard. It wasn't only prisoners on the road, but also civilians running from the Russians. It ended up being about 250 miles. Have you ever walked all day on cobblestones? I don't recommend it. There's nothing smooth about a cobblestone road. It beats mud, but not by much.

I was in Rostock when the Russians came through. The Germans were trying to get out of there, and the Russians were coming in. The guards begged us to go with them, but we refused to go. So they left us to our own devices. When the Russians finally got into the camp, they came in there with their tanks, right through the barbed wire.

I was afraid of the Russians more than the Germans. They were crazy, just absolutely crazy. They didn't know if there were Germans there or not, so they were shooting at this, that and the other thing. We all stayed in our barracks. I was in my barracks, in my bunk, and saw Russian tracer bullets come through the barracks — in one side and out the other — random shooting to try and draw fire.

They pretty much ignored us after they figured out that there was nothing but prisoners here. They didn't want anything to do with us; they didn't want to feed us or anything. So they pretty much left us alone. It was several days after we were liberated when they sent a convoy of trucks in to pick us up. The Russians moved us part of the way and turned us over to the British, and we were with the British a few days, and finally they got an American convoy in there to pick us up.

We were a pretty rag-tag looking bunch. We didn't have much left for clothing by the time we got liberated. We were getting pretty slim. It had been 21 months since I'd slept between a pair of sheets.

I think a lot of us survived because we never gave up hope at all. There was never a doubt. You had to go through a bunch of crap and some hard times, but you knew that eventually you were going to get back home. You were going to get that big meal you've been dreaming about. It just carried you through. You had to have something like that or it would have been very easy to just go crazy over this whole thing. ☆

Most of Davis' postwar years were spent working as an electrician for South Dakota State University in Brookings.

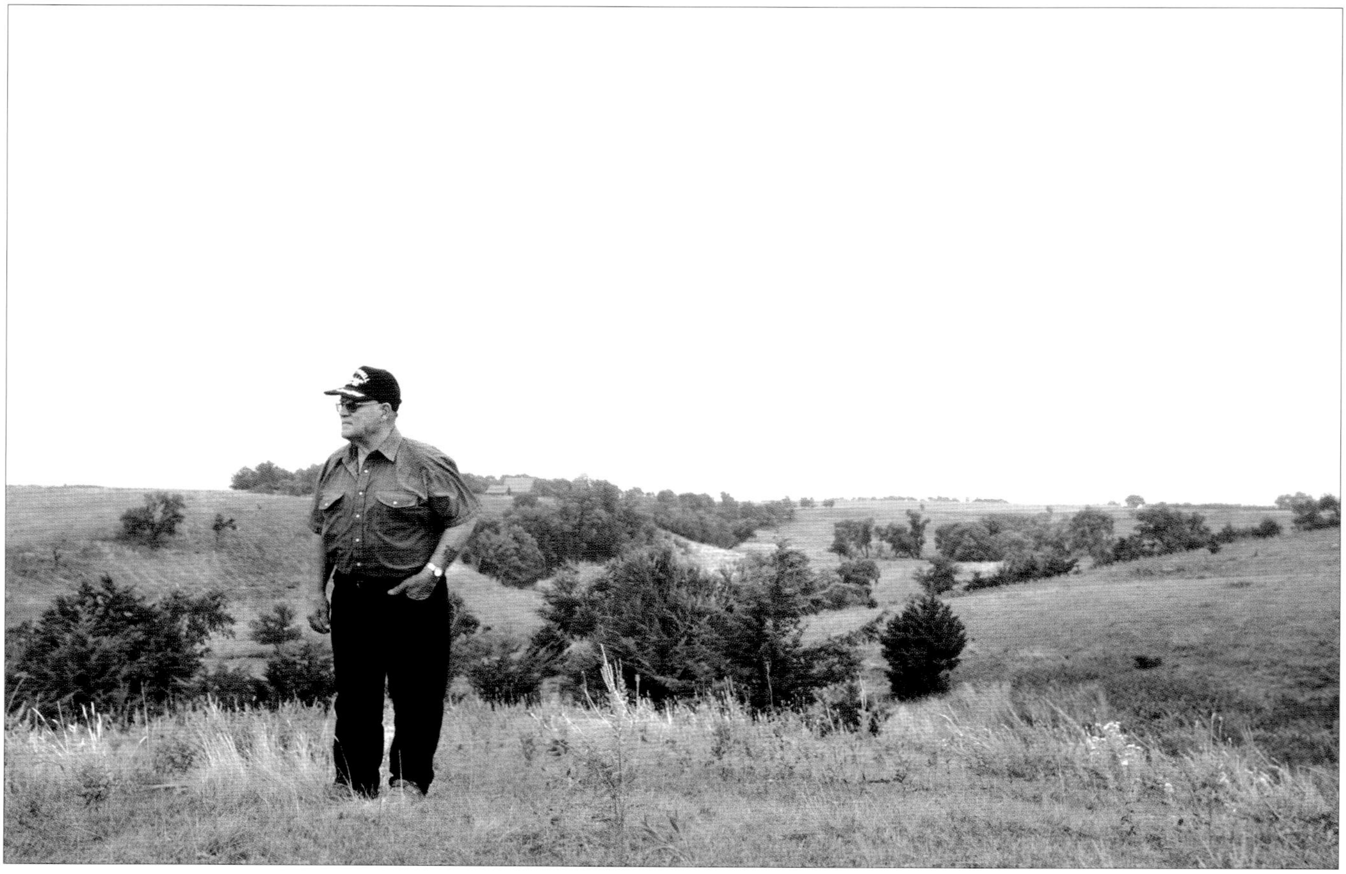

Rudy Bohlmann ☆ *Menno*

When the atomic bombs were dropped on Japan, Bohlmann was floating offshore aboard the U.S.S. Tyrell. *The attack cargo ship was waiting to participate in the first wave of the planned invasion of Japan. When Japan surrendered, the* Tyrell *was the first ship to dock at Nagasaki and offer relief. Bohlmann boarded the* Tyrell *at port in San Francisco.*

It was the first time I'd ever seen a ship, and I couldn't believe they made them that big. It was just like a big old barn sitting there in the water.

Pretty soon the tugboats took us away. We went underneath the Golden Gate Bridge. I was standing on the tail end of the ship, and I could still see that darn bridge. And I was throwing up already, seasick like a dog.

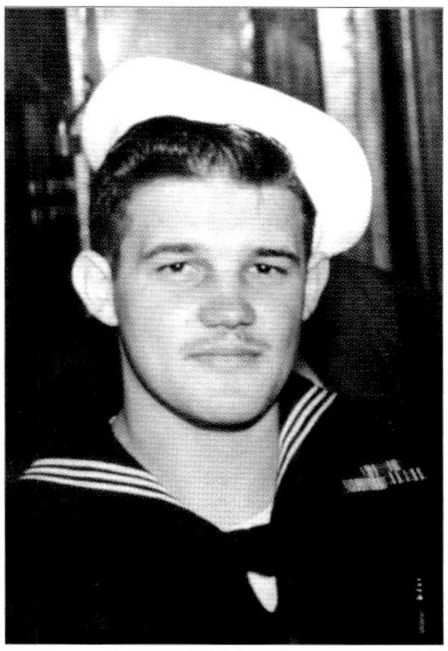

On the ship, they called me Plowboy. That was my nickname. Making soft water, that's what I was doing — salt water evaporators. We used steam and boiled that salt water to condense it, just like a still. The brine is pumped out into the ocean again, and the good water goes into a tank. You had four hours on, eight hours off, all around the clock.

They said, "They just bombed Hiroshima, Japan, with an atomic bomb." Nobody knew what an atomic bomb was, and nobody knew what Hiroshima was. Three days later, they told us that they bombed Nagasaki with another one.

Our ship was in the first line *(to invade)* Japan, and that's why we were the first ship to go in. They had been congregating ships there — I would say thousands of them, not hundreds — as far as you could see. We were the only ship moving. We went through the night.

The next morning at 8 o'clock, I was up and off my watch and I went up topside to get some fresh air. We were just tying up in Nagasaki harbor. They had stopped and picked up an old Japanese fisherman. He guided them in. He knew where to go — there were underground reefs.

The town was absolutely flat, as far as I could see. Stinking to high heaven. Oh my gosh, that stink. Dead human bodies. If you smell it, you never forget it. As far as you could see with binoculars, there wasn't a thing moving. Nagasaki was on flat ground, but *(two mountains were adjacent to it)*. The blast in front of the first mountain cut off the heat from the second one. Where the heat wasn't cut off, it was all brown. Big, nice trees — all brown. Steel booms — that's where they put those two-man suicide submarines into the water, they were about a block away from our ship, towards the front end — they were just like a pretzel from the heat, all rusted.

I tell you, I couldn't sleep that night. Mostly from the smell, the decaying bodies. We put on some troops — Army guys — and a dozer. They were supposed to doze down a flat spot and set up some tents for the next ship to come in. We were there five days, and no more ships came in behind us.

We couldn't see any roads, either. You could see some streets off in the distance. I imagine I could see a half a mile, and there was nothing standing up. No trees, no color. Anything that was iron, the paint was gone and it was rusty. It wasn't like a tornado went through there, piled up and junked up.

There came two little boys. I thought they were about 7 or 8 years old, maybe 10. They were the first Japanese people I'd ever seen. The captain threw them each some fruit — I can't remember now if it was an orange or an apple — and them little kids were just starved to death. I looked close — I was about 20 feet away from them — their eyes were running matter, their ears were all red and festering, their nose was festering, the corners of their mouths were just festering. They had been in the outer edge of that bomb, I think.

Radiation is what it was. They wouldn't live a couple more weeks; I was sure they wouldn't. That's the only living thing we'd seen.

I didn't get into any action, just that I saw Nagasaki and what one bomb can do. ☆

While exact figures are impossible to confirm, it is generally accepted that about 74,000 Japanese citizens were killed in Nagasaki, and another 73,000 were injured. Slightly higher figures have been estimated for Hiroshima's population. Bohlmann has farmed near Menno since the war's end.

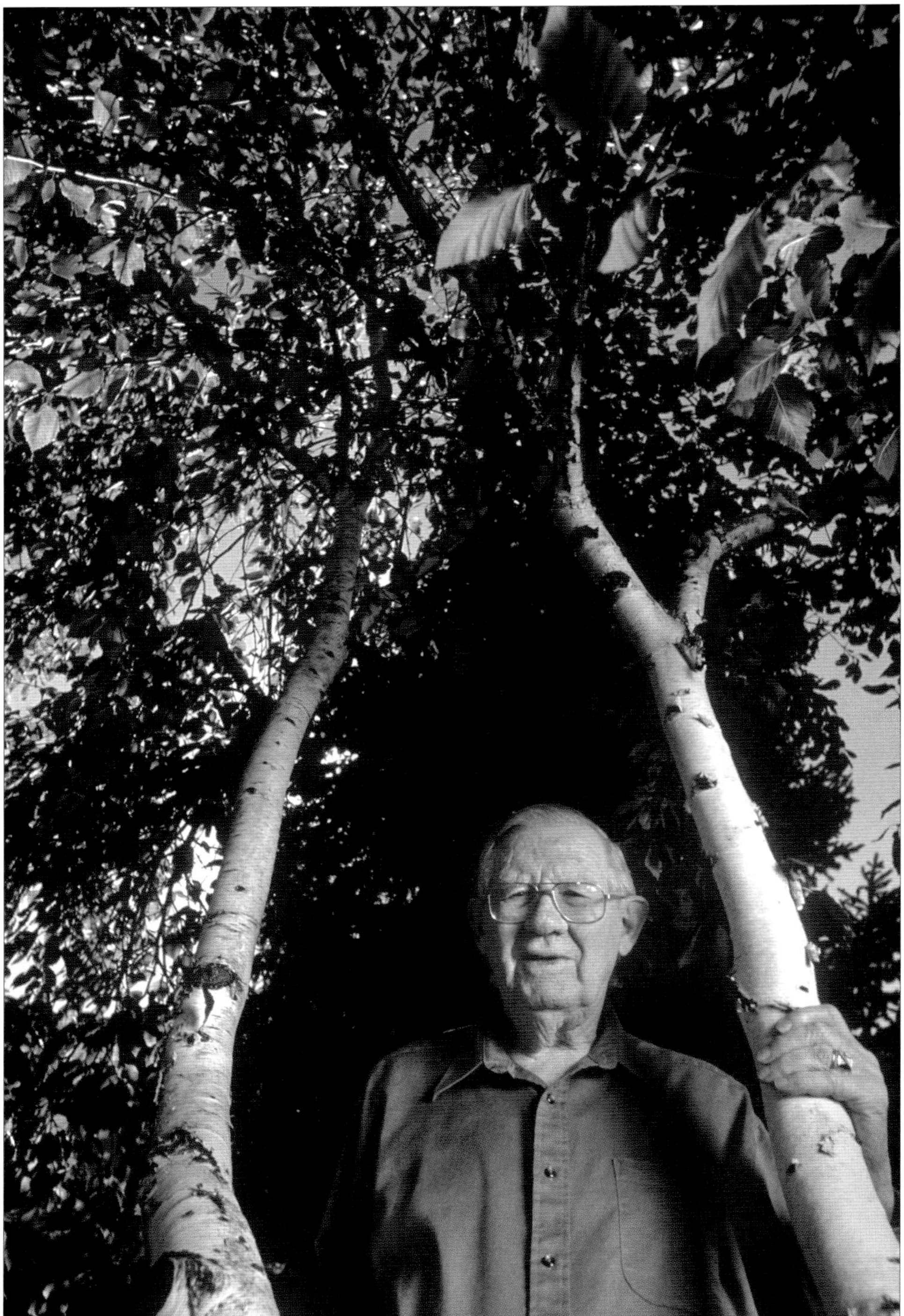

ARTHUR DAVIS ☆ *Rapid City*

For Davis, combat in Italy and France did not involve firepower, but rather the power of information. He served in the Army primarily as an information officer, disseminating news and protocol guidelines to troops about what they could or could not say and do. His department afforded assistance to the Stars and Stripes *newspaper, and when the war ended, he was stationed in Berlin as an educator.*

Since there wasn't combat or active duty for us at the front lines, there wasn't much said about *(our work)*. It was all backyard stuff, you might say. I was always just behind the campaign, but never in it. We were close enough to be active in part of it, and yet far enough back so we didn't get hurt, which was a nice place to be.

You always put your own twist on a piece of news. I don't think anybody can get away from that. We weren't in a position to originate news; we were given information. We didn't have much trouble finding subjects that we could give to the troops that they wanted. The point system, for instance — we had to have information on that, how it was governed. We were concerned with what the troops were concerned about, and that's always, "When do I go home and what'll I do when I get there?"

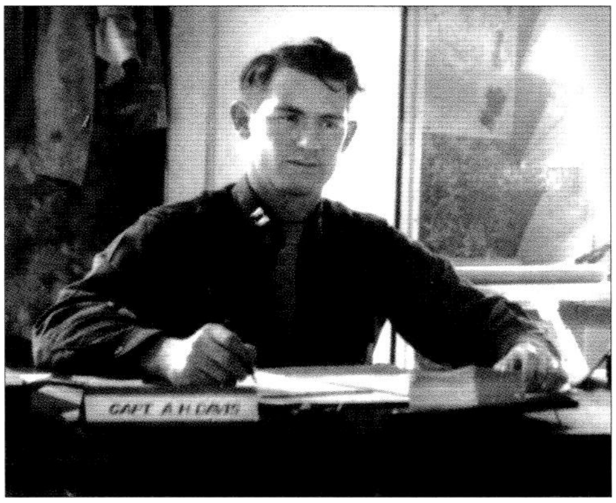

They accused us of being a propaganda instrument. It depends on your definition of propaganda. We disseminated information. That's propaganda, isn't it? Could be, but on the other hand, it served its purpose of letting the troops know what was going on.

There was no one more independent than the *Stars and Stripes*. They did what they wanted to and went where they wanted to. They were a different body entirely. We weren't in competition at all, because we went for the dead news, and they went for the active news. *Stars and Stripes* did their job pretty darn well. They are to be congratulated.

We were winding down in Sicily, and General Patton was in command there with his headquarters, and he was moving troops out all the time. One day a second lieutenant came in and wanted to speak to the general, got permission, and he says, "Well, general, I understand your troops are going into England. They'll be located at such and such a place, will be doing this and that," and gave him a whole rundown on what his operation — the highly secret organization of moving from Sicily to England — was all about. And of course, the general kind of blew his top clear out of the place and says, "Where'd you get that information?" *(The lieutenant then replied)*, "Out of your troops' mail, general. I'm on the censor department at the general post office, and this is what we learned through our censorship." No more mail out of Palermo at all. It was cut off. Gone.

I think everyone has heard of the $64,000 question, which was fraternization. And that was a common topic of information on what not to do. Information as to the conduct of the troops with the nationals of the country in which we were involved.

We were always telling them not to fraternize with the local population. There was one quartermaster unit that was stationed down at the docks in Palermo, and they were quartered in a row of buildings along one side of the street, and the Italians were on the other side of the street. Well, there was no fence down the middle, so there was, let us say, a lot of fraternization going on. They got orders to move out, and they even had a celebration with the people, and goodbye and all that sort of thing, so that the word that they were leaving was pretty active on the street. They sailed out, and that was pretty well known too. The ship was torpedoed, and there were black bodies washed ashore all the next day. So this was the type of thing we had to combat to keep people informed, but yet keep it secret. Certain things couldn't be used, certain things could be used. It served as a good example of what not to do.

It was never publicized in the papers at all, but the fact is that a German submarine was laying offshore waiting for them to come because they knew they were coming. It served as a very costly lesson. ☆

Davis worked as a banker in Lead after the war.

Arvid Ambur ☆ *Presho*

As flight engineer on a B-24 Liberator, Ambur's duties also included serving as a medic when necessary. He needed both skills to survive the Daisy Mae's *final flight, an unforgettable bombing run from Midway to Wake Island on July 24, 1943.*

We had at least 50 missions besides all the sea searches over there. I think we had 1,600 hours over water. It started out with 25 *(missions required before going home)*, and then it got to be more and more. We probably put in more time than any other crew, because we laid up and we changed pilots and we waited for the group to get organized.

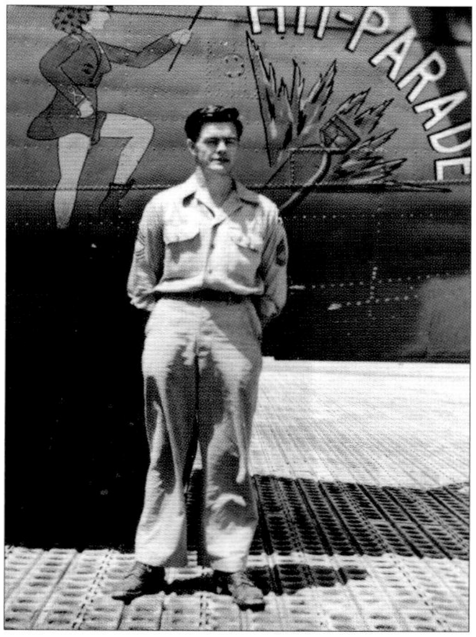

We ended up all the way from the Hawaiian Islands to Guam, so we had the islands up to Japan, pretty near.

You don't really get acquainted with the other crews that much, though we knew them and we drank beer with them and all that stuff. The crew stuck together like a family.

The Wake one, that was definitely the worst mission. There were five planes on this mission. We were the lead plane in the second wing. We made the bomb run, and the ack-ack *(anti-aircraft flak)* was pretty heavy. They had about 26 or 30 Zeroes in the air before we got there. The lead pilot in the first flight — he got shot in the leg or something — and that plane kind of nosed down. The other two planes, they followed him to keep close. And then our wing plane — a Zero took a wing off of it and dove into it. I saw the wing go off, and the plane just kind of slid to the side and went down and we saw it go in the water. No parachutes. So that left us.

I was up in front with the pilots when it started. I saw the Zeroes coming in, and then the other things started to happen in the back end. You don't really see that much except just what you're looking at.

We had an engine knocked out then. That left us back behind, so the Zeroes pretty much picked on us. That's why we got shot up pretty bad. We might have gotten a couple of Zeroes. They were coming in from both sides. I don't know why they didn't get us. With that many holes, they could easily have got the pilots, or more gas, or more engines. If we'd have lost one more engine ....

As Pop, our photographer, was raising his camera, anti-aircraft fire burst at the exact spot and he got it in his left leg. A second later, the bombardier who was on the left waist gun got hit three times by .30-caliber fire — one through his left wrist, one in the shoulder and one in the stomach. He came through the bomb bay to the flight deck, and the navigator gave him first aid. I think after the first hit, you don't have much feeling. You cry over a little hurt a lot quicker than you cry over a real bad one, I think. He didn't have much of a chance. There was nothing a fella could do.

I went back to his position, and I found the gun jammed by pieces of his watch and the cartridge shot loose from the gun. There were still Zeroes around, so I went ahead and put the gun into condition. I was still watching for Zeroes and I started cutting Pop's clothes from his left leg. He had a ragged hole bigger than a goose egg high on his leg, just below the hip — it never went clear through. No doubt a big piece of ack-ack got in there and lodged. He was laying there and I was going to do something with him, and he said, "No, no. You take care of them. Leave me alone."

The waist gunner on the other side, he got a little flak in his back. His ammunition carrier *(attached to the gun)* got kind of shot off or loose, so I got that patched up and going. So I'd go to one side to shoot, go to the other side to shoot. Every fifth bullet was a tracer, you know, so kind of like a garden hose you just spray them — you knew about how close you was. It don't take long for them to come in, they come in so fast. You don't have much time to shoot.

The top turret gunner got shot up a little bit. The belly gunner, he come out of there with a bloody face and he had a spot in his forehead that looked like a bullet hole, but it was just a bunch of blood.

We had quite a few of them that needed attention. You give them a bunch of morphine and sulfa on the wounds, talk to them and that's all you can do.

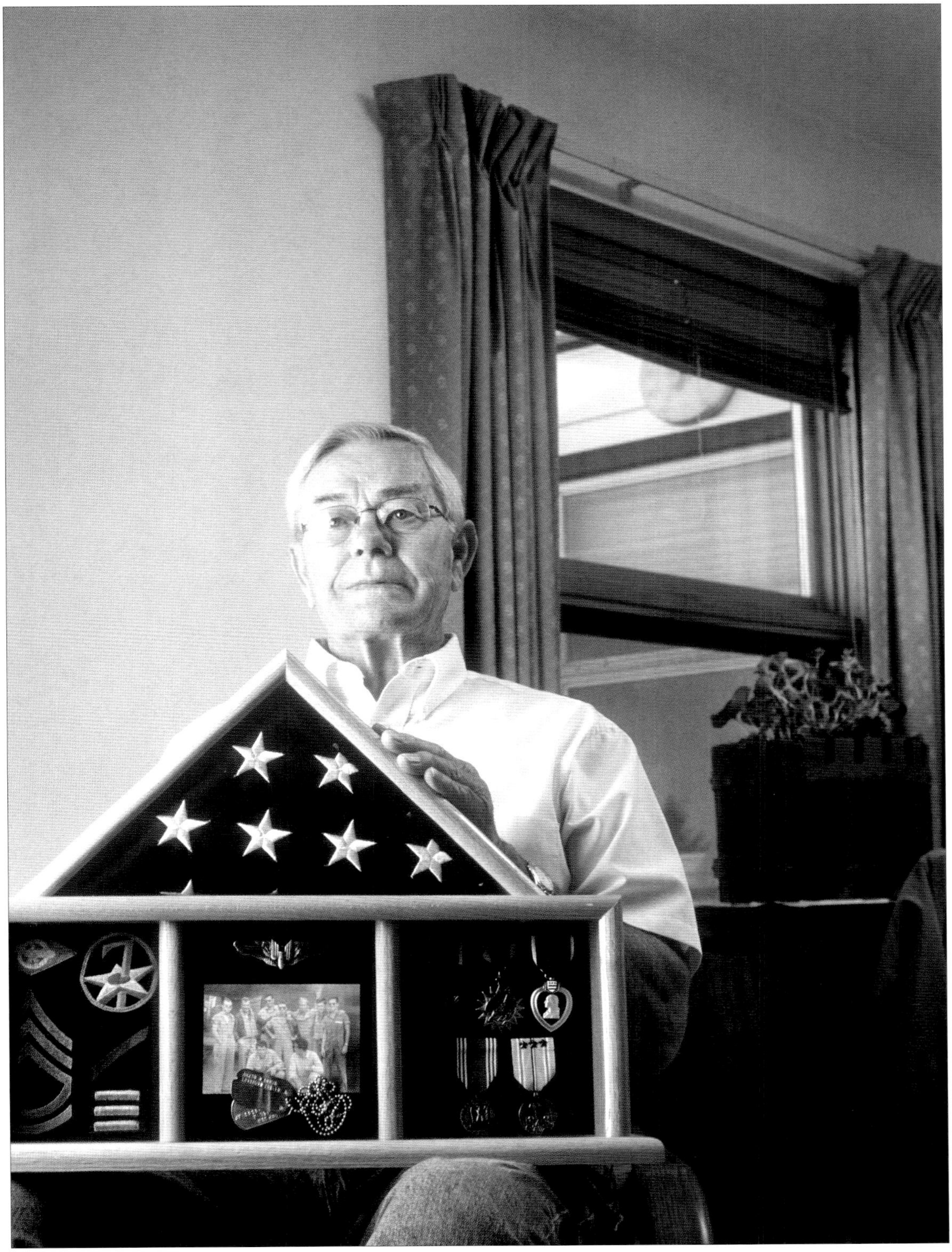

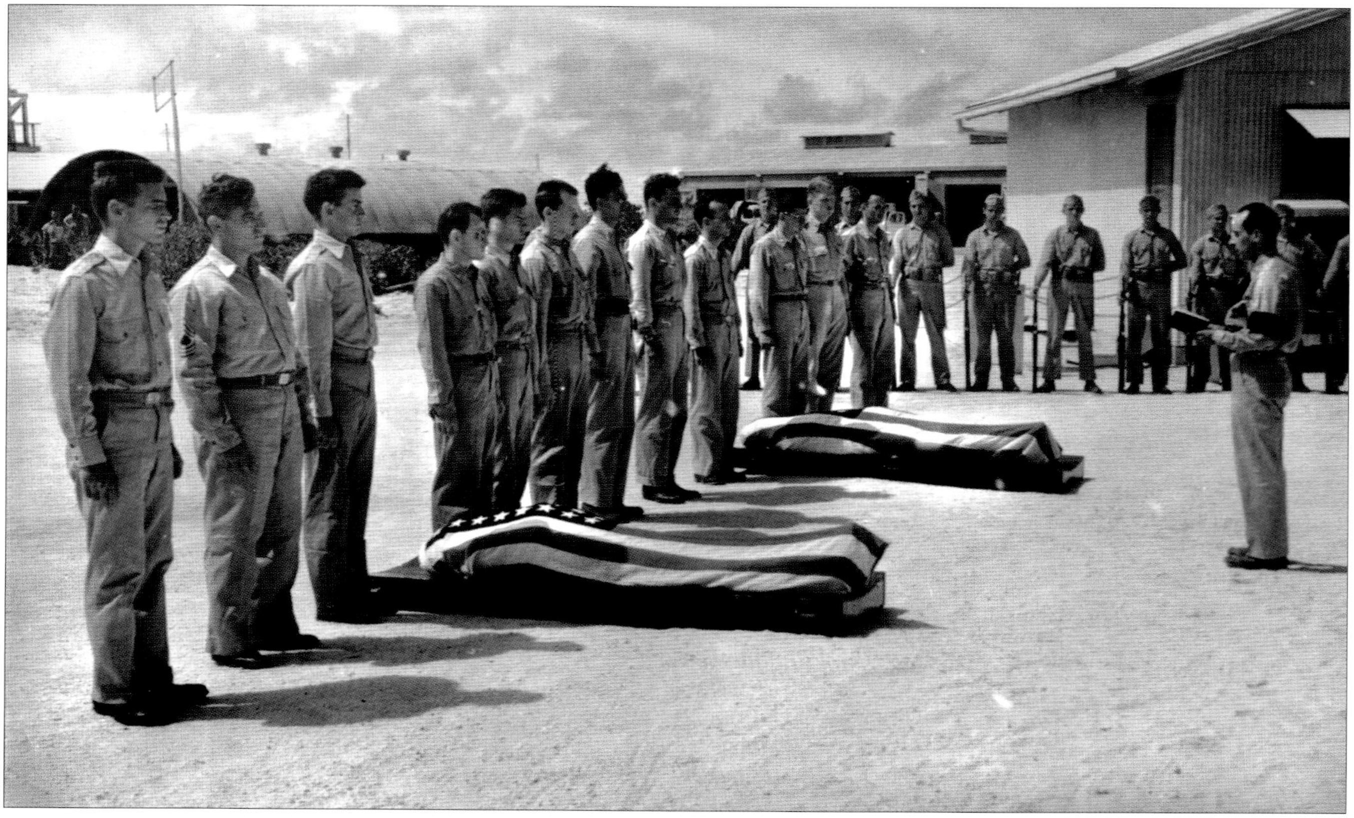

Above: The Daisy Mae's *surviving crewmen prepare for a burial at sea shortly after the fateful Wake Island mission. Ambur is fifth from the left.*

Right: The battered Daisy Mae *rests on the beach next to the runway at Midway Island after returning her crew to safety. She would never fly again.*

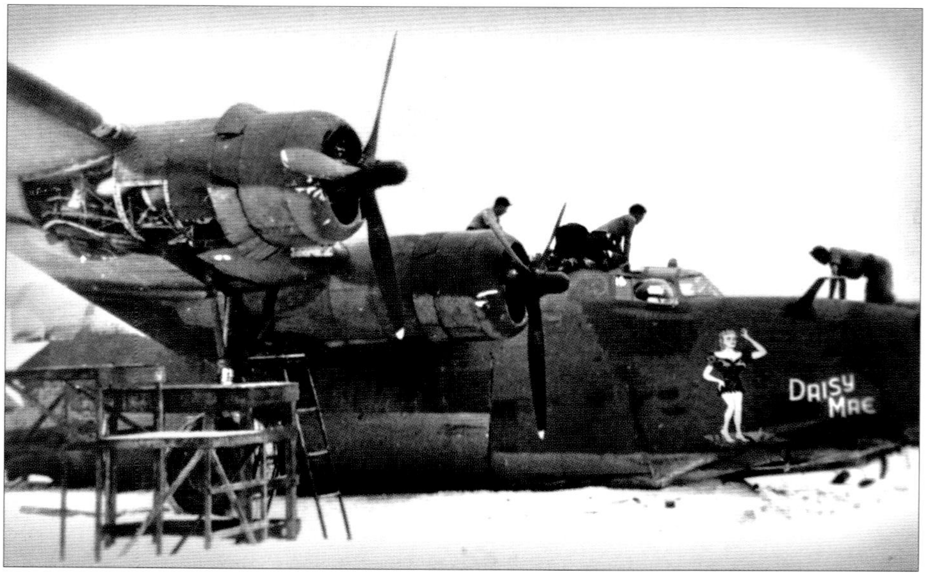

We had two 20mm *(shells)* go into the gas tanks inside the fuselage. Somebody discovered we had a fire, so they got me back there right away. I went up and they handed me a fire extinguisher. I had radio equipment and wires and all that stuff to crawl through to get up there. By that time *(the extinguisher)* was out of stuff. They finally sent up a bug deodorizer, and that didn't work.
I hollered back, "Give me a couple of leather jackets!"
I took these two leather jackets and I shoved one in each hole, and the fire went out.

Whether I should have did what I did, I don't know, but anyhow it worked out. I did have a little fear when I was doing it: Is this going to blow? What's going to happen? The oxygen tank is right there by it, and so forth. There had to be heat — it burned probably 500 gallons of gas. Whether we should have bailed out and let it burn, I don't know. I don't know what some other crew or other outfit might have done.

We came back on three engines and threw everything out of the plane. I carried this high-priced bomb sight, and it was clear through to the nose. I had to take it through the bomb bay to the back end of the plane to throw it out. I don't know if I handed it to someone else or if I threw it out the window, but somebody did. All the guns we threw out. We threw out everything in there.

There was supposed to be a submarine halfway in between, and if our radio equipment had been working good, we'd have had communication with them. If we needed a water landing, we'd have tried to get close to them. We finally did get it going. We got in contact with the Midway tower, so they knew we were coming in.

We were pretty near out of gas. We were pretty sure we were going to have a water landing. But it seemed like the farther we went, we'd gain a little more gas. I had to transfer fuel from one side to the other.

When we landed, we had 13 gallons left on the plane. We burned 50 gallons an hour in each engine, so that's 200 gallons an hour. Sixteen hours times 200 is what? Three thousand or so?

There was a lot of holes. Some say 800, some 700. I know there were two big holes in the wing up there where the fire was! Of course, those .50-calibers, if you go in the right place, you aren't doing no damage to speak of. We had hydraulics knocked out, and the radio equipment up there was knocked out. The tail gunner, he got a lot of holes back around him. He was just about sitting on a piece of tin back there. I know when we landed, the tail gunner dove out of the waist window because he thought we were out on the water.

I went out where they dismantled her, and they had the skin off. The one fuel cell — the whole top had burned off and about 6 or 8 inches on the side. And the fuel cell on the other side — the top had burned off and just strings were hanging across. So it was quite a fire.

The photographer, he was dead when we got there, and the bombardier was dead the next morning. We had a burial at sea. That was quite an experience to put those guys on a boat and paddle out in the ocean and slip them off of the side.

Our *Daisy Mae* got all dismantled and pushed out to sea. They didn't have no place to put it, so it floated out there. One night they had an air raid; "There's a submarine coming in!" They had a look around and it was *Daisy Mae* out there floating around. *(The* Daisy Mae *actually sank, but not far enough below the surface to avoid sonar detection.)*

I think what helped me a lot when we got back from this mission and got to Midway, was that I started writing about it. That let it off, rather than holding all that stuff and not talking about it and not writing it down. It released a lot.

It isn't often that I think about it, but there are some nights that I go through the thing again. ☆

Ambur returned to Presho to grow wheat and raise cattle. Unbeknownst to the crew, a Marine on Midway had cut a square piece of metal from Daisy Mae's *fuselage after her crash landing and kept it in an album for the next 50 years. He then discovered it, returned it to the pilot, and the surviving crew members took turns passing it between them until it was lost.*

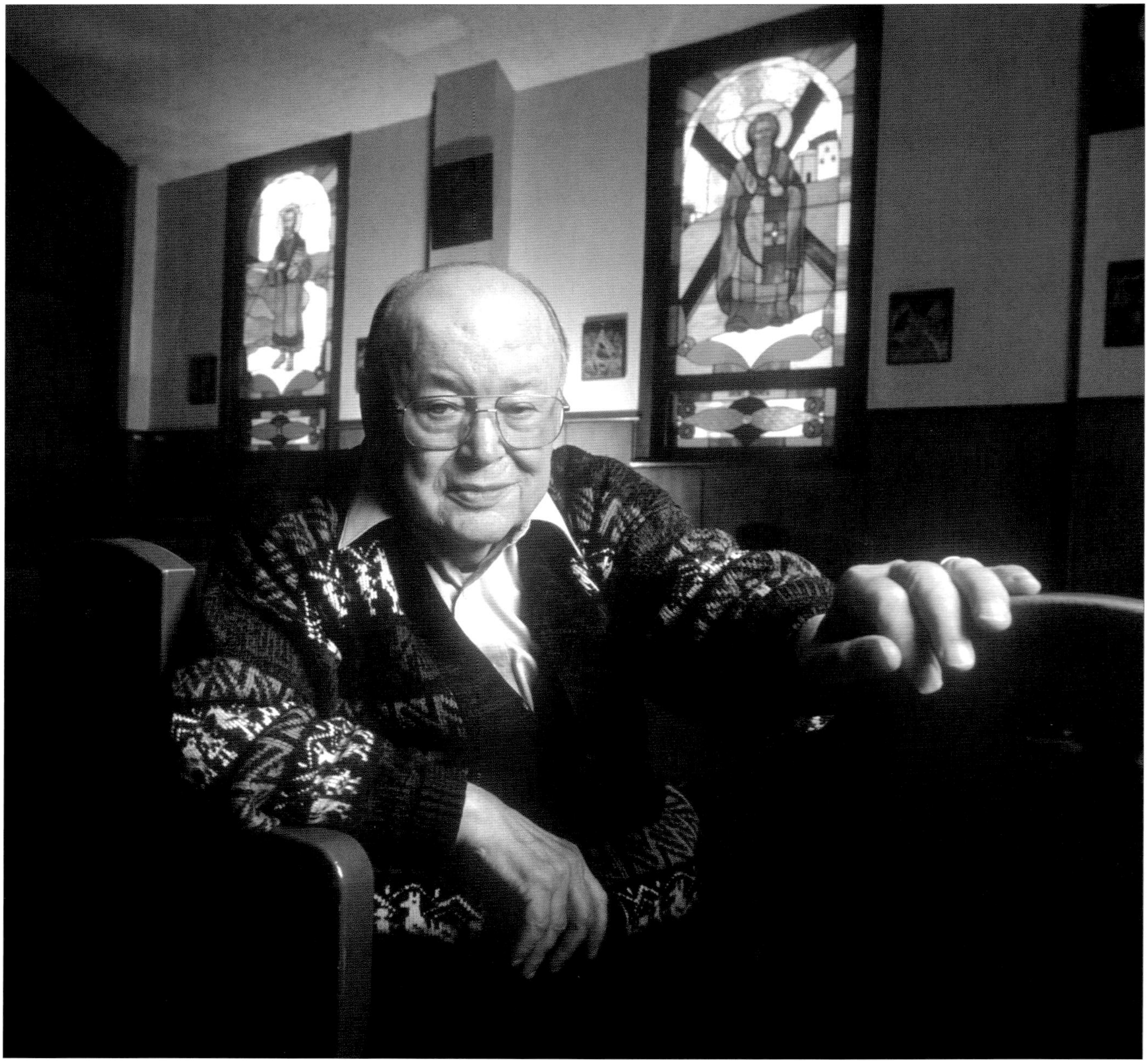

LARRY KIRK ☆ *Sioux Falls*

Arriving on Omaha beach in a follow-up wave during the Normandy invasion, Kirk was not required to face the gore his predecessors did. However, the following months brought a string of near-death experiences as he made his way through France, Luxembourg and Belgium.

During one of those intervals *(in France)*, I was in a halftrack. Eight men and a driver. I got on the hood, my back based against the steel uprise, and a mortar shell came in. The concussion threw me outside of the roadbed, and just shattered the eight guys to pieces.

We kept on going. I was in a jeep with four guys. Hit a mine, blew the jeep apart, three of them were killed. I was shaken up, slightly wounded.

We came to the German lines and set up in Luxembourg. We were doing light patrol action between the Germans. One time we had those sleeping bags, and we got off a patrol and another patrol took over. We zipped up and a German patrol came through and stabbed or shot seven of us. I escaped, and from then on I cut holes in *(the bag)*.

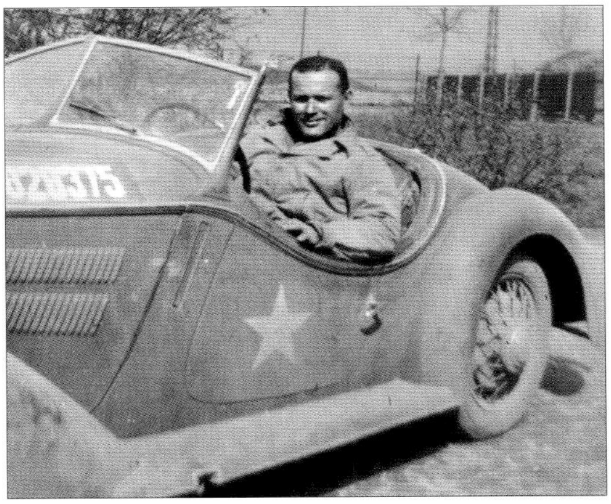

I was liaison between Division and Corps, which was in Liege, Belgium. Coming back, the Battle of the Bulge broke. I was cut off. Everybody for himself. I took off and was surrounded — in fact, I was less than a kilometer away when they massacred those boys in Malmedy. I heard the firing but didn't see the shooting. *(Nearly 100 American prisoners were murdered in cold blood by SS troops there on Dec. 17, 1944.)* I was five days and five nights behind the German lines; they overran me. I hid by day and traveled by night with compass directions. I had two chocolate military bars to eat and snow *(to drink)*. And then I came across a couple of German corpses and took their blood sausage rations.

The 101st pulled in, so I went under the 101st jurisdiction. I came up to them on the German side. At that time the Germans were trying to infiltrate us with American speakers, if you remember your history. *(Upon seeing me approach the perimeter)*, some outpost of the 502nd Regiment in the 101st Airborne yelled, "Shoot the Kraut son of a bitch!" *(So I hurriedly said in return)*, "Joe DiMaggio, Babe Ruth, Bob Hope, blah blah blah." *(German infiltrators were customarily asked questions, most often pertaining to American sports or entertainment, to which only Americans would know the answers.)*

I got attached to the 502nd on the same outpost *(outside of Bastogne)*. The Germans captured a whole medical battalion; we had no medics. Two doctors per regiment, and two combat medics per regiment.

It was Christmas Eve. No hopes, shellfire coming over just like a movie scene. I was in a bombed-out Catholic church *(in Bastogne)*. Protestant, Jew and Catholic praying together. Nobody arguing denominations. It was like a movie scene. I'll never forget it.

On an outpost, it means you're ahead of the regular lines. Now this was blizzard weather. A column of tanks came up. I picked up the bazooka and two shells. They wounded my bazooka man, and I got the boogie wheels of the first tank and stopped them. A guy popped out of the turret. I shot him, and then I threw a grenade in. Another one comes, trying to angle away, and the same thing — I jumped up and threw another grenade in. And the whole column backed up.

I got wounded by shrapnel, up here on my face. A couple in the groin — only flesh wounds, nothing serious — and I think one in my back. They put sulfa powder and paste on it, and I went back to fighting — there were many men more wounded than me.

You never know what you're going to do. Nobody gets a medal to be a hero. That's stupid. Nobody, I don't care what theater. Conditions and timing — if you had to do it a half hour later, you wouldn't do it — that's my personal experience. War does one thing: It brings the worst of mankind, and the best. ☆

After the war, Kirk returned to Sioux Falls and went into the restaurant business with his brothers. He was nominated for the Distinguished Service Cross for his Bastogne heroics, but the paperwork got lost in the shuffle of the war.

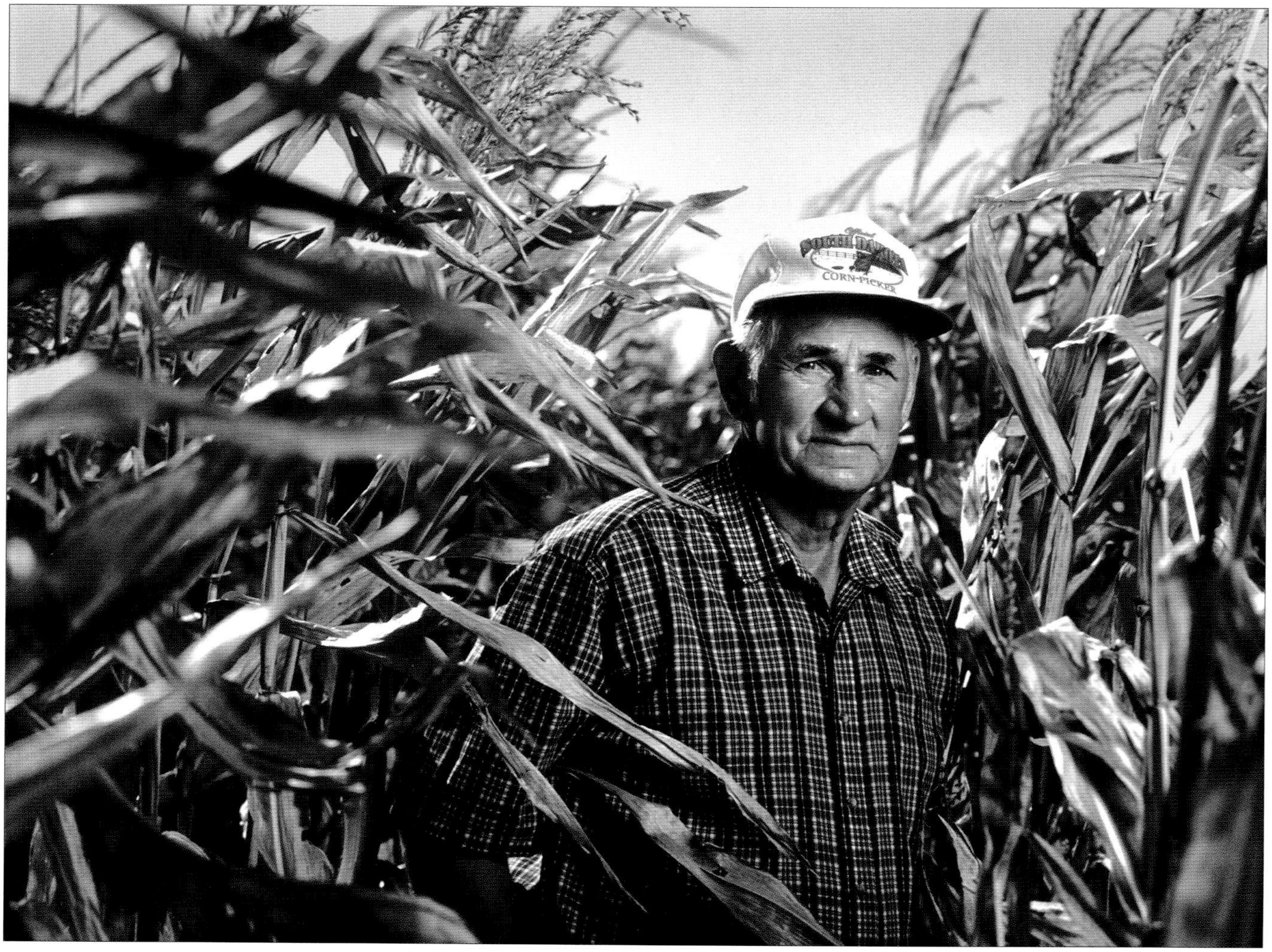
CORN-PICKER

JOHN VAN LIERE ☆ *Colton*

The Pacific war ended just as Van Liere finished boot camp. He spent the next year in the Army's occupation force.

World War II started, and I just got into high school. So I was pretty young and really didn't understand what being in a war was. During those first years, a lot of our neighbors got drafted real quick. A lot of the guys. They ended up with a lot of combat time in the service.

I graduated in '44 and I just turned 18. I was home one year with my dad on the farm, and then I was classified 1-A and got drafted.

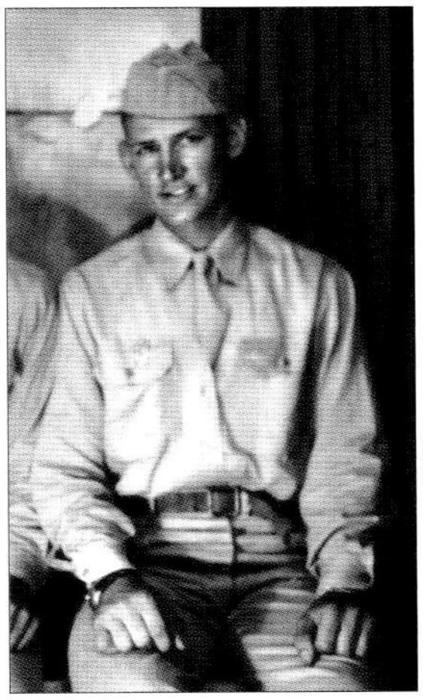

When we started our infantry training, Germany quit and that was in May. Two of my hut mates were a pair of Japanese brothers. They were from California, originally, but they had been expatriated from the coast to Arkansas with their family. They took the same infantry training I did, and they got told to "bayonet those Japs" just like I did. And they were full-blooded Japanese people! They didn't seem to rebel against that at all. They were the best, toughest little soldiers. I wouldn't be afraid to be in a war next to those guys anytime. They knew how to handle that rifle and bayonet.

At the end of our training period, which was the first part of August, Japan quit. Don't think that we weren't a happy bunch of soldiers to hear that news! In the last part of October, we boarded ship out of Seattle to spend a full year in Japan as part of the occupation force.

The Japanese people were ready to quit. They were just as happy as we were that the war was over. The American soldiers we replaced in Japan were the combat veterans that came up through the Philippines and had been through the fighting. Some of them had been in the war three years. They were tough cookies! They had no love for the Japanese people.

Never once in that whole year in Japan did we have any problems with the Japanese people. Most of them were so busy trying to get things put back together. A lot of them were trying to put some housing back together. Their houses were blown apart. Their cities were bombed so terrible. We were in several cities that looked like they were bombed flat.

Because it was a peacetime Army, there were a lot of things allowed, such as sport teams. The Army thought that was the best morale builder there was.

One day, there was some information that came to our company about signing up for this track team. The U.S. Army wanted to hold what they called the Pacific Army Olympics.

So I signed up. Then I never heard nothing for a month or so. I got on a basketball team then, and all of a sudden here come some orders through my company to the commander: cut orders for me to go to this track meet. I had kind of lost interest in it at that time, but the commander says, "We'd sure like to have you go because you're the only one from this area that signed up."

I got on a Japanese train and I traveled from the south part of Japan by myself up to Nagoya, and they held this track meet — in January. And that's winter there!

I had a big coat on and stuff, and I hadn't practiced any track. I threw the discus, and I won my event. So I got picked to be on this 30-man track team that was going to be sent from Japan to Manila.

It was a great experience. I got to meet some super athletes. We had two national champions on our track team — the top pole vaulter in the nation at that time, then we also had the national decathlon champion — but I could beat him in the discus. So I was kind of proud of myself. Here I was just out of high school and they were through college, and we're on the track team together. They run it just like the Olympics. In the final meet, I got sixth — I was inches from fifth. If I'd got fifth, I'd have got me a new wristwatch.

I think if I had never gone to Japan, I would never have realized what war really can do to a country.

I call it my million-dollar vacation, because I never could afford to take a trip and see as much as I did in that year. I never regretted it. ☆

Van Liere farmed near Colton after the war and has competed in corn picking contests around the country. He was national corn picking champion in 1995, and was runner-up six times.

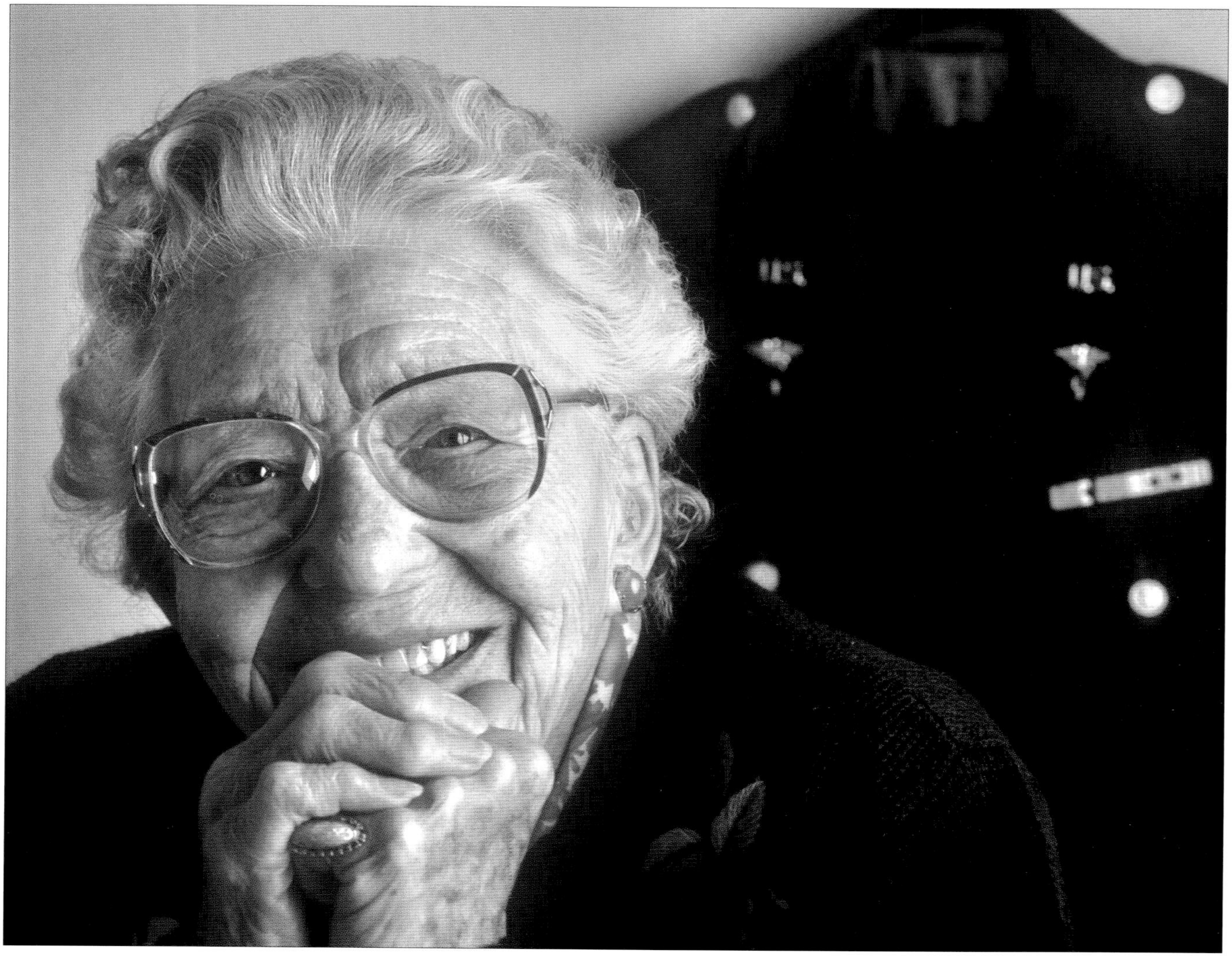

Edna Basler ☆ *Rapid City*

Growing up on a ranch near Hereford, Edna Reichert learned how to be tough at a young age. After the Pearl Harbor attack, she channeled her anger at the Japanese into a career in medicine, joining the Army Nurse Corps the following day. She served with the 116th Station Hospital first in New Guinea, then at Leyte in the Philippines, helping wounded and dying Marines as quickly as they were delivered to her from the front. Her first taste of danger came en route to Leyte.

We were going along, all sitting up in the sun on the top deck, with the big red cross on a white deck, and all of a sudden I heard this funny motor. I knew it was a Japanese plane because our planes didn't sound like that. I looked up and here's this little plane coming straight at us. The ship just blew its whistles and ring-rang bells and just leaped ahead.

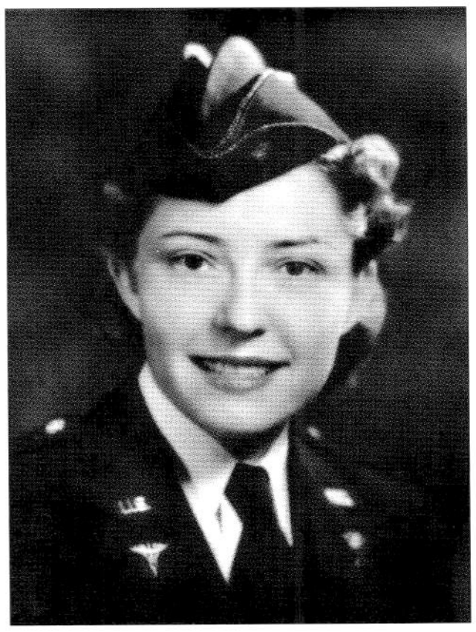

I was standing at the rail and I saw this plane drop the torpedo. It hit the water just behind us and just sizzled along under the surface. Of course, everyone was scared. I was just petrified. When he went past and missed us, I thought, "He'll be back and will strafe us with his machine guns." Luckily, the guy didn't come back.

When we first landed, the men came up ahead of us. They had the hospital set up, and they were holding us girls down at Hollandia, New Guinea, until we could get up into the hospital. The fighting got so close to their hospital, they had to move back quite a few miles away. When they started to set up again, they sent for us because there were so many wounded coming in.

Christmas Eve *(1944)* they came in so fast. They were all muddy and bloody; it was really pathetic the things those men went through. You take boots off of them, and they didn't have any socks, and some of the skin would come off their feet because they were wet in the trenches so long. We couldn't feed them all in the mess hall, there were so many. Bing Crosby was singing *I'll Be Home for Christmas* on the loudspeaker.

We were feeding them, and I was carrying trays to them, and one kid asked for some more white meat from the turkey. I actually cried because they didn't have any extra. I thought, "After all this kid's been through, and all he wants is a little piece of white meat from the turkey!"

There was a lot of water, a lot of floods. Water ran through our tents, sometimes 4 inches deep. They didn't have any floors. We slept on canvas cots for quite a bit of the time there. You just had to keep your feet above water. Everything molded — the jungle was all around us.

Have you ever heard of Tokyo Rose? They were bringing her back to prison on the ship that I came home on. She was not a very attractive woman — tall, kind of plump. She always stood by the railing by herself. I went over and talked to her a couple of times. I was afraid she was going to jump overboard. I think I would have if I'd been her.

When you're a nurse, you're prepared for anything. I was always responsible around the ranch, and so I was kind of a leader in our hospital. I was older than the other girls, and I didn't have to be reconciled to where I was.

It was hard for anybody to be a Marine, I tell you. They're my favorites of the guys that were there. I just dearly loved all hundreds of them. They fought like tigers. They were so cocky. They just knew what they could do, and they did it.

I've told people since then, if it wasn't for the soldiers we took care of, and all the other soldiers, and all the other nurses, and whoever worked there, we would be speaking German or Japanese right now, or both. So I've always felt like I could be proud of myself for being there. I sometimes wonder how we ever did it. We had a lot bigger heart then and a lot less machinery, and I don't think we lost any more patients than they do now with all their technology.

It was exciting, and interesting, and crazy. We did a lot of good, I think. People say, "How do you remember it?" I say, "How can you forget it?" ☆

After the war, Edna returned to Rapid City and worked at St. John's Hospital. She married Pat Basler, a World War II veteran himself, in 1948 and still lives in the house he built for them.

Back Stories

Bernie and Katie Hunhoff provided **Bill Abernathy's** (p. 46) name when they shared their plans for a *South Dakota Magazine* article featuring the few surviving Buffalo County WWII veterans. Photographed at his Gann Valley ranch, Bill downplayed his role in WWII — just like a typical cowboy would — even though he was involved in some of the war's most well-documented events.

☆

Lucy Halverson at the *Lyman County Herald* supplied me with **Arvid Ambur's** (p. 112) name after I solicited the state's daily and weekly newspaper editors for names of local veterans. As I listened to Arvid's account of the Wake Island mission, it was as if he were reading from a movie script.

☆

I found **Alvin Anderson's** (p. 90) name listed on a South Dakota World War II Memorial Internet database dedicated to veterans. He is pictured with a commemorative map given to members of the 2nd Armored Division before they came back to America in late 1945. He had never spoken of his service much, but he proved to be a wonderful interview.

☆

Terry Woster and I visited **Dave Bald Eagle** (p. 32) at his remote Cheyenne River Reservation ranch during the rough winter of 1997 for an *Argus Leader* story. During that interview, Dave mentioned that he'd been a paratrooper, and I made a mental note of it. He was photographed with a ceremonial headdress — notice his paratrooper jump wings affixed to his hat. Dave is also chief of the United Native Nations of the Americas.

☆

In late 2001, when Steve Miller wrote several profiles about WWII veterans for the *Rapid City Journal*, **Edna Basler** (p. 120) was featured among them. We hung her uniform on the wall behind her for the portrait. After I sent her a complete copy of our interview, she called me with some additional comments. She also paid me the finest compliment I received during the making of *Blue Stars*. She told me, "When you left that day and we shook hands, I felt like I was saying goodbye to an old friend." The honor was mine, Edna.

For the 50th anniversary of V-J Day in 1995, the *Argus Leader* conducted a write-in campaign so people could share their memories of that happy time. **Rudy Bohlmann** (p. 108) sent a letter that told of his Nagasaki visit. Here was a quiet farmer nestled in the middle of South Dakota who just happened to witness the dawn of the Cold War. Incredible. He is pictured at his farm in rural Menno.

☆

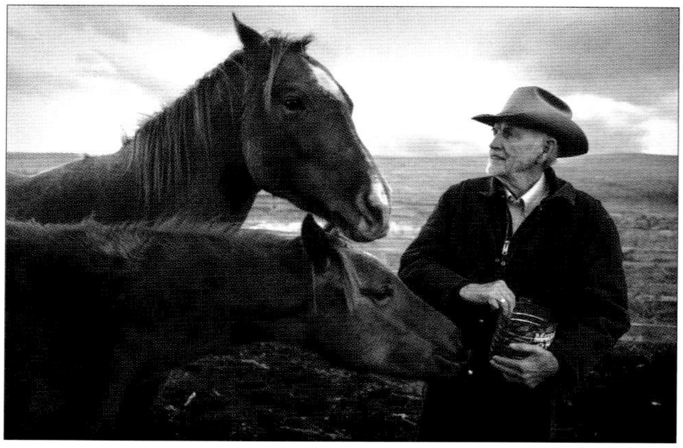

Bill Abernathy feeds some eager horses on his Gann Valley ranch.

☆

I can't remember exactly how I first heard about **Frank Branaugh** (p. 54). Although nearly blind and deaf, and missing part of his left arm, he sat and patiently recounted his war experiences for almost two hours. His failing eyes seemed to dance as he remembered several humorous accounts of his duty. After the interview, his wife Mildred drove him to Memorial Park so I could photograph him with the memorial plaque he helped to create. Despite his disability, he has become a successful businessman and remains lighthearted. Truly, he is an inspiration.

☆

When I visited **Jack Brookens** (p. 18), another veteran gleaned from a Steve Miller story in the *Rapid City Journal*, he had recently lost his wife Marie to cancer. I wanted to photograph him in his Veterans of Foreign Wars uniform because of his longtime involvement with the VFW funeral color guard. In the 1940s photo he is holding his niece Sandra on the Pacific coast near Seattle.

When the 50th anniversary of D-Day rolled around in 1994 and the *Argus Leader* provided a forum for D-Day veterans to tell their stories, **Oliver Carlson's** (p. 28) account caught my eye. He's still extremely active; in fact, we had to interrupt our interview so he could haul a load of cattle. I photographed him in the backyard of his rural Beresford home, holding a 105mm casing similar to the ones he handled in WWII. The lyrics to *When a Blue Star Turns to Gold* were included in a program Oliver had kept from a service for returning Beresford veterans held at the Brooklyn Evangelical Free Church.

☆

I saw **Darrel Christopherson's** (p. 42) account of the Pearl Harbor attack on the Digital Dakota Network Web site, hosted by the South Dakota Department of Education. We conducted our interview in the Clay County courthouse, where I photographed him among the hundreds of veterans' photos hanging in the Clay County Veterans Service Office.

☆

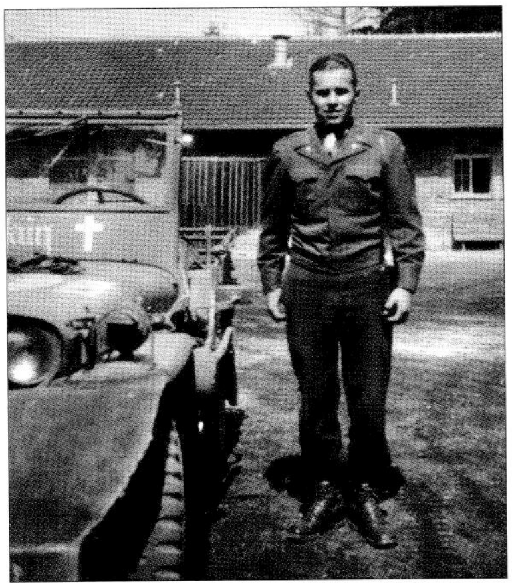

Richard Diede stands with his chaplain jeep during a visit to the Dachau concentration camp after the war.

☆

Upon discovering the existence of a compilation of Belle Fourche area veteran profiles, I solicited one of the co-authors, Peggy Davis, for a copy (the other co-author is Billie Jane Hamblin). In it I found a wealth of information about dozens of veterans, and decided to focus on **LeRoy Clarkson** (p. 60), Arthur Davis and Don Fuhrmann. LeRoy seemed to delight in recollecting his service days as we talked in his office at Pioneer Bank & Trust. In his vintage photo, he is pictured at the Ingersoll School east of Belle Fourche, where he attended as a youngster.

I found **Dale Coughlin's** (p. 98) name when searching for veterans on the South Dakota World War II Memorial Web site. All his entry said was that he spent 21 months on a PT boat. I knew there had to be more to his story, and he obliged my visit. He is pictured at his Lake Poinsett home, and his WWII photo shows him on the deck of PT-344, leaning on the 40mm cannon.

☆

Arthur Davis (p. 110) was culled from the same Belle Fourche book as LeRoy Clarkson and Don Fuhrmann. I found him to be a very smart man, and it seemed obvious that he was destined to work in intelligence during the war. His portrait was taken in the courtyard of the Westhills Village Retirement Community where he lives.

☆

Chuck Cecil wrote a lengthy story about **Lyle Davis** (p. 104) and his P.O.W. journal for *Remember the Time*, a book of stories about Brookings County people and places. Leave it to Chuck to find all the interesting people. Lyle was photographed with the journal in his Brookings home.

☆

Richard Diede (p. 48) was featured in a newspaper article written by Gale Pifer. He happily donned his original chaplain vestment for the portrait and opened the battered suitcase containing the objects he needed for spontaneous services in the field. I laughed when I realized I was handling the suitcase like a Ming vase — it probably endured more bumps and bangs in the war than most modern-day luggage does.

☆

While reading about him in the aforementioned Belle Fourche veterans book, I was stunned to discover that **Don Fuhrmann** (p. 74) was involved in the Okinawa flag-raising. The flag in his portrait is the one flown on the Fuhrmann house in Spearfish. A professional photojournalist shot the 1945 picture of Don on Okinawa.

☆

I got **Arnie Gibson's** (p. 20) name from Hughes County CVSO Jim Melgaard. Arnie's vintage photo shows he and wife Margaret on their wedding day, March 26, 1945. A great sport, Arnie stood in a stiff November breeze for his portrait at the World War II memorial at Capitol Lake in Pierre.

I was introduced to **Joe Habeger** (p. 76) after I spoke at a South Dakota Ag Heritage Museum Brown Bag Luncheon in Brookings. I was getting all set to contact him a few months later when I heard a shocking item on the 6 o'clock news: Madison pilot crash-lands his WWII-era plane near Brookings. I was relieved to hear Joe was okay, and we ended up shooting his portrait with the AT-6 trainer he had crashed in. This is one of the planes used for training pilots in WWII, and Joe had recently acquired it for pleasure flying. After the crash he said to me, "I was real embarrassed because I had run out of gas, but I was proud of the landing I made." Joe is 83.

☆

Peggy Gibson brought her father, **Jack Hyde** (p. 36), to my attention after a presentation I made to the Huron Camera Club. I always mention upcoming projects whenever I speak to groups, and it paid off again! He is pictured holding the .25-caliber Japanese bullet that shattered his shoulder.

☆

I got **Charlie Johnson's** (p. 64) name from Jim Black, another submariner from Yankton. A great storyteller, Charlie had me entranced at his dining room table for about two hours. All I needed for his portrait was the reminiscent look on his face. He is shown holding son Charlie in his 1940s snapshot.

☆

I got **Larry Kirk's** (p. 116) name from an *Argus Leader* story that commemorated the 50th anniversary of the Battle of the Bulge. We conducted our interview and portrait session at the Transfiguration Greek Orthodox Church in Sioux Falls, which provided a great backdrop as he recounted that unforgettable 1944 Christmas service in Bastogne.

☆

My solicitation to the state's weekly newspapers provoked a great response from Kim Olson at the *Lemmon Leader,* who sent a booklet of stories about area World War II veterans written by *Leader* reporters Jeri Lynn Bakken and Kathy Larson. As I read through the stories, **Monte LaBarge's** (p. 80) Alaska duty caught my eye. He was photographed in the same kitchen chair where he was interviewed. The 1940s portrait shows him at the edge of the Alaskan wilderness.

While searching for *Blue Stars* veterans, I contacted county and tribal veterans service officers throughout the state. Sisseton-Wahpeton TVSO Lisa Gonsalvez answered my request and helped me arrange an interview with 90-year-old **Reuben LaBatte** (p. 58). He was extremely proud of his uniform and his war staff, which was presented to him by the tribe after he returned home.

☆

Nelson Lagendyk's (p. 40) interview was conducted in his "war room," a den full of memorabilia saved from his Air Force career. He sat patiently as I arranged four separate strobes to make his portrait with a Waco Glider model. At least three of the other vets I interviewed mentioned their admiration for glider pilots; their missions were some of the most dangerous of the war. I discovered his story after reading about it in a Randy Dockendorf article in the *Yankton Daily Press & Dakotan.*

☆

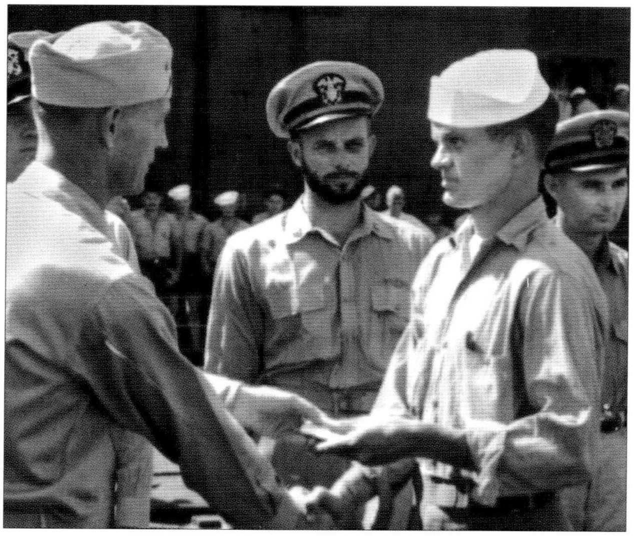

Charlie Johnson, right, receives his "dolphins," a silver pin depicting a submarine flanked by two dolphins. The prized insignia symbolized his formal submarine certification.

☆

I read an article about **Marcella LeBeau** (p. 86) written by Dottie Potter in a copy of the *Lakota Journal* back in 2001. A very classy lady, Marcella represents all Lakota veterans well. She was photographed with one of her beautiful star quilts in the Rose Room, an Eagle Butte workshop she owns and operates with her granddaughter Bonnie.

I interviewed **Howard Lee** (p. 26) at the Brookings County Historical Society Museum in Volga. I first tried photographing him at the cemetery that afternoon, but the light was too harsh. I returned and made his portrait on the morning of Veterans Day, November 11, 2003. His brother Leonard is buried there at Volga, while Walter is interred in a beautiful American cemetery in the Philippines. I contacted Howard after reading about him in a Chuck Cecil story.

☆

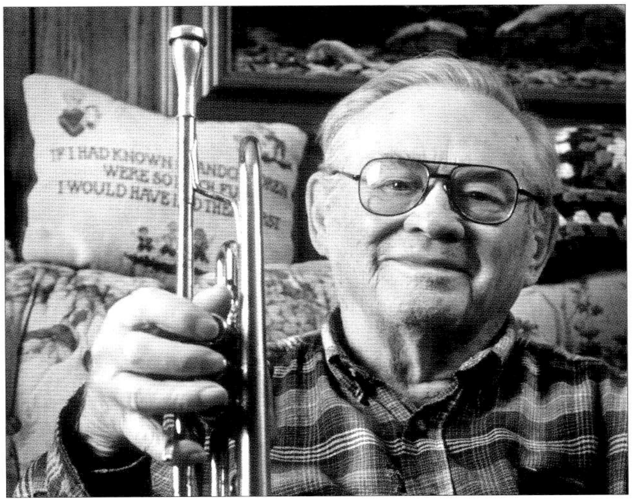

Homer Parce doesn't play his trumpet much anymore, but he can still muster a good rendition of Taps *when needed.*

☆

Steve Young wrote a story about **Morris Magnuson** (p. 66) for the *Argus Leader*, briefly detailing his fateful mission and subsequent capture. Morris did a superb job of telling the story. When I began to transcribe the audio from our interview, I couldn't bring myself to edit it down to two or four or even six pages, and that's why it spans an eight page spread in the book. He is pictured at one of the old Big Sioux River bridges near Western Avenue in Sioux Falls.

☆

John Maher (p. 92) owns a quarter of land just west of our family farm near Letcher. We started farming it for him in the 1980s, but I didn't realize he was a WWII veteran until he shared some stories with my dad while they rode together in the combine. He is pictured near a stock dam on the quarter.

Finding a Bataan Death March survivor who will talk about his experiences is rare, so I felt lucky to find **Tom McDill** (p. 50). I don't think he ever talked about it much after the war, so I appreciated his candor with me. He is photographed on his rural Custer ranch with the Black Hills spreading out behind him.

☆

I interviewed **Dave Moore** (p. 52) at his kitchen table in Vivian. We then walked down to the former Vivian State Bank, where he'd worked for 36 years, and made the portrait there. I think his amusement at all the attention shows on his face. Dave's name was provided to me by Jones County CVSO Gary Sletto.

☆

While reviewing some of Yankton historian Bob Karolevitz's archived articles, I ran across a reference to **Hod Nielsen** (p. 82) and his brothers serving in WWII. I was amazed to learn of his unique wartime duty and that he'd already been mentioned by fellow Yanktonian Tom Brokaw in his book *The Greatest Generation*. He is photographed in his front yard with a P-38 model plane.

☆

Elmer Olson (p. 102) was the first veteran I interviewed for the book. He is the father of Lyle Olson, a journalism professor at South Dakota State University who first taught typography to Jodi and me. Elmer really provided a spark for the rest of the project. Our interview was conducted nearly 18 months before I spoke with the rest of the vets in late 2003. He is pictured in the Westside Wesleyan Church in Bristol, which he built. He lives across the street.

☆

On numerous occasions I've heard **Homer Parce** (p. 38) play *Taps* at the Letcher cemetery, and his wife Norma fed me for 13 years as a cook on the Letcher school cafeteria crew. It was really fun to include a veteran from my hometown, and I was reminded of his and the Stach brothers' service by fellow Letcherite John O'Connell. He is pictured playing in the living room of his Letcher home.

I photographed **Jim Peacock** (p. 14) admiring the WWII memorial in Pierre during the September 15, 2001 dedication ceremony, and I was pleased to cross paths with him again for *Blue Stars*. Struggling to think of a way to photograph him after our interview, I tried shooting his profile against my black backdrop. It turned out to be one of my favorite portraits in the book.

☆

I was very pleased to find **Victor Peterson** (p. 100) after Deuel County CVSO Dennis Evenson included him on a list of Deuel County veterans. At 85, Victor is still quite active, and he still lives on the farm.

☆

Cecil Sanderson (p. 44) donated several pieces of WWII memorabilia to the Brookings County Historical Society Museum in Volga, and Chuck Cecil wrote about it. I interviewed and photographed Sanderson at the museum — the portrait was taken just outside the back door. During our interview, his wife Grace helped "translate" at times when I wasn't asking questions loudly enough. Howard Lee opened the museum for us and was a great help in making the pistol and Nazi flag available for the photograph. Cecil is holding his son Reed in his 1940s photograph.

☆

Albert Schamens (p. 88) was very candid about the most frightening episode of his life, and it never ceases to amaze me when a veteran can freely talk about that type of experience. I took his photo in front of a weathered shed across from his house in Hazel. I first discovered his name in a collection of short veteran profiles in the *Pierre Capital Journal*.

☆

When I mailed a request to all of the state's county veterans service officers for potential WWII interviewees, **Floyd Short** (p. 34) responded with a list that included several notable veterans around Lemmon. I ended up interviewing HIM. He is pictured with a 1948 Chrysler limousine owned by the Lemmon Masonic Temple, of which he is a member.

I had photographed **Bob Swift** (p. 94) for an *Argus Leader* story in 1997 and was very impressed by him. When I called to arrange our interview at his Waterford apartment, I mentioned that he lived near our old neighborhood (we had moved to a new house in 2002). He asked me where we had lived, and I gave my pat answer: on First Avenue, between 18th and 19th Streets. He said, "Which house?" I answered, "1017." After a long pause he said, "Greg, I used to live in that house." I was speechless. As it turned out, Bob had spent some of his boyhood years there, and had moved out in 1932. He is pictured at The Waterford with some remnants of the former All Saints School behind him. In his 1940s portrait he is holding his son Richard.

☆

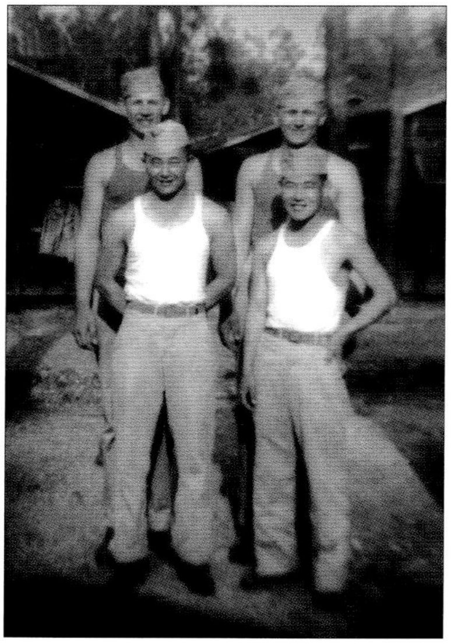

John Van Liere (top left) and Harlen Voigt of Avon pose with their bunkmates: Japanese brothers they trained and roomed with toward the end of WWII.

☆

Harold Thune (p. 22) was recommended to me by Troy Larson, a former congressional staffer for Harold's son, John Thune. I interviewed Harold in his Murdo home, just across the street from the school. In keeping with his 20-year history in Murdo athletics, I photographed him on the outdoor basketball courts there.

☆

I first photographed **John Van Liere** (p. 118) when he was competing at the McCrossan Boys Ranch corn picking contest near Crooks. He didn't mind when I asked him for another photograph — this time in a cornfield outside of Colton. Following the shoot, we spent 10 minutes scraping sand burrs off of each other's clothing.

Acknowledgments

One of the names offered by Floyd Short was Bison's **Steve Vetter** (p. 96). Despite his near-complete disability in both hands, he can do pretty much anything. Steve is pictured with a Japanese 7.7mm rifle like the one that was used to shoot him.

☆

From the beginning, it was my desire to interview a Lakota code-talker for *Blue Stars*. **Clarence Wolf Guts** (p. 78) graciously agreed to sit down in an Oglala Lakota College extension center classroom in Wanblee, where I photographed him in front of a Chief Red Cloud mural painted by student Eugene Swift Hawk. Unfortunately, a war-era photo of Clarence could not be found.

☆

I interviewed **Albert (Red) Zarecky** (p. 62) in his basement workshop, and he requested to be photographed there as well. "This is where I belong," he said. I was impressed by his woodworking talent. He even gave me one of his handmade picture frames, which I treasure. I found out about Red's story while reading a WWII commemorative issue of the *Pierre Capital Journal*.

☆ ☆ ☆

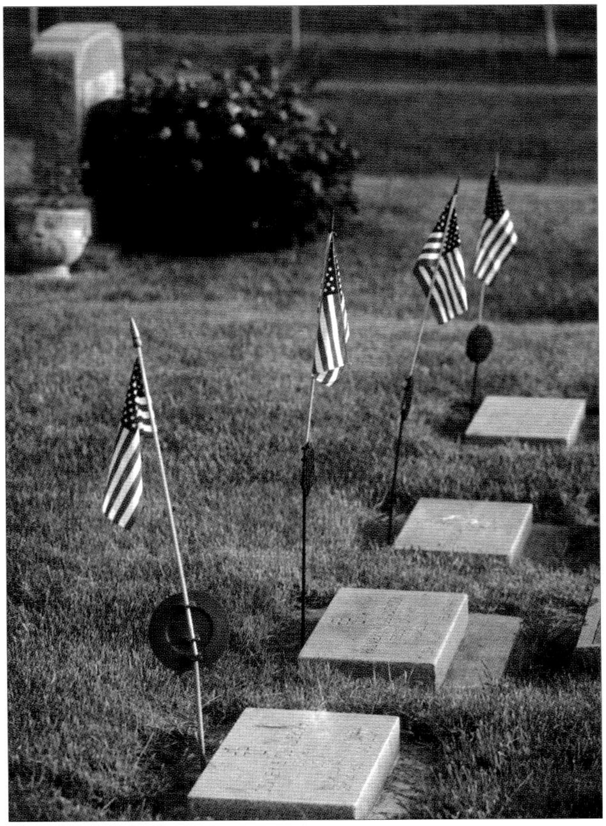

Since a project like *Blue Stars* cannot be done alone, I'd like to acknowledge several people who played large and small parts in the production of this, our fifth book.

First and foremost, I want to thank my wife Jodi. Her design and editing work were crucial to *Blue Stars'* success. But perhaps more importantly, she was the first person to whom I told this idea and she never wavered in her support of it. She stayed home with our children Anna, Luke and Jack, while I drove to all corners of the state interviewing veterans, and she did a wonderful job looking after the office in my absence. I can't say enough about being able to work with my best friend every day.

Thank you to the 44 men and women featured in these pages. Each person was a pleasure to visit with, and though I was a stranger in their homes, each one of them treated me to their best hospitality. I am grateful for their time and their willingness to share their amazing stories and vintage photos with us. Truly, they are an inspiration to us all.

I'd like to thank Curt Nickisch for his assistance with the audio portion of *Blue Stars*. Curt advised me about what audio equipment I needed, how to properly record the interviews and how to best prepare the finished audio before I handed the interviews over to him. His talent and help were invaluable.

Thank you to the many people who provided veteran contacts: several of the state's county and tribal veterans service officers, various weekly and daily newspaper editors and reporters and all of the individuals mentioned in the back stories.

Thanks to all of our family and friends who provided support (and babysitting!) in our times of need.

And finally, deepest thanks to the 2,200 South Dakotans who made the ultimate sacrifice during WWII. They never got the chance to share their stories, but their spirit is alive in the hearts and minds of everyone who enjoys the freedoms they provided for us.

☆ ☆ ☆

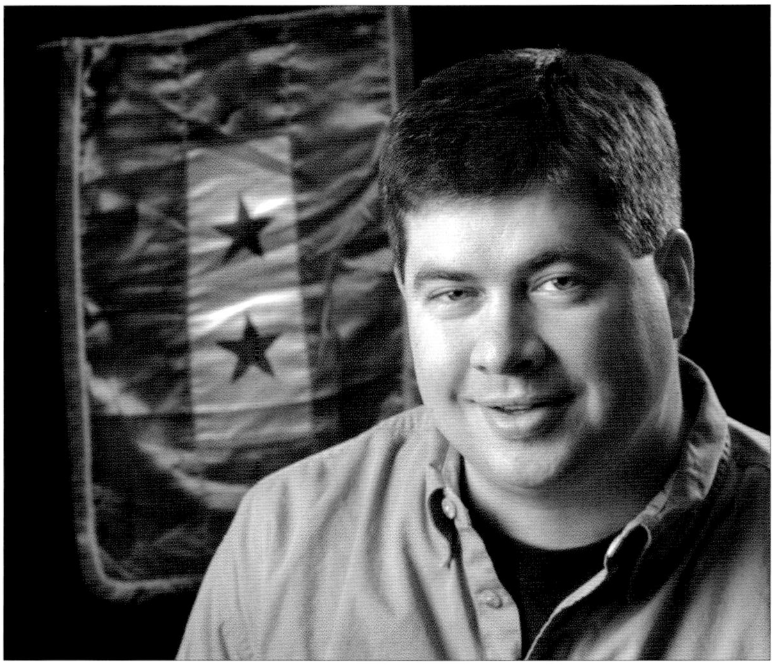

Greg Latza grew up on a farm near Letcher and earned journalism and geography degrees from South Dakota State University. After working as a photojournalist at newspapers in Minnesota, Wisconsin and Kansas, he returned to South Dakota in 1994 to work at the Sioux Falls *Argus Leader*. In 1997, Greg and his wife Jodi started PeopleScapes, a freelance photography and graphic design company in Sioux Falls. They have published four other books to date: *Back on the Farm, Hometown, S.D., The Missouri,* and a children's book, *South Dakota: An Alphabetical Scrapbook*. Greg and Jodi have three children: Anna, Luke and Jack.